Pocket

BUSINESS
SPANISH
DICTIONARY

second edition

English-Spanish/Spanish-English

Inglés-Español/Español-Inglés

General Editor
P. H. Collin

Spanish Editor
Lourdes Melcion

BLOOMSBURY

A BLOOMSBURY REFERENCE BOOK

Originally published by Peter Collin Publishing

First published in Great Britain 1995
Second edition published 2003
This edition published in the United States of America 2004

Bloomsbury Publishing Plc
38 Soho Square
London W1D 3HB

Bloomsbury Reference titles are distributed
in the United States of America by
Independent Publishers Group,
814 N. Franklin St., Chicago, IL 60610
1-800-888-4741
www.ipgbook.com

Copyright © P. H. Collin 1995
This edition copyright © Bloomsbury Publishing 2003, 2004

All rights reserved. No part of this publication may be reproduced
in any form or by any means without the prior written permission
of the publishers.

ISBN 1 904970 03 6

All papers used by Bloomsbury Publishing are natural, recyclable
products made from wood grown in well-managed forests.
The manufacturing processes conform to the environmental regulations
of the country of origin.

Text computer typeset by Bloomsbury
Printed in the United States of America by Quebecor World Fairfield

Preface

This pocket dictionary is designed for any business person, business student, or traveler who needs to deal with the language of business. It contains over 5,000 essential business terms in Spanish and English with clear and accurate translations.

Abbreviations

adj	adjective
adv	adverb
f	feminine
fpl	feminine plural
m	masculine
mf	masculine or feminine
mpl	masculine plural
n	noun
v	verb

Prefacio

Este diccionario tiene como objetivo facilitar la comunicación a toda persona que se relacione o viaje por asuntos de negocios. Contiene más de 5.000 términos básicos de negocios con sus correspondientes traducciones.

Abreviaturas

adj	adjetivo
adv	adverbio
f	femenino
fpl	femenino plural
m	masculino
mf	masculino o femenino
mpl	masculino plural
n	nombre
v	verbo

Contents

Índice

English-Spanish
Inglés-Español

A

A1 *adj* de primera clase
abandon *v* abandonar; renunciar a
abandon an action *v* desistir de una acción
abatement *n* disminución *f*
abroad *n* (en el) extranjero *m*
absence *n* ausencia *f*
absent *adj* ausente
absolute monopoly *n* monopolio *m* absoluto
abundance *n* abundancia *f*
accelerated depreciation *n* amortización *f* acelerada
accept *v* aceptar
accept a bill *v* aceptar una letra
acceptable *adj* aceptable; admisible
acceptance *n* aceptación *f*
acceptance of an offer *n* aceptación *f* de una oferta
acceptance sampling *n* muestreo *m* de aceptación
accept delivery of a shipment *v* aceptar la entrega de mercancías
accept liability for something *v* aceptar la responsabilidad de algo
access *n* acceso *m*
accessible *adj* accesible
accommodation address *n* dirección *f* postal
accommodation bill *n* pagaré *m*; efecto *m* de favor
according to *prep* según
account *n* cuenta
accountant *n* contable *mf*
account executive *n* ejecutivo *m* de cuentas
account for *v* justificar; responder de

account in credit *n* cuenta *f* con saldo positivo; cuenta *f* acreedora
accounting *n* contabilidad *f*
accounting department *n* departamento *m* de contabilidad
account: on account *phrase* cuenta: a cuenta
account on stop *n* cuenta *f* bloqueada
accounts department *n U.K.* departamento *m* de contabilidad
accounts payable *npl* cuentas *fpl* a pagar; por pagar
accounts receivable *npl* cuentas *fpl* a cobrar; cuentas *fpl* por cobrar
accrual *n* acumulación *f*
accrual of interest *n* acumulación *f* de interés
accrue *v* acumularse; devengar
accrued interest *n* interés *m* acumulado
accumulate *v* acumular; acumularse
accurate *adj* exacto *or* -ta; correcto *or* -ta
accusation *n* acusación *f*
accuse *v* acusar
acknowledgement *n* acuse *m* de recibo
acknowledge receipt of a letter *v* acusar recibo de una carta
acquire *v* adquirir
acquisition *n* adquisición *f*
across-the-board *adj* general
act *v* 1. actuar 2. (*do something*) tomar medidas
acting *adj* interino *or* -na; en funciones
acting manager *n* director *m* en funciones
action *n* 1. acción *f* 2. (*lawsuit*) acción *f* legal
action for damages *n* demanda *f* por daños y perjuicios
active *adj* activo *or* -va
activity *n* actividad *f*
act of God *n* fuerza *f* mayor
actual *adj* real; efectivo *or* -va
actuals *npl* cifras *fpl* reales

actuarial tables *npl* tablas *fpl* actuariales; tablas *fpl* de mortalidad

actuary *n* actuario *or* -ria

add *v* añadir

addition *n* suma *f*; adición *f*

additional *adj* adicional; suplementario *or* -ria

additional charges *npl* cargos *mpl* adicionales

additional premium *n* sobreprima *f*

add on 10% for service *v* añadir el 10% por el servicio

address *n* dirección *f*; señas *fpl* ■ *v* dirigir

address a letter, a package *v* poner las señas; poner la dirección

addressee *n* destinatario *or* -ria

address label *n* etiqueta *f* (de señas)

address list *n* lista *f* de direcciones

add up a column of figures *v* sumar una columna de cifras

adequate *adj* adecuado *or* -da

adjourn *v* aplazar; diferir

adjourn a meeting *v* aplazar una reunión

adjudicate in a dispute *v* arbitrar un litigio

adjudication *n* adjudicación *f*

adjudication tribunal *n* tribunal *m* de justicia

adjudicator *n* árbitro *mf*; juez *mf*

adjust *v* ajustar; reajustar

adjustment *n* ajuste *m*; reajuste *m*

administration *n* administración *f*

administrative *adj* administrativo *or* -va

administrative body, authority *n* órgano *m* administrativo

administrative expenses *npl* gastos *mpl* administrativos

admission *n* entrada *f*; ingreso *m*

admission charge *n* precio *m* de entrada

admit *v* admitir

ad valorem *adj, adv* ad valorem

ad valorem tax *n* impuesto *m* ad valorem

advance *n* 1. (*loan*) anticipo *m* 2. (*progress*) avance *m* ■ *v* 1. (*lend*) anticipar 2. (*progress*) avanzar

advance booking *n* reserva *f* anticipada

advanced *adj* anticipado *or* -a; adelantado *or* -a

advance on account *n* anticipo *m* a cuenta

advance payment *n* pago *m* anticipado

advertise *v* anunciar; publicar

advertise a new product *v* anunciar un nuevo producto

advertise a vacancy *v* anunciar una vacante

advertisement *n* anuncio *m*

advertiser *n* anunciante *mf*

advertising *n* publicidad *f*

advertising agency *n* agencia *f* de publicidad

advertising budget *n* presupuesto *m* de publicidad

advertising campaign *n* campaña *f* publicitaria

advertising manager *n* jefe *m* de publicidad

advertising rates *n* tarifas *fpl* publicitarias

advertising space *n* espacio *m* publicitario

advice note *n* nota *f* de aviso

advise *v* 1. (*suggest*) aconsejar 2. (*tell what happened*) informar

advise against *v* desaconsejar; disuadir

adviser, advisor *n* asesor *or* -ra; consejero *or* -ra

affidavit *n* acta *f* notarial

affiliated *adj* afiliado *or* -da; filial

affiliation *n* afiliación *f*

affirmative *adj* afirmativo *or* -va

afford *v* permitirse un gasto; tener tiempo

after-sales service *n* servicio *m* posventa; de post-venta

after-tax profit n beneficios mpl netos de impuestos

agency n agencia f

agenda n orden m del día

agent n 1. (in an agency) agente mf 2. (representative) representante mf

AGM abbr (annual general meeting) junta f general anual

agree v 1. (accept) aceptar 2. (approve) acordar 3. (be same as) corresponder; coincidir

agreed adj acordado or -da; convenido or -da

agreed price n precio m acordado; precio m convenido

agreement n convenio m; acuerdo m; contrato m; pacto m

agree to do something v aceptar hacer algo

agree with v 1. (be same as) corresponder; coincidir con 2. (of same opinion) estar de acuerdo

agricultural adj agrícola; agropecuario or -ria; agrario or -ria

aim n objetivo m; propósito m ■ v proponerse; aspirar a

air n aire m

air freight n flete m aéreo; carga f aérea

airfreight v enviar por carga aérea

air freight charges, rates n tarifas fpl de carga aérea

air letter n aerograma m

airline n línea f aérea

airmail n correo m aéreo ■ v enviar por correo aéreo

airmail sticker n etiqueta f de correo aéreo

airport n aeropuerto m

airport bus n autobús m del aeropuerto

airport tax n tasas fpl de aeropuerto

airport terminal n terminal f del aeropuerto

air terminal n terminal f de aeropuerto

airtight packaging n embalaje m hermético

all expenses paid phrase todos los gastos pagados

all-in adv U.K. todo incluido

all-inclusive adv todo incluido

all-inclusive price n precio m todo incluido

all-in price n U.K. precio m todo incluido

allocate v asignar

allocation of funds n provisión f de fondos

allow v 1. permitir 2. (accept) aceptar 3. (give) conceder; dar

allow 10% for shipping v dejar un margen del 10% para el porte

allowance for depreciation n cuota f de depreciación

allow for v dejar un margen; tener en cuenta

all-risks policy n póliza f a todo riesgo

alphabetical order n orden m alfabético

alter v modificar

alteration n modificación f

alternative adj alternativo or -va ■ n alternativa f

amend v enmendar

amendment n enmienda f

American adj americano or -na; estadounidense ■ n americano or -na; estadounidense mf

amortization n amortización f

amortize v amortizar

amount n (of money) importe m; cantidad f

amount owing n importe m debido

amount paid n importe m pagado

amount to v ascender a

analysis n análisis m

analyze v analizar

analyze the market potential v analizar las posibilidades del mercado

annex n anexo m

announce v anunciar; comunicar

announcement n anuncio m; declaración f

annual adj anual

annual accounts npl cuentas fpl anuales

annual general meeting n U.K. junta f general anual

annually adv anualmente

annual meeting n junta f general anual

annual report n informe m anual

answer n contestación f; respuesta f ■ v contestar; responder

answer a letter v contestar una carta

answering machine n contestador m automático

answering service n servicio m de contestación

answer the telephone v contestar el teléfono

antedate v antedatar

anticipate v anticipar; prever

apartment n apartamento m; piso m

apologize v disculparse; presentar excusas; pedir perdón

apology n disculpa f; excusa f

appeal n 1. (against a decision) apelación f 2. (attraction) atractivo m; interés m ■ v (against a decision) apelar

appeal to v (attract) atraer; interesar

appear v parecer

appendix n apéndice m

applicant for a job n candidato m a un puesto de trabajo or -ta

application n 1. aplicación f 2. (request) solicitud f 3. (for a job) solicitud f de trabajo

application form n impreso m de solicitud; formulario m de solicitud

apply v aplicar

apply for v (ask for) solicitar

apply for a job v solicitar un trabajo

apply in writing v solicitar por escrito

apply to v (affect) referirse a

appoint v nombrar

appointment n 1. (job) empleo m 2. (meeting) cita f; compromiso m 3. (to a job) nombramiento m

appointments book n agenda f

appointments vacant n ofertas fpl de trabajo

appreciate v 1. (how good something is) apreciar; valorar 2. (increase in value) subir (en valor)

appreciation n 1. (how good something is) apreciación f; aprecio m; valoración f 2. (in value) aumento m; subida f

apprentice n aprendiz or -za

appropriate adj apropiado or -da ■ v (funds) asignar; consignar

approval n aprobación f

approval: on approval phrase prueba: a prueba

approve the terms of a contract v aprobar los términos de un contrato

approximate adj aproximado or -da

approximately adv aproximadamente

arbitrate v arbitrar

arbitrate in a dispute v arbitrar un litigio; en una disputa

arbitration n arbitraje m

arbitration board, arbitration tribunal n comisión f de arbitraje; tribunal m de arbitraje

arbitrator n árbitro mf

area n 1. área f 2. (of town) distrito m; zona f 3. (region) región f; zona f 4. (subject) campo m

area code n U.K. (for mail) código m postal; código m territorial; (for telephone) prefijo m

area manager n director m regional

argument n discusión f; argumento m

arrange v 1. (meeting) organizar; fijar 2. (set out) ordenar; disponer; acomodar

arrangement n 1. acuerdo m; acomodo m; arreglo m 2. (system) plan m

arrears *npl* atrasos *mpl*
arrival *n* llegada *f*
arrivals *npl* llegadas *fpl*
arrive *v* llegar
article *n* 1. artículo *m* 2. (*clause*) cláusula *f*
articles of association *npl* estatutos *mpl*; escritura *f* de constitución
articulated lorry, articulated vehicle *n* U.K. camión *m* con remolque; camión *m* articulado
asap *abbr* (*as soon as possible*) lo antes posible
ask *v* 1. (*inquire*) preguntar 2. (*request*) pedir
ask for *v* solicitar; pedir
ask for a refund *v* exigir el reembolso
ask for further details, particulars *v* pedir más detalles
as per advice *phrase* según nota de expedición
as per invoice *phrase* según factura
as per sample *phrase* según muestra
assembly *n* 1. asamblea *f*; reunión *f* 2. (*putting together*) montaje *m*
assembly line *n* cadena *f* de montaje
assess *v* valorar; evaluar
assess damages *v* fijar los daños
assessment *n* valoración *f*
assessment of damages *n* valoración *f* de daños
asset *n* activo *m*
assets and liabilities *npl* activo *m* y pasivo *m*
asset value *n* valor *m* de activo
assign *v* asignar
assign a right to someone *v* adjudicar un derecho a alguien
assignee *n* cesionario *or* -ria
assignment *n* 1. asignación *f* 2. (*work*) tarea *f*
assignor *n* cedente *mf*
assist *v* asistir; ayudar
assistance *n* asistencia *f*; ayuda *f*

assistant *n* ayudante *mf*; auxiliar *mf*
assistant manager *n* subdirector *or* -ra
assisted: computer-assisted *phrase* asistido por ordenador
associate *adj* asociado *or* -da; afiliado *or* -da ■ *n* socio *or* -cia
associate company *n* compañía *f* afiliada
association *n* asociación *f*
assurance *n* U.K. seguro *m* (de vida)
assurance company *n* U.K. compañía *f* de seguros
assurance policy *n* U.K. póliza *f* de seguros
assure someone's life *v* U.K. asegurar la vida de alguien
ATM *n* cajero *m* automático
ATM card *n* tarjeta *f* de cajero automático; tarjeta *f* de dinero
attach *v* adjuntar; sujetar
attachment *n* (*email*) adjunto *m*
attack *v* atacar
attend *v* (*meeting*) asistir
attended *adj* asistido *or* -da
attend to *v* ocuparse de
attention *n* atención *f*
attorney *n* apoderado *or* -da; procurador *or* -ra
attract *v* atraer; interesar
attraction *n* atractivo *m*
attractive salary *n* salario *m* interesante
attrition *n* pérdida *f* de trabajadores por jubilación
auction *n* subasta *f* ■ *v* subastar
auction rooms *n* sala *f* de subastas
audit *n* auditoría *f*; intervención *f*; revisión *f* de cuentas ■ *v* auditar; intervenir
auditing *n* auditoría *f*
auditor *n* auditor *m or* -ra; censor *or* -ra; interventor *or* -ra
audit the accounts *v* revisar las cuentas

authenticate *v* autentificar; legalizar

authority *n* autoridad *f*

authorization *n* autorización *f*

authorize *v* autorizar

authorized *adj* autorizado *or* -da

authorize payment *v* autorizar el pago

availability *n* disponibilidad *f*

available *adj* disponible; asequible

available capital *n* capital *m* disponible

average *adj* medio *or* -dia; mediano *or* -na ■ *n* 1. promedio *m* 2. (*insurance*) avería *f* ■ *v* calcular el promedio

average price *n* precio *m* medio; precio *m* corriente

avoid *v* evitar

await instructions *v* esperar instrucciones

award *n* premio *m* ■ *v* conceder; adjudicar; otorgar

award a contract to someone *v* adjudicar un contrato a alguien

B

back *n* dorso *m*; reverso *m*

backdate *v* antedatar

backer *n* garante *mf*

backhander *n* *U.K.* soborno *m*

backing *n* respaldo *m*; apoyo *m* financiero

backlog *n* acumulación *f* de trabajo atrasado

back orders *npl* pedidos *mpl* pendientes

back payment *n* pago *m* atrasado

back tax *n* impuesto *m* atrasado

back up *v* 1. respaldar; apoyar 2. (*computer file*) archivar; guardar

backup *adj* (*computer*) de reserva

backup copy *n* copia *f* de reserva; de seguridad

backwardation *n* margen *m* de cobertura

bad buy *n* mala compra *f*

bad debt *n* deuda *f* morosa; incobrable

bag *n* saco *m*; bolsa *f*

baggage *n* equipaje *m*; maletas *fpl*

baggage check *n* consigna *f*

bail someone out *v* obtener la libertad de alguien bajo fianza

balance *n* 1. equilibrio *m* 2. (*accounts*) balance *m*; saldo *m* ■ *v* 1. equilibrar 2. (*accounts*) cuadrar; saldar

balance brought down, balance brought forward *n* saldo *m*

balance carried down, balance carried forward *n* saldo *m* a cuenta nueva

balance due to us *n* saldo *m* a (nuestro) favor

balance of payments *n* balanza *f* de pagos

balance of trade *n* balanza *f* comercial

balance sheet *n* balance *m* general; de situación

ban *n* prohibición *f* ■ *v* prohibir

bank *n* banco *m* ■ *v* ingresar; depositar

bankable paper *n* efecto *m* negociable

bank account *n* cuenta *f* bancaria

bank balance *n* estado *m* de cuenta

bank base rate *n* tipo *m* base de interés bancario

bank bill *n* 1. *U.K.* letra *f* bancaria; giro *m* bancario 2. billete *m* de banco

bank book *n* libreta *f* de ahorros

bank borrowings *n* préstamos *mpl* bancarios

bank charges *npl* gastos *mpl* bancarios

bank credit *n* crédito *m* bancario

bank deposits *npl* depósitos *mpl* bancarios

bank draft *n* giro *m* bancario

banker *n* banquero *or* -ra

banker's draft *n* giro *m* bancario

banker's order *n* orden *f* de domiciliación (bancaria)

bank holiday *n* fiesta *f* oficial

banking *n* banca *f*

banking hours *npl* horario *m* bancario

bank loan *n* préstamo *m* bancario

bank manager *n* director *m* de banco

banknote *n* billete *m*; billete *m* de banco

bankrupt *adj* en bancarrota; en quiebra; insolvente ■ *n* quebrado *m* ■ *v* arruinar

bankruptcy *n* quiebra *f*; insolvencia *f*; bancarrota *f*

bank statement *n* extracto *m* de cuentas

bank transfer *n* transferencia *f* bancaria

bar chart *n* gráfico *m* de barras

bar code *n* código *m* de barras

bargain *n* 1. (*cheaper than usual*) ganga *f* 2. (*deal*) trato *m*; negocio *m* 3. (*Stock Exchange*) venta *f* en la bolsa ■ *v* negociar; regatear

bargaining *n* negociación *f*

bargaining position *n* postura *f* negociadora

bargaining power *n* poder *m* de negociación

bargain offer *n* oferta *f* de ocasión

bargain price *n* precio *m* de ocasión; precio *m* irrisorio

barrier *n* barrera *f*

barter *n* trueque *m* ■ *v* trocar

bartering *n* trueque *m*; cambio *m* en especie

base *n* base *f* ■ *v* 1. basar 2. (*in a place*) radicar; establecer

base year *n* año *m* base

basic *adj* 1. básico *or* -ca 2. (*most important*) fundamental

basic discount *n* descuento *m* básico

basic tax *n* impuesto *m* básico

basis *n* base *f*

batch *n* 1. (*of orders*) serie *f*; remesa *f*; partida *f* 2. (*of products*) lote *m* ■ *v* agrupar

batch number *n* número *m* de lote

batch processing *n* procesamiento *m* por lotes

bear *n* (*Stock Exchange*) bajista *mf* ■ *v* 1. (*carry*) llevar 2. (*interest*) devengar; rendir 3. (*pay for*) pagar (costes)

bearer *n* portador *or* -ra

bearer bond *n* título *m* al portador

bear market *n* mercado *m* bajista

begin *v* empezar; comenzar

beginning *n* comienzo *m*

beginning inventory *n* existencias *fpl* iniciales

behalf: on behalf of *phrase* nombre: en nombre de

belong to *v* pertenecer

below *prep* abajo

benchmark *n* punto *m* de referencia

beneficiary *n* beneficiario *or* -ria

benefit *n* beneficio *m*; subsidio *m*

benefit from *v* beneficiarse de

berth *n* amarradero *m* ■ *v* atracar

best *adj* lo mejor ■ *n* (el/la) mejor

best-selling car *n* coche *m* en gran demanda

bid *n* oferta *f*; (*at an auction*) puja *f*

bidder *n* postor *m*; licitador *m*

bidding *n* ofertas *fpl*; subasta *f*; licitación *f*

big *adj* grande

bilateral *adj* bilateral

bill *n* 1. (*draft*) letra *f* 2. *U.K.* (*in a restaurant*) cuenta *f* 3. (*in Parliament*) proyecto *m* de ley 4. (*invoice*) factura *f* 5. billete *m*; billete *m* de banco ■ *v* facturar

billboard *n* valla *f* publicitaria; cartelera *f*

billing *n* facturación *f*

billion *n* mil millones *mpl*

bill of exchange *n* letra *f* de cambio

bill of lading *n* conocimiento *m* de embarque

bill of sale *n* contrato *m* de venta

bills for collection *n* letras *fpl* por cobrar

bills payable *n* letras *fpl* a pagar

bills receivable *n* letras *fpl* a cobrar

binding *adj* obligatorio *or* -ria; vinculante

black economy *n* economía *f* sumergida

black list *n* lista *f* negra

blacklist *v* poner en la lista negra

black market *n* mercado *m* negro

blame *n* culpa *f* ■ *v* culpar; echar la culpa

blank *adj* en blanco ■ *n* blanco *m*; espacio *m* en blanco

blank check *n* cheque *m* en blanco

blister pack *n* embalaje *m* de plástico tipo burbuja

block *n* 1. (*building*) manzana *f* 2. (*of shares*) paquete *m* ■ *v* bloquear

block booking *n* reserva *f* en bloque

blocked currency *n* moneda *f* bloqueada

blue chip *n* acción *f* de primera categoría

blue-chip investments *npl* inversiones *fpl* en valores seguros

board *n* (*group of people*) consejo *m* (de administración) ■ *v* abordar; embarcarse

boarding pass *n* tarjeta *f* de embarque

board meeting *n* reunión *f* del consejo de administración

board of directors *n* junta *f* directiva

board: on board *phrase* a bordo

boardroom *n* sala *f* de juntas

bona fide *adj* de buena fe

bond *n* bono *m*; título *m*

bonded warehouse *n* depósito *m* aduanero

bonus *n* prima *f*; bonificación *f*

bonus issue *n* emisión *f* gratuita

book *n* libro *m* ■ *v* reservar

booking *n* reserva *f*

booking clerk *n* taquillero *or* -ra

booking office *n* *U.K.* taquilla *f*; despacho *m* de billetes

bookkeeper *n* contable *mf*

bookkeeping *n* contabilidad *f*

book sales *n* ventas *fpl* registradas

book value *n* valor *m* contable

boom *n* auge *m*; "boom" *m* ■ *v* prosperar; aumentar

boom industry *n* industria *f* próspera; en pleno auge

booming *adj* próspero *or* -ra; floreciente

boost *n* estímulo *m*; impulso *m* ■ *v* estimular; impulsar

border *n* frontera *f*

borrow *v* pedir prestado; tomar prestado

borrower *n* prestatario *or* -ria

borrowing *n* préstamo *m*

borrowing power *n* capacidad *f* de endeudamiento

boss *n* *informal* jefe *or* -fa; amo *m*

bottleneck *n* atasco *m*; embotellamiento *m*

bottom *n* fondo *m*

bottom line *n* saldo *m* final; saldo *m* total

bought ledger *n* *U.K.* libro *m* mayor de compras

bought ledger clerk *n* *U.K.* encargado *m* del libro de compras

bounce *v* (*check*) devolver por falta de fondos

boxed set *n* juego *m* completo en caja de presentación

box number *n* número *m* de apartado de correos

boycott *n* boicot *m* ■ *v* boicotear

bracket n (tax) categoría f; clase f

bracket together v agrupar

brake n freno m

branch n sucursal f; rama f

branch manager n director m de sucursal

branch office n sucursal f

brand n marca f

brand image n imagen f de marca

brand loyalty n fidelidad f a la marca

brand name n marca f comercial; nombre m comercial

brand new adj completamente nuevo or -va

breach of contract n violación f de contrato

breach of warranty n violación f de garantía

break n descanso m ■ v (contract) infringir; incumplir

breakages npl roturas fpl; desperfectos mpl

break an agreement v romper un acuerdo

break down v 1. (itemize) desglosar; detallar 2. (machine) estropearse; averiarse 3. (talks) romperse

breakdown n 1. (items) desglose m 2. (machine) avería f 3. (talks) ruptura f; interrupción f

break even v cubrir gastos

break-even point n punto m muerto

break off negotiations v romper las negociaciones

break the law v infringir la ley

bribe n soborno m ■ v sobornar

brief v informar; dar instrucciones

briefcase n cartera f; maletín m

bring v traer

bring a civil action v constituirse parte civil

bring in v producir

bring out v lanzar al mercado

British adj británico or -ca; inglés or -esa

brochure n folleto m publicitario

broke adj informal sin dinero; arruinado or -da

broker n agente mf; intermediario or -ria

broker's commission, brokerage n corretaje m; comisión f

brown paper n papel m de estraza

bubble pack n embalaje m de plástico tipo burbuja

budget n 1. presupuesto m 2. (government) presupuesto m del Estado ■ v presupuestar

budget account n (in bank) cuenta f presupuestaria

budgetary adj presupuestario or -ria

budgetary control n control m presupuestario

budgetary policy n política f presupuestaria

budgeting n preparación f de presupuestos

build v construir

building v edificio m

building society n U.K. sociedad f hipotecaria; sociedad f de crédito hipotecario

built-in adj incorporado or -da

bulk n volumen m

bulk buying n compra f a granel

bulk shipments npl envíos mpl a granel

bulky adj voluminoso or -sa

bull n (Stock Exchange) alcista mf

bulletin n boletín m

bullion n oro m; plata f en lingotes

bull market n mercado m alcista

bureaucracy n burocracia f

bureau de change n U.K. agencia f de cambio

bus n autobús m

business n 1. negocios mpl 2. (company) empresa f; negocio m 3. (discussion) asunto m

business address n dirección f comercial

business call n visita f de negocios

business card n tarjeta f

business center n centro m comercial

business class n clase f preferente (en aviones)

business equipment n equipos mpl de oficina

business hours npl horas fpl de oficina

business letter n carta f comercial

business lunch n almuerzo m de negocios

businessman n hombre m de negocios

business: on business phrase negocios: por asuntos de negocios

business premises npl local m comercial

business school n escuela f empresarial

business strategy n estrategia f comercial

business transaction n transacción f; trámite m

business trip n viaje m de negocios

businesswoman n mujer f de negocios

busy adj ocupado or -da

buy v comprar; adquirir

buy back v volver a comprar; rescatar

buyer n 1. (for a store) encargado m de compras 2. (person) comprador or -ra

buyer's market n mercado m de compradores

buy for cash v comprar en efectivo; comprar al contado

buy forward v comprar a futuros

buying n compra f

buying department n departamento m de compras

byproduct n subproducto m; producto m derivado

C

cable address n dirección f telegráfica

calculate v calcular

calculation n cálculo m

calculator n calculadora f

calendar n agenda f

calendar month n mes m civil

calendar year n año m civil

call n 1. (for money) demanda f de pago 2. (phone) llamada f 3. (Stock Exchange) petición f de pago (de acciones); demanda f de pago de acciones 4. (visit) visita f ■ v 1. (meeting) convocar (una reunión) 2. (phone) llamar (por teléfono)

callable bond n obligación f redimible

call collect v llamar a cobro revertido

call off a deal v suspender un acuerdo; anular un acuerdo

call on v (visit) visitar

call rate n frecuencia f de visitas de un representante

campaign n campaña f

cancel v cancelar; suspender; anular

cancel a check v anular un cheque

cancel a contract v rescindir un contrato; anular un contrato

canceled adj cancelado or -da

cancellation n 1. cancelación f; anulación f 2. (of an appointment) cancelación f de una cita

cancellation clause n cláusula f de rescisión

candidate n candidato or -ta; aspirante mf

canvass v solicitar votos

canvasser n persona f que busca clientes; solicita votos

canvassing n búsqueda f de clientes; solicitación f de votos

canvassing techniques n técnicas fpl de sondeo

capable adj capaz; competente

capable of adj capaz de

capacity n 1. capacidad f 2. (ability) aptitud f 3. (output) rendimiento m

capacity utilization n empleo m de la capacidad

capital adj capital m ■ n (heritage) patrimonio m

capital account n cuenta f de capital

capital assets npl bienes mpl de capital

capital equipment n bienes mpl de equipo

capital expenditure n gastos mpl de capital

capital gains npl plusvalía f

capital gains tax n impuesto m sobre las plusvalías

capital goods npl bienes mpl de capital

capital-intensive industry n industria f con alto coeficiente de capital

capitalist n capitalista mf

capitalization n capitalización f

capitalization of reserves n capitalización f de las reservas

capitalize v capitalizar

capitalize on v aprovechar

capital loss n pérdidas fpl de capital; minusvalías fpl

captive market n mercado m cautivo

capture v acaparar

carbon copy n copia f carbón

carbonless adj sin papel carbón

carbon paper n papel m carbón

card n 1. (business card) tarjeta f 2. (material) cartulina f 3. (postcard) postal f; tarjeta f postal

cardboard n cartón m

cardboard box n caja f de cartón

card catalog n fichero m

card-index v pasar información a un fichero

card-index file n fichero m de tarjetas

card-indexing n paso m de información a un fichero

card phone n teléfono m de tarjeta

care of adv para entregar a

cargo n carga f

cargo ship n barco m de carga

carnet n (document) carnet m

carriage n U.K. porte m; transporte m

carriage forward n U.K. porte m debido

carriage free adj U.K. franco de porte

carriage paid n U.K. porte m pagado; franco m a domicilio

carrier n 1. empresa f de transportes; transportista mf 2. (vehicle) vehículo m de transporte

carry v 1. llevar; transportar 2. (a motion) aprobar 3. (have in stock) tener en existencia 4. (yield) producir

carry forward v pasar a cuenta nueva

carry on a business v llevar un negocio

carry out v (fulfil) cumplir

carry over a balance v pasar a cuenta nueva

cartel n cartel m

carton n 1. cartón m 2. (box) caja f de cartón

case n 1. (box) caja f 2. (suitcase) maleta f ■ v (put in boxes) poner en una caja; embalar

cash adv en efectivo; al contado ■ n (money) dinero m efectivo

cashable adj cobrable

cash account n cuenta f de caja

cash a check v cobrar un cheque

cash advance n anticipo m de caja a cuenta

cash-and-carry n autoservicio m mayorista

cash balance n saldo m de caja

cash book n libro m de caja

cash card n U.K. tarjeta f de cajero automático; tarjeta f de dinero

cash deal n transacción f en efectivo

cash deposit n imposición f en efectivo

cash desk n caja f

cash discount n descuento m por pago al contado

cash dispenser n U.K. cajero m automático

cash float n fondo m de caja

cash flow n flujo m de caja; "cash flow" m

cash flow statement n estado m de flujo de caja

cashier n cajero or -ra

cashier's check n cheque m de administración

cash in hand n efectivo m en caja

cash offer n oferta f en metálico

cash on delivery n cobro m a la entrega; contra reembolso

cash payment n pago m en efectivo

cash price n precio m al contado

cash purchase n compra f al contado

cash register n caja f registradora

cash reserves n reservas fpl de caja

cash sale n venta f al contado

cash terms npl pago m al contado

cash transaction n operación f al contado

cash voucher n vale m de caja

casting vote n voto m de calidad

casual work n trabajo m eventual

casual worker n trabajador m eventual; temporero or -ra

catalog n catálogo m

catalog price n precio m de catálogo

category n categoría f

cater to v abastecer

caveat emptor phrase por cuenta y riesgo del comprador

ceiling n techo m; límite m

ceiling price n precio m tope; precio m máximo autorizado

cell phone n teléfono m móvil

cellular telephone n teléfono m celular; móvil

center n centro m

central adj central

central bank n banco m central

centralization n centralización f

centralize v centralizar

central purchasing n centralización f de las compras

CEO abbr (chief executive officer) jefe m ejecutivo; director m general

certificate n certificado m

certificated adj titulado or -da; diplomado or -da

certificated bankrupt n quebrado m rehabilitado

certificate of approval n certificado m de aprobación

certificate of deposit n certificado m de depósito

certificate of guarantee n certificado m de garantía

certificate of origin n certificado m de origen

certificate of registration n certificado m de registro

certified accountant n U.K. censor jurado de cuentas

certified check n cheque m conformado

certified copy n compulsa f; copia f auténtica; certificada

certified mail n entrega f con acuse de recibo

certified public accountant n censor jurado de cuentas

certify v certificar

cession n cesión f

chain n cadena f

chain store n tienda f de una cadena; sucursal f

chairman *n* presidente *or* -ta

chairman and managing director *n* presidente y director gerente

Chamber of Commerce *n* Cámara *f* de Comercio

change *n* **1.** cambio *m* **2.** (*cash*) dinero *m* suelto; moneda *f* suelta **3.** (*in a shop*) vuelta *f* ■ *v* cambiar

change hands *v* cambiar de dueño

change machine *n* máquina *f* de cambio

channel *n* canal *m* ■ *v* dirigir; encauzar

channels of distribution *npl* canales *mpl* de distribución

charge *n* **1.** coste *m*; precio *m*; cargo *m* **2.** (*in court*) acusación *f*; cargo *m* **3.** (*on account*) débito *m* ■ *v* **1.** cargar **2.** (*in court*) acusar **3.** (*price*) cobrar

chargeable (to) *adj* a cargo de

charge account *n* cuenta *f* abierta; cuenta *f* de crédito

charge a purchase *v* cargar una compra en cuenta

charge card *n* tarjeta *f* de crédito

charges forward *n* gastos *mpl* a cobrar a la entrega

chart *n* gráfico *m*; gráfica *f*

charter *n* flete *m*; alquiler *m* ■ *v* fletar; alquilar

charter an aircraft *v* fletar un avión

charterer *n* fletador *or* -ra

charter flight *n* vuelo *m* chárter

charter plane *n* avión *m* chárter

chase *v* **1.** perseguir **2.** (*an order*) apremiar

cheap *adj* barato *or* -ta

cheap labor *n* mano *f* de obra barata

cheap money *n* dinero *m* barato; crédito *m* barato

cheap rate *n* tarifa *f* reducida

check *n* **1.** (*examination*) control *m*; comprobación *f* **2.** cheque *m* **3.** (*stop*) freno *m* **4.** (*in a restaurant*)

cuenta *f* ■ *v* **1.** (*examine*) comprobar; cotejar **2.** (*stop*) parar; contener

check account *n* cuenta *f* corriente

check book *n* talonario *m* de cheques

check (guarantee) card *n* tarjeta *f* de crédito

check in *v* **1.** (*at airport*) facturar el equipaje **2.** (*at hotel*) registrarse

check-in (counter) *n* (*at airport*) mostrador *m* de facturación

checking account *n* cuenta *f* corriente

check-in time *n* horario *m* de presentación en el aeropuerto

check number *n* número *m* de cheque

check out *v* (*of hotel*) pagar la cuenta y marcharse

checkout *n* (*in supermarket*) caja *f*

check sample *n* muestra *f* de inspección

check stub *n* matriz *f* de un talonario

check to bearer *n* cheque *m* al portador

cheque *n U.K.* cheque *m*

chief *adj* principal; jefe

chief clerk *n* jefe *m* de oficina

chief executive *n* jefe *m* ejecutivo

choice *adj* escogido *or* -da; selecto *or* -ta ■ *n* **1.** (*choosing*) elección *f*; selección *f* **2.** (*items to choose from*) surtido *m* **3.** (*thing chosen*) preferencia *f*

choose *v* elegir

Christmas bonus *n* paga *f* extraordinaria de Navidad

chronic *adj* crónico *or* -ca; endémico *or* -ca

chronological order *n* orden *m* cronológico

c.i.f. *abbr* (*cost, insurance and freight*) cif

circular *n* circular letter circular *f*

circular letter of credit *n* carta *f* de crédito general

circulation n 1. circulación f; difusión f 2. (*newspaper*) tirada f

city center n centro m de la ciudad

civil law n derecho m civil

civil servant n funcionario or -ria

claim n reclamación f; demanda f; reivindicación f ■ v 1. exigir; reclamar; reivindicar 2. (*suggest*) alegar; pretender

claimant n demandante mf

claims department n departamento m de reclamaciones

claims manager n director m de reclamaciones

clarify v aclarar; clarificar

class n clase f; categoría f

classification n clasificación f

classified ads, advertisements npl anuncios mpl por palabras

classified directory n directorio m comercial

classify v clasificar

clause n cláusula f

clawback n devolución f (de impuestos)

clear adj claro or -ra ■ v 1. aclarar; clarificar 2. (*stock*) liquidar existencias

clear a check v tramitar el pago de un cheque

clear a debt v liquidar una deuda

clearance certificate n certificado m de aduana

clearance of a check n tramitación f del pago de un cheque

clearing n (*paying*) liquidación f de una deuda; pago m de una deuda

clearing bank n banco m comercial

clear profit n ganancia f neta

clerical adj de oficina

clerical error n error m de copia; error m de oficina

clerical staff n personal m de oficina

clerical work n trabajo m de oficina

clerk n oficinista mf; empleado m de oficina

client n cliente mf

clientele n clientela f

climb v subir; aumentar

clinch v cerrar un trato

clipping service n servicio m de recortes de prensa

close n (*end*) cierre m ■ v (*after work*) cerrar

close a bank account v cerrar una cuenta bancaria

close a meeting v clausurar; levantar una sesión

close an account v cerrar una cuenta

closed adj cerrado or -da

closed circuit TV n circuito cerrado

closed market n mercado m cerrado

close down v cerrar

close to adj cercano or -na; próximo or -ma

closing adj final; al cierre ■ n cierre m

closing balance n saldo m final

closing bid n oferta f final

closing date n fecha f tope; fecha f límite

closing-down sale n U.K. liquidación f total por cierre

closing price n precio m al cierre

closing stock n existencias fpl finales

closing time n hora f de cierre

closure n clausura f; cierre m

c/o abbr (*care of*) para entregar a

co-creditor n coacreedor or -ra

COD, c.o.d. abbr (*cash on delivery*) cobro m a la entrega; contra reembolso

code n código m

code of practice n normas fpl de conducta

coding n codificación f

co-director n codirector or -ra

coin n moneda f

co-insurance n coaseguro m

cold call n visita f comercial sin cita previa

cold start v empezar un negocio a cero

cold storage n almacenaje m frigorífico

cold store n almacén m frigorífico

collaborate v colaborar

collaboration n colaboración f

collapse n hundimiento m; derrumbamiento m ■ v hundirse; derrumbarse

collateral adj colateral ■ n garantía f

collect v 1. (fetch) recoger 2. (money) cobrar

collect a debt v cobrar una deuda

collect call n llamada f a cobro revertido

collection n 1. recogida f 2. (of money) cobro m

collection charges, collection rates npl cobro m por recogida

collective adj colectivo or -va

collective ownership n propiedad f colectiva

collective wage agreement n convenio m salarial colectivo

collector n cobrador or -ra; recaudador or -ra

commerce n comercio m

commercial adj comercial ■ n (TV) emisión f publicitaria; anuncio m

commercial attaché n agregado or -da comercial

commercial college n escuela f superior de comercio

commercial course n curso m comercial

commercial directory n guía f comercial

commercial district n distrito m comercial

commercial failure n quiebra f comercial

commercialization n comercialización f

commercialize v comercializar

commercial law n derecho m mercantil

commercial traveler n representante mf

commercial undertaking n empresa f comercial

commission n 1. (committee) comisión f; comité m 2. (money) comisión f

commission agent n comisionista mf

commission rep n representante mf a comisión

commit v (crime) cometer

commit funds to a project v asignar fondos a un proyecto

commitment n compromiso m

commitments npl compromisos mpl

commodity n mercancía f

commodity exchange n lonja f; bolsa f de contratación; de comercio

commodity futures npl materias fpl primas cotizadas en el mercado de futuros

commodity market n lonja f; bolsa f de contratación

common adj 1. (frequent) corriente; frecuente 2. (to more than one) común; público or -ca

common carrier n empresa f de transporte público

Common Market n Mercado Común Europeo

common ownership n propiedad f colectiva

common pricing n fijación f colectiva de precios

communicate v comunicar; comunicarse

communication n 1. comunicación f 2. (message) comunicado m

communications npl comunicaciones fpl

community n comunidad f

commute v 1. (exchange) conmutar 2. (travel) viajar diariamente al trabajo

commuter n viajero diario m; viajera diaria f

companies' register n registro m de compañías

company n compañía f; sociedad f

company director n director m de una empresa

company law n ley f de sociedades anónimas

company secretary n secretario m de una empresa

comparability n posibilidad f de comparación

comparable adj comparable

compare v comparar; cotejar

compare with v comparar con

comparison n comparación f

compensate v compensar; indemnizar; resarcir

compensation n compensación f

compensation for damage n indemnización f por daños y perjuicios

compete (with) v competir (con)

competent adj competente

competing adj competitivo or -va

competing firms npl empresas fpl rivales

competing products n productos mpl en competencia

competition n competencia f

competitive adj competitivo or -va

competitively priced adj con precio competitivo

competitiveness n competitividad f

competitive price n precio m competitivo

competitive pricing n fijación f de precios competitivos

competitive products n productos mpl competitivos

competitor n competidor or -ra

complain (about) v quejarse

complaint n queja f

complaints department n oficina f de reclamaciones

complementary adj complementario or -ria

complete adj completo or -ta ■ v completar; acabar

completion n finalización f

completion date n fecha f de cumplimiento

completion of a contract n firma f de un contrato

compliance n conformidad f; acuerdo m

complimentary adj de favor

complimentary ticket n entrada f de favor

compliments slip n saluda m; tarjeta f de saludo

comply with v obedecer

composition n (with creditors) acomodamiento m

compound interest n interés m compuesto

comprehensive adj completo or -ta; global

comprehensive insurance n seguro m a todo riesgo

compromise n compromiso m; acuerdo m ■ v transigir

compulsory adj obligatorio or -ria

compulsory liquidation n liquidación f forzosa

compulsory purchase n expropiación f forzosa

computer n ordenador m

computer bureau n oficina f de informática

computer department n departamento m de informática

computer error n error m de ordenador

computer file n archivo m; fichero m

computerize v informatizar

computerized adj informatizado or -da; informático or -ca

computer language n lenguaje m informático; de ordenador

computer listing n listado m de ordenador

computer printer n impresora f

computer printout n copia f impresa (de ordenador)

computer program n programa m de ordenador

computer programmer n programador m de ordenadores

computer programming n programación f de ordenador

computer-readable adj legible por ordenador

computer-readable codes npl códigos mpl legibles por ordenador

computer services n servicios mpl de informática

computer system n sistema m informático

computer terminal n terminal m de ordenador

computer time n tiempo m invertido por el ordenador

concealment of assets n encubrimiento m de activos

concern n 1. (business) negocio m; empresa f 2. (worry) preocupación f; inquietud f ■ v (deal with) concernir

concession n 1. (reduction) desgravación f 2. (right) concesión f; agencia f exclusiva

concessionaire n concesionario or -ria

conciliation n conciliación f

conclude v (agreement) concluir

conclusion n conclusión f

condition n condición f

conditional adj condicional

conditions of employment n condiciones fpl de empleo

conditions of sale n condiciones fpl de venta

conduct negotiations v llevar negociaciones

conference n 1. (large) congreso m 2. (small) asamblea f; conferencia f

conference phone n teléfono m de conferencias

conference room n sala f de conferencias

confess v confesar

confidence n confianza f

confidential adj confidencial

confidentiality n confidencialidad f

confidential report n informe m confidencial

confirm v confirmar

confirm a reservation v confirmar una reserva

confirmation n confirmación f

confirm someone in a job v confirmar a alguien en su puesto de trabajo

conflict of interest n conflicto m de intereses

conglomerate n conglomerado m

congress n congreso m

connect v conectar; relacionar

connecting flight n vuelo m de correspondencia

connection n vínculo m; relación f; enchufe m; conexión f

consider v considerar

consign v consignar

consignee n consignatario or -ria

consignment n 1. (sending) consignación f; envío m; expedición f 2. (things sent) envío m; remesa f

consignment note n nota f de expedición; nota f de envío

consignment sale n venta f en depósito

consignor n remitente mf; consignador or -ra

consist of v constar de

consolidate v 1. consolidar 2. (shipments) agrupar

consolidated v consolidado or -da

consolidated shipment n envío m agrupado de mercancías

consolidation n agrupación f

consortium n consorcio m

constant n constante; invariable; continuo or -nua

consult v consultar

consultancy n asesoría f

consultant n asesor or -ra; consejero or -ra

consulting engineer n técnico m asesor; técnica f asesora

consulting firm, consultancy firm n asesoría f; consultoría f

consumables npl bienes mpl de consumo

consumer n consumidor or -ra

consumer credit n crédito m al consumidor

consumer durables npl bienes mpl de consumo duraderos

consumer goods npl bienes mpl de consumo

consumer panel n equipo m de consumidores

consumer price index n índice m de precios al consumo (IPC)

consumer protection n protección f al consumidor

consumer research n investigación f sobre el consumo

consumer spending n gastos mpl del consumidor; gastos mpl de consumo

consumption n consumo m

contact n contacto m; (useful contact) enchufe m ■ v contactar

contain v contener

container n 1. (box, tin) recipiente m; envase m 2. (for shipping) contenedor m

containerization n 1. contenerización f 2. (shipping) transporte m en contenedores

containerize v 1. poner en contenedores 2. (ship in containers) transportar en contenedores

container port n puerto m de contenedores

container ship n buque m de contenedores; portacontenedores

container terminal n terminal f de contenedores

content n significado m

contents n contenido m

contested takeover n oferta f de adquisición disputada; rebatida

contingency n eventualidad f; contingencia f

contingency fund n fondo m para imprevistos

contingency plan n plan m de emergencia

continual adj continuo or -nua

continually adv continuamente

continuation n continuación f

continue v continuar; proseguir

continuous adj continuo or -nua

continuous feed n alimentación f continua

continuous stationery n papel m continuo

contra account n cuenta f compensada

contra an entry v anotar una contrapartida; anotar un contraasiento

contract n contrato m ■ v contratar

contracting party n parte f contratante

contract law n derecho m de contratos; de obligaciones

contract note n contrato m de Bolsa

contract of employment n contrato m de empleo

contractor n contratista mf

contractual adj contractual

contractual liability n responsabilidad f contractual

contractually adv según contrato; por contrato

contract work n trabajo m a contrata

contra entry adv contrapartida f; contraasiento m

contrary adj contrario or -ria

contrast n contraste m

contribute v contribuir; cotizar

contribution n contribución f; colaboración f

contribution of capital n contribución f de capital

contributor n contribuyente mf

control n 1. (check) control m 2. (power) control m; mando m ■ v controlar

control a business v controlar un negocio; dirigir un negocio

control key n tecla f de control

controlled economy n economía f dirigida

controller n 1. (who checks) inspector or -ra 2. contable mf jefe

controlling adj dominante

control systems n sistemas mpl de control

convene v convocar

convenient adj cómodo or -da; conveniente

conversion n conversión f

conversion of funds n apropiación f indebida de fondos

conversion price, conversion rate n precio m de conversión; tasa f de conversión

convert v convertir

convertibility n convertibilidad f

convertible currency n moneda f convertible

convertible loan stock n valores mpl convertibles en acciones

conveyance n transmisión f del título de propiedad

conveyancer n notario m especialista en escrituras de trapaso

conveyancing n transmisión f de títulos de propiedad

cooling off period (after purchase) n periodo m de reflexión

co-operate v cooperar

co-operation n cooperación f

co-operative adj cooperativo or -va ■ n cooperativa f

cooperative society n sociedad f cooperativa

co-opt someone v nombrar por coopción

co-owner n copropietario or -ria

co-ownership n copropiedad f

copartner n socio or -cia

copartnership n coparticipación f

cope v arreglárselas; hacer frente (a)

copier n fotocopiadora f

copy n 1. copia f 2. (book, newspaper) ejemplar m; número m ■ v copiar

corner n 1. (inside angle) rincón m 2. (outside angle) esquina f 3. (monopoly) monopolio

corner store n tienda f de barrio; de la esquina

corner the market v acaparar el mercado

corporate image n imagen f pública de una empresa

corporate name n razón f social

corporate plan n plan m de trabajo de una empresa

corporate planning n planificación f empresarial

corporate profits npl beneficios mpl de la empresa

corporation n corporación f; sociedad f mercantil

corporation tax n impuesto m de sociedades

correct adj correcto or -ta ■ v corregir; rectificar

correction n corrección f; rectificación f

correspondence n correspondencia f

correspondent n 1. (journalist) corresponsal mf 2. (who writes letters) correspondiente mf

correspond with someone v escribir a alguien

correspond with something v corresponder a algo

cost n costo m; coste m ■ v costar; valer

cost, insurance and freight n coste, seguro y flete; cif

cost accountant n contable mf de costes

cost accounting n contabilidad f de costes

cost analysis n análisis m de costes

cost-benefit analysis n análisis m coste-beneficio

cost center n centro m de costes

cost-cutting *n* reducción *f* de costes

cost-effective *adj* rentable

cost-effectiveness *n* rentabilidad *f*

cost factor *n* factor *m* del coste

costing *n* cálculo *m* de costos

costly *adj* costoso *or* -sa

cost of living *n* coste *m* de vida

cost-of-living allowance *n* subsidio *m* de carestía de vida

cost-of-living bonus *n* plus *m* de carestía de vida

cost-of-living increase *n* aumento *m* de sueldo por coste de vida

cost-of-living index *n* índice *m* del coste de vida

cost of sales *n* coste *m* de ventas

cost plus *n* costo *m* más honorarios; porcentaje *m* de comisión

cost price *n* precio *m* de coste

cost-push inflation *n* inflación *f* de costes

costs *npl* costas *fpl*

counsel *n* abogado *or* -da

count *v* (*add*) contar; calcular

counter *n* mostrador *m*; ventanilla *f*

counter-claim *n* reconvención *f* ■ *v* presentar una reconvención

counterfeit *adj* falso *or* -sa; falsificado *or* -da ■ *v* falsificar dinero

counterfoil *n* matriz *f* (de un talonario)

countermand *v* revocar

counter-offer, counterbid *n* contraoferta *f*

countersign *v* refrendar

counter staff *n* personal *m* de atención al público

country *n* **1.** país *m* **2.** (*not town*) campo *m*

country of origin *n* país *m* de origen

coupon *n* cupón *m*

coupon ad *n* cupón *m* de anuncio

courier *n* **1.** (*guide*) guía *mf* de turismo **2.** (*messenger*) mensajero *or* -ra

court *n* tribunal *m*; juzgado *m*

court case *n* proceso *m*; causa *f*; juicio *m*

covenant *n* pacto *m*; convenio *m* ■ *v* pactar

cover *n* **1.** cubierta *f*; funda *f* **2.** (*insurance*) cobertura *f* ■ *v* cubrir

cover a risk *v* cubrir un riesgo

cover charge *n* (*restaurant*) (precio del) cubierto *m*

cover costs *v* cubrir gastos

covering letter *n* carta *f* adjunta; carta *f* explicatoria

covering note *n* carta *f* adjunta; carta *f* explicatoria

cover note *n* póliza *f* provisional; nota *f* de cobertura

crane *n* grúa *f*

crash *n* **1.** (*accident*) choque *m*; colisión *f* **2.** (*financial*) "crack" *m* ■ *v* **1.** chocar **2.** (*fail*) quebrar

crate *n* cajón *m* ■ *v* embalar

credit *n* crédito *m* ■ *v* abonar; acreditar

credit account *n* cuenta *f* de crédito

credit agency *n* agencia *f* de informes comerciales

credit balance *n* haber *m*; saldo *m* acreedor; saldo *m* a favor

credit bank *n* banco *m* de crédito

credit card *n* tarjeta *f* de crédito

credit card sale *n* venta *f* con tarjeta de crédito

credit ceiling *n* techo *m* crediticio

credit column *n* columna *f* del haber

credit control *n* control *m* de crédito

credit entry *n* abono *m*

credit facilities *npl* facilidades *fpl* de crédito

credit freeze *n* congelación *f* de créditos

credit limit *n* límite *m* de crédito

credit note *n* nota *f* de abono; nota *f* de crédito

credit: on credit *phrase* crédito: a crédito

creditor *n* acreedor *or* -ra

credit policy *n* política *f* crediticia

credit rating *n* clasificación *f* crediticia

credit side *v* haber *m*

credit-worthy *adj* solvente

cross a check *v* U.K. cruzar un cheque

crossed check *n* U.K. cheque *m* cruzado

cross off, cross out *v* tachar

cross rate *n* tipo *m* de cambio cruzado

crowd *n* multitud *f*

cubic *adj* cúbico *or* -ca

cubic measure *n* medida *f* de volumen; de capacidad

cum coupon *n* con cupón de interés

cum dividend *adv* con dividendo

cumulative *adj* acumulativo *or* -va

cumulative interest *n* interés *m* acumulativo

cumulative preference share *n* acción *f* preferente acumulativa

currency *n* moneda *f*

currency conversion *n* conversión *f* de divisas

currency note *n* billete *m* de banco

currency reserves *n* reservas *fpl* de divisas

current *adj* actual; corriente

current account *n* U.K. cuenta *f* corriente

current assets *npl* activo *m* circulante

current cost accounting *n* contabilidad *f* de costes actuales

current liabilities *npl* pasivo *m* circulante; obligaciones *fpl* a corto plazo

current price *n* precio *m* actual

current rate of exchange *n* tipo *m* de cambio actual

current yield *n* rendimiento *m* corriente

curriculum vitae *n* U.K. curriculum (vitae) *m*

curve *n* curva *f*

custom *n* clientela *f*

custom-built, custom-made *adj* hecho a medida; a la orden

customer *n* cliente *mf*

customer appeal *n* atractivo *m* para los clientes

customer loyalty *n* fidelidad *f* a un establecimiento

customer satisfaction *n* satisfacción *f* del cliente

customer service department *n* departamento *m* de atención al cliente

customs *n* aduana *f*

Customs and Excise *n* Aduanas y Arbitrios

customs barriers *n* barreras *fpl* arancelarias

customs broker *n* agente *mf* de aduanas

customs clearance *n* despacho *m* aduanero; de aduanas

customs declaration *n* declaración *f* de aduana

customs declaration form *n* impreso *m* de declaración de aduana

customs duty *n* derecho *m* de aduana

customs entry point *n* puesto *m* aduanero

customs examination *n* inspección *f* aduanera

customs formalities *n* formalidades *fpl* aduaneras

customs officer, customs official *n* aduanero *or* -ra; funcionario *f* de aduanas

customs receipt *n* recibo *m* de aduana

customs seal *n* precinto *m* de aduana

customs tariff n arancel m aduanero

customs union n unión f aduanera

cut n recorte m; rebaja f ■ v recortar

cut down on expenses v reducir gastos

cut price n precio m reducido

cut-price adj a precio reducido

cut-price gasoline n gasolina a precio reducido

cut-price goods npl mercancías fpl a precio reducido

cut-price store n tienda f de rebajas

cut-throat competition n competencia f encarnizada

CV abbr (curriculum vitae) curriculum (vitae) m

cycle n ciclo m

cyclical adj cíclico or -a

cyclical factors npl factores mpl cíclicos

D

daily adj diario or -ria

daisy-wheel printer n impresora f de rueda de margarita

damage n daño m ■ v dañar

damaged adj dañado or -da; tarado or -da; deteriorado or -da

damages npl daños mpl y perjuicios

damage survey n inspección f de daños

damage to property n daños mpl materiales

data n datos mpl

database n base f de datos

data processing n elaboración f; proceso m de datos

data retrieval n recuperación f de datos

date n fecha f ■ v fechar

dated adj 1. (with date) con fecha de 2. (old) anticuado or -da

date of receipt n fecha f de recepción

date stamp n fechador m

day n 1. día m 2. (working day) jornada f

day shift n turno m de día

day-to-day adj cotidiano or -na; diario or -ria

DCF abbr (discounted cash flow) cash flow actualizado; flujo de caja descontado

dead adj (person) muerto or -ta; fallecido or -da

dead account n cuenta f inactiva

deadline n fecha f tope; plazo m límite m

deadlock n punto m muerto ■ v estar en punto muerto

dead loss n siniestro m; pérdida f total

deadweight n peso m muerto

deadweight cargo n carga f por peso muerto

deadweight tonnage n toneladas fpl de peso muerto

deal n transacción f; negocio m; trato m

dealer n comerciante mf; tratante mf; concesionario or -a

deal in v comerciar (en); negociar (en)

dealing n (Stock Exchange) operaciones fpl en bolsa

deal with an order v servir un pedido

deal with someone v tratar con alguien; comerciar con alguien

dear adj U.K. caro or -ra

debate n debate m; discusión f

debenture n bono m; pagaré m de interés fijo

debenture holder *n* obligacionista *mf*

debit *n* débito *m*; debe *m*

debit an account *v* adeudar; cargar en cuenta

debit balance *n* saldo *m* deudor

debit column *n* columna *f* del debe

debit entry *n* asiento *m* de débito; adeudo

debit note *n* nota *f* de adeudo

debits and credits *v* debe y haber

debt *n* deuda *f*

debt collection *n* cobro *m* de morosos

debt collection agency *n* agencia *f* de cobro de morosos

debt collector *n* cobrador *m* de morosos

debtor *n* deudor *or* -ra; prestatario *or* -ria

debtor side *n* debe *m*

debts due *n* deudas *fpl* a pagar

decentralization *n* descentralización *f*

decentralize *v* descentralizar

decide *v* decidir; optar

decide on a course of action *v* optar por una línea de conducta

deciding *adj* decisivo *or* -va

deciding factor *n* factor *m* decisivo

decimal *n* decimal *m*

decimal point *n* punto *m* decimal

decision *n* decisión *f*

decision maker *n* persona *f* que toma las decisiones

decision making *n* toma *f* de decisiones

decision-making body *n* órgano *m* decisorio

decision-making processes *n* procesos *mpl* decisorios

deck *n* cubierta *f*

deck cargo *n* carga *f* en cubierta

declaration *n* declaración *f*

declaration of bankruptcy *n* declaración *f* de quiebra

declaration of income *n* declaración *f* de renta

declare *v* declarar; confesar

declared *adj* declarado *or* -da

declared value *n* valor *m* declarado

declare goods to customs *v* declarar mercancías en la aduana

declare someone bankrupt *v* declarar a alguien en quiebra

decline *n* baja *f*; descenso *m* ■ *v* (*fall*) disminuir; bajar

decontrol *v* liberalizar; suprimir controles

decrease *n* descenso *m*; reducción *f*; disminución *f* ■ *v* disminuir; reducir

decrease in price *n* bajada *f* de precio

decrease in value *n* disminución *f* de valor

decreasing *adj* decreciente

deduce *v* deducir

deduct *v* deducir; descontar; rebajar

deductible *adj* deducible

deduction *n* deducción *f*

deed *n* título *m*; escritura *f*

deed of assignment *n* escritura *f* de cesión

deed of covenant *n* escritura *f* de convenio

deed of partnership *n* escritura *f* de sociedad

deed of transfer *n* escritura *f* de transferencia

default *n* incumplimiento *m* ■ *v* incumplir

defaulter *n* deudor *or* -ra

default on payments *v* incumplir los pagos

defect *n* defecto *m*; tara *f*

defective *adj* 1. (*faulty*) defectuoso *or* -sa 2. (*not valid*) defectivo *or* -va

defend *v* defender; proteger

defend a lawsuit *v* defenderse en juicio

defendant *n* demandado *or* -da; acusado *or* -da; parte *f* demandada

defense n defensa f; protección f

defense counsel n abogado m defensor

defer v aplazar; diferir

deferment n aplazamiento m

deferment of payment n aplazamiento m de pago

defer payment v diferir el pago

deferred adj diferido or -da; aplazado or -da

deferred creditor n acreedor m diferido

deferred payment n pago m aplazado

deficit n déficit m

deficit financing n financiación f del déficit presupuestario

deflation n deflación f

deflationary adj deflacionista

defray v (costs) pagar; sufragar

defray someone's expenses v costear los gastos de alguien

delay n demora f; retraso m ■ v demorar; retrasar

del credere n prima f al comisionista

del credere agent n agente mf del credere

delegate n delegado mf or -da ■ v delegar

delegation n delegación f

delete v suprimir

deliver v entregar; repartir

delivered price n precio m de entrega

delivery n entrega f; reparto m

delivery date n fecha f de entrega

deliveryman n recadero m

delivery note n albarán m

delivery of goods n reparto m de mercancías

delivery order n orden f de expedición

delivery time n plazo m de entrega

delivery van, delivery truck n furgoneta f de reparto

demand n 1. demanda f 2. (for payment) reclamación f; requerimiento m de pago ■ v exigir; reclamar

demand deposit n depósito m a la vista

demonstrate v demostrar; mostrar (el funcionamiento de algo)

demonstration n demostración f; prueba f

demonstration model n modelo m de prueba

demonstrator n exhibidor or -ra

demurrage n gastos mpl de demora

department n 1. departamento m; sección f 2. (in government) Departamento m de Estado; ministerio m 3. (in shop) sección (de tienda)

departmental adj departamental

departmental manager n jefe m de departamento or -fa; jefe m de sección or -a

department store n grandes almacenes mpl

departure n 1. (going away) salida f 2. (new venture) novedad f

departure lounge n sala f de embarque

departures n salidas fpl

depending on adv según

depend on v depender de

deposit n 1. (in bank) depósito m; ingreso m; imposición f 2. (paid in advance) depósito m; señal f; entrada f ■ v depositar; ingresar

deposit account n cuenta f de depósito; cuenta f a plazo

depositor n depositante mf; impositor or -ra

depository n (place) almacén m

deposit slip n recibo m (de depósito)

depot n almacén m central; centro m de transporte

depreciate v 1. (amortize) amortizar; depreciar 2. (lose value) depreciarse; perder valor

depreciation n 1. (amortizing) amortización f; depreciación f 2.

(*loss of value*) depreciación *f*; pérdida *f* de valor

depreciation rate *n* coeficiente *m* de amortización; tasa *f* de amortización

depression *n* depresión *f*; crisis *f* económica

dept *abbr* (*department*) dpto. (= departamento)

deputize for someone *v* sustituir a alguien

deputy *n* delegado *mf or* -da; adjunto *or* -ta; suplente *mf*

deputy manager *n* subdirector *or* -ra; director *m* adjunto

deputy managing director *n* director *m* general adjunto

deregulation *n* liberalización *f*; desregulación *f*

describe *v* describir; exponer

description *n* descripción *f*

design *n* diseño *m* ■ *v* diseñar; proyectar

design department *n* departamento *m* de diseño

desk *n* escritorio *m*; mesa *f* de despacho

desk diary *n* agenda *f* de mesa (de despacho)

desk-top publishing *n* autoedición *f*; publicación *f* asistida por ordenador

destination *n* destino *m*

detail *n* detalle *m* ■ *v* detallar

detailed *adj* detallado *or* -da

detailed account *n* cuenta *f* detallada; factura *f* detallada

determine *v* determinar

deutsche mark *n* marco *m* alemán

devaluation *n* devaluación *f*; desvalorización *f*

devalue *v* devaluar; desvalorizar

develop *v* 1. (*build*) construir 2. (*plan*) desarrollar

developing country *n* país *m* en vías de desarrollo

development *n* desarrollo *m*

device *n* aparato *m*; dispositivo *m*; estratagema *f*

diagram *n* diagrama *m*

dial *v* marcar

dial a number *v* marcar un número

dial direct *v* marcar directamente

dialing *n* acto *m* de marcar

dialling code *n* U.K. prefijo *m*

dial tone *n* señal *f* de línea

diary *n* U.K. agenda *f*

dictate *v* dictar

dictating machine *n* dictáfono *m*

dictation *n* dictado *m*

differ *v* diferir; ser distinto

difference *n* diferencia *f*

differences in price *n* diferencias *fpl* de precio

different *adj* distinto *or* -ta; diferente

differential *adj* diferencial

differential tariffs *n* tarifas *fpl* diferenciadas

difficult *adj* difícil

difficulty *n* dificultad *f*

digit *n* dígito *m*

dilution of equity *n* dilución *f* del capital

dimensions *npl* dimensiones *fpl*

direct *adj* directo *or* -ta ■ *adv* directamente ■ *v* dirigir

direct cost *n* coste *m* directo

direct debit *n* domiciliación *f* bancaria

direction *n* dirección *f*

directions for use *npl* instrucciones *fpl*; modo *m* de empleo

directive *n* directriz *f*; directiva *f*; instrucción *f*

direct mail *n* venta *f* por correo

direct-mail advertising *n* publicidad *f* por correo

direct mailing *n* envío *m* de publicidad por correo

director *n* director *or* -ra; consejero *or* -ra

directory *n* directorio *m*

direct selling *n* venta *f* directa

direct tax *n* impuesto *m* directo

direct taxation n imposición f directa

disagreement n desacuerdo m

disburse v desembolsar

disbursement n desembolso m

discharge n (of debt) pago m; descargo m ■ v (employee) despedir

discharge a debt v pagar una deuda

disclaimer n renuncia f; abandono m de responsabilidad

disclose v revelar; divulgar

disclose a piece of information v revelar una información

disclosure n divulgación f; revelación f

disclosure of confidential information n revelación f de información confidencial

discontinue v suspender; interrumpir

discount n descuento m; rebaja f ■ v descontar

discountable adj descontable

discounted cash flow n cash flow actualizado; flujo m de caja descontado

discounter n banco m de descuento

discount house n 1. (bank) banco m de descuento 2. (store) tienda f de rebajas

discount price n precio m de descuento

discount rate n tipo m; tasa f de descuento

discount store n tienda f de rebajas

discredit v desacreditar

discrepancy n discrepancia f; diferencia f

discuss v discutir

discussion n discusión f; debate m

dishonor v deshonorar

dishonor a bill v devolver una letra

disk n disco m

disk drive n disquetera f

diskette n disquete m; diskette

dismissal n despido m

dismiss an employee v despedir a un empleado

dispatch n 1. (goods sent) envío m 2. (sending) despacho m; envío m ■ v enviar; consignar; despachar; expedir

dispatch department n oficina f de expedición

dispatch note n nota f de expedición; de envío

display n exposición f; exhibición f ■ v exhibir; exponer

display case n vitrina f

display material n material m de exposición

display pack n embalaje m de exposición

display stand, display unit n estantería f; vitrina f de exposición

disposable v desechable; de usar y tirar

disposal n venta f

dispose of excess stock v deshacerse de las existencias sobrantes; vender las existencias sobrantes

dissolve v disolver

dissolve a partnership v disolver una sociedad

distressed merchandise n efectos mpl embargados (vendidos a bajo precio)

distress sale n venta f forzosa; remate m

distributable profit n beneficios mpl distribuibles

distribute v distribuir; repartir

distribution n distribución f; reparto m

distribution channels npl canales mpl de distribución

distribution costs npl costes mpl de distribución

distribution manager n jefe m de distribución

distribution network n red f de distribución

distributor n distribuidor or -ra

distributorship n distribución f exclusiva

district n distrito m

diversification n diversificación f

diversify v diversificar

divide v dividir

dividend n dividendo m

dividend cover n cobertura f del dividendo

dividend warrant n cheque m en pago de dividendos

dividend yield n rentabilidad f del dividendo

division n 1. (part of a company) sección f; departamento m 2. (part of a group) división f; sucursal f

do v hacer

do business with v comerciar con

dock n muelle m; dique m ■ v 1. (remove money) deducir del sueldo; descontar del sueldo 2. (ship) entrar en dársena; atracar

docket n lista f del contenido de un paquete

doctor's certificate n parte f de baja

document n documento m

documentary adj documental

documentary evidence n pruebas fpl documentales

documentary proof n prueba f documentada

documentation n documentación f

documents npl documentos mpl

dollar n dólar m

dollar area n zona f del dólar

dollar balance n reserva f en dólares

dollar crisis n crisis f del dólar

domestic adj interior; nacional

domestic market n mercado m interior; mercado m nacional

domestic production n producción f interior; producción f nacional

domestic sales n ventas fpl nacionales

domestic trade n comercio m interior

domicile n domicilio m

door n puerta f

door-to-door adj de puerta en puerta; a domicilio

door-to-door salesman n vendedor m a domicilio

door-to-door selling n venta f a domicilio

dossier n expediente m

dot-matrix printer n impresora f matricial

double adj doble ■ v duplicar; duplicarse

double book v reservar la misma plaza a dos personas

double booking n doble reserva f

double taxation n doble imposición f

double taxation agreement n acuerdo m de doble imposición

down prep abajo

down-market adj dirigido a un mercado popular

down payment n entrada f; depósito m; pago m inicial

downside factor n factor m de riesgo (en una inversión)

down time n tiempo m muerto

downtown adv en el centro de la ciudad; hacia el centro ■ n centro m de la ciudad

downturn n descenso m

downward adv hacia abajo

dozen n docena f

draft n 1. (money) letra f; giro m 2. (rough plan) borrador m; proyecto m ■ v hacer un borrador; redactar

draft a contract v redactar un contrato

draft a letter v redactar una carta

draft plan, draft project n anteproyecto m

draw v 1. (a check) girar 2. (money) sacar

drawee n librado or -da

drawer n librador or -ra

drawing account n cuenta f corriente

draw up v preparar; redactar

draw up a contract v preparar un contrato; redactar un contrato

drive n 1. (*energy*) energía f; empuje m 2. (*part of machine*) motor m ■ v (*a car*) conducir

driver n conductor m; chófer m

drop n caída f; baja f ■ v descender; bajar; caer

drop in sales n caída f de las ventas

DTP abbr (*desk-top publishing*) autoedición f; publicación f asistida por ordenador

due adj 1. (*awaited*) que está por llegar 2. (*owing*) debido or -da; vencido or -da

dues npl (*orders*) pedidos mpl por servir

dull adj átono or -na

duly adv 1. (*in time*) oportunamente 2. (*legally*) debidamente

dummy n producto m ficticio

dummy pack n embalaje m vacío; ficticio

dump bin n caja f de artículos sueltos para la venta

dump goods on a market v practicar el "dumping"

dumping n "dumping" m

duplicate n duplicado m; copia f ■ v copiar; duplicar

duplicate an invoice v copiar una factura

duplicate of a receipt n duplicado m de una factura

duplicate receipt n factura f por duplicado

duplication n duplicación f

durables npl bienes mpl duraderos

duty n 1. (*obligation*) obligación f 2. (*tax*) impuestos mpl; arancel m

duty-free adj libre de impuestos

duty-free store n tienda f libre de impuestos

duty-paid goods npl mercancías fpl con impuestos aduaneros pagados

E

e. & o.e. salvo error u omisión

early adj pronto; temprano

earmark funds for a project v asignar fondos a un proyecto

earn v 1. ganar 2. (*interest*) devengar

earning capacity n escala f de rendimiento

earnings npl 1. ingresos mpl 2. (*profit*) ganancias fpl; beneficios mpl

earnings per share, earnings yield n dividendo m por acción

easy adj fácil

easy terms npl facilidades fpl de pago

e-commerce n comercio m electrónico

economic adj económico or -ca

economical adj económico or -ca

economic cycle n ciclo m económico

economic development n desarrollo m económico

economic growth n crecimiento m económico

economic indicators npl indicadores mpl económicos

economic model n modelo m económico

economic planning n planificación f económica

economics n economía f

economic system n sistema m económico

economic trends n tendencias fpl económicas

economies of scale n economías fpl de escala

economist n economista mf

economize v economizar

economy n 1. economía f 2. (system) sistema m económico

economy class n clase f económica; clase f turista

effect n efecto m ■ v efectuar

effective adj efectivo or -va

effective date n fecha f de entrada en vigor

effective demand n demanda f efectiva

effectiveness n eficiencia f; eficacia f

effective yield n rendimiento m efectivo

efficiency n eficiencia f; eficacia f

efficient adj eficaz; eficiente

effort n esfuerzo m

elasticity n elasticidad f

elect v elegir

election n elección f

electronic mail n correo m electrónico

electronic point of sale n puntos mpl de venta electrónicos

elevator n 1. (goods) montacargas m 2. (grain) elevador m de granos

email n (message) correo m electrónico; e-mail ■ v mandar por correo electrónico; mandar por e-mail

embargo n embargo m; prohibición f ■ v embargar; prohibir

embark v embarcar

embarkation n embarque m

embarkation card n tarjeta f de embarque

embark on v embarcarse en

embezzle v malversar; desfalcar

embezzlement n malversación f; desfalco m

embezzler n malversador or -ra; desfalcador or -ra

emergency n emergencia f; urgencia f

emergency reserves n reservas fpl para imprevistos

employ v emplear; dar empleo

employed n 1. (in job) empleado or -da 2. (used) en uso; utilizado or -da

employee n empleado or -da

employer n empresario or -ria

employment n empleo m; ocupación f

employment agency, employment bureau n oficina f de colocación

empty adj vacío or -cía ■ v vaciar

EMS abbr (European Monetary System) SME (Sistema Monetario Europeo)

encash v U.K. hacer efectivo; cobrar

encashment n U.K. cobro m en metálico

enclose v adjuntar; remitir adjunto

enclosure n documento m adjunto

end n fin m; final m ■ v terminar; finalizar

end of season sale n rebajas fpl de fin de temporada

endorse a check v endosar un cheque

endorsee n endosatario or -ria

endorsement n 1. (action) endoso m 2. (on insurance) suplemento m de póliza

endorser n endosante mf

end product n producto m final

end user n usuario m final

energy n 1. (electricity) energía f 2. (human) energía f; vigor m

energy-saving adj que ahorra energía

enforce v hacer cumplir; ejecutar

enforcement n ejecución f

engaged adj 1. ocupado or -da 2. (telephone) (línea) ocupada

engaged tone n señal f de comunicar

English adj inglés or -esa

enter v 1. (go in) entrar en 2. (write in) inscribir

entering n entrada f; inscripción f

enter into v (discussion) entablar

enterprise n empresa f
entitle v autorizar
entitlement n derecho m
entrance n entrada f
entrepot port n puerto m distribuidor
entrepreneur n empresario or -ria
entrepreneurial adj empresarial
entrust v encargar; confiar
entry n 1. (going in) ingreso m; entrada f 2. (to market) acceso m 3. (writing) asiento m; anotación f
entry visa n visado m de entrada
environmentally friendly adj ecológico
epos, EPOS abbr (electronic point of sale) puntos mpl de venta electrónicos
equal adj igual ■ v igualar; ser igual a
equality n igualdad f
equalization n equiparación f
equip v equipar
equipment n equipo m
equities npl títulos mpl; acciones fpl ordinarias
equity n beneficios mpl; participación f de beneficios
equity capital n capital m en acciones
erode v erosionar; desgastar
erroneous adj erróneo or -nea
error n error m; equivocación f
error rate n coeficiente m de errores; tasa f de errores
errors and omissions excepted salvo error u omisión
escalate v escalar
escape clause n cláusula f de excepción
escrow account n cuenta f de garantía bloqueada
escudo n (Portuguese currency) escudo m
essential adj esencial; imprescindible
establish v establecer; consolidar

establishment n 1. (business) establecimiento m 2. (staff) personal m; plantilla f
estimate n 1. (calculation) estimación f; cálculo m; valoración f 2. (quote) presupuesto m ■ v estimar; calcular; valorar
estimated adj estimado or -da
estimated figures npl cifras fpl estimadas
estimated sales n ventas fpl estimadas
estimation n estimación f; valoración f
EU abbr (European Union) UE (= Unión Europea)
euro n euro m
Eurocheque n eurocheque m
Eurocurrency n eurodivisa f
Eurodollar n eurodólar m
Euromarket n euromercado m
European adj europeo or -a
European Investment Bank (EIB) n Banco Europeo de Inversiones (BEI)
European Monetary System (EMS) n Sistema Monetario Europeo (SME)
European Union (EU) n Unión Europea (UE)
eurozone n zona f euro
evade v evadir; eludir
evade tax v evadir impuestos
evaluate v evaluar; calcular
evaluate costs v evaluar los costes
evaluation n evaluación f
evasion n evasión f; elusión f
exact adj exacto or -ta
exactly adv exactamente
examination n 1. (inspection) examen m; registro m; inspección f 2. (test) examen m
examine v examinar
exceed v exceder; sobrepasar; superar
excellent adj excelente
except prep excepto; salvo
exceptional adj excepcional

exceptional items *npl* partidas *fpl* excepcionales

excess *n* exceso *m*; excedente *m*

excess baggage *n* exceso *m* de equipaje

excess capacity *n* exceso *m* de capacidad

excessive *adj* excesivo *or* -va

excessive costs *npl* costes *mpl* excesivos

excess profits *npl* beneficios *mpl* extraordinarios

exchange *n* cambio *m*; intercambio *m* ■ *v* **1.** (*currency*) cambiar divisas; moneda extranjera **2.** (*one thing for another*) canjear; intercambiar

exchangeable *adj* intercambiable; cambiable

exchange control *n* control *m* de divisas

exchange rate *n* tipo *m* de cambio; tasa *f* de cambio

Exchequer *n* ministerio *m* de Hacienda

excise *v* (*cut out*) extirpar; suprimir

excise duty *n* impuesto *m* sobre el consumo

Excise officer *n* recaudador *m* de impuestos *or* -ra

exclude *v* excluir

excluding *prep* excepto; con excepción de

exclusion *n* exclusión *f*

exclusion clause *n* cláusula *f* de exclusión

exclusive agreement *n* contrato *m* en exclusiva

exclusive of *phrase* no incluido

exclusive of tax *n* impuesto *m* no incluido

exclusivity *n* exclusividad *f*

ex coupon *adj* sin cupón de interés

ex-directory *adj* U.K. que no figura en la guía telefónica

ex dividend *adv*, *adj* sin dividendo

execute *v* ejecutar; cumplir

execution *n* ejecución *f*; cumplimiento *m*

executive *adj* ejecutivo *or* -va ■ *n* ejecutivo *or* -va

executive director *n* director *m* ejecutivo

exempt *adj* exento *or* -ta ■ *v* eximir

exempt from tax *adj* exento de impuestos *or* -ta

exemption *n* exención *f*

exemption from tax *n* exención fiscal

exercise *n* ejercicio *m* ■ *v* ejercer

exercise an option *v* ejercer derecho de opción

exercise of an option *n* ejercicio *m* del derecho de opción

exhibit *v* exponer

exhibition *n* exhibición *f*; exposición *f*

exhibition hall *n* salón *m*; sala *f* de exposiciones

exhibitor *n* expositor *or* -ra

expand *v* ampliar; expandir

expansion *n* expansión *f*; ampliación *f*

expenditure *n* gasto *m*; desembolso *m*

expense *n* gasto *m*

expense account *n* cuenta *f* de gastos de representación

expenses *npl* gastos *mpl*

expensive *adj* caro *or* -ra; costoso *or* -sa

experienced *adj* experto *or* -ta; experimentado *or* -da

expertise *n* pericia *f*; competencia *f*

expiration *n* expiración *f*; terminación *f*; vencimiento *m*

expiration date *n* fecha *f* de caducidad

expire *v* caducar; expirar; vencer

expiry *n* caducidad *f*; expiración *f*; vencimiento *m*

expiry date *n* U.K. fecha *f* de caducidad

explain *v* explicar

explanation n explicación f; aclaración f

exploit v explotar; aprovechar

explore v explorar

export n exportación f; mercancía f exportada ■ v exportar

export department n departamento m de exportación

export duty n derechos mpl de exportación

exporter n exportador or -ra

exporting adj de exportación; exportador or -ra

export license, export permit n licencia f de exportación; permiso m de exportación

export manager n director m de exportación

exports npl exportaciones fpl

export trade n comercio m de exportación

exposure n exposición f; riesgo m

express adj 1. (fast) rápido or -da; urgente 2. (stated clearly) expreso or -sa ■ v 1. (send fast) enviar por correo; transporte urgente 2. (state) expresar

express delivery n entrega f urgente

express letter n carta f urgente

extend v 1. extender; ampliar 2. (grant) conceder 3. (make longer) prolongar; prorrogar

extended credit n crédito m a largo plazo

extension n 1. ampliación f; prolongación f; prórroga f 2. (telephone) extensión f

external adj 1. (foreign) exterior 2. (outside a company) externo or -na

external account n cuenta f de no residente

external audit n auditoría f externa

external auditor n auditor m externo

external trade n comercio m exterior

extra adj extra; no incluido

extra charges npl gastos mpl adicionales y complementarios

extraordinary adj extraordinario or -ria

extraordinary items npl partidas fpl extraordinarias

extras npl gastos mpl aparte; extras mpl

F

face value n valor m nominal

facilities npl instalaciones fpl; medios mpl

facility n 1. facilidad f 2. (building) edificio m

factor n 1. (influence) factor m; elemento m 2. (person, company) comisionista mf al por mayor ■ v gestionar deudas con descuento

factoring n gestión f de deudas con descuento

factoring charges npl coste m de la gestión de deudas

factors of production n factores mpl de producción

factory n fábrica f

factory inspector n inspector m de fábrica

factory outlet n tienda f de fábrica

factory price n precio m de fábrica

fail v 1. (go bust) quebrar 2. (to do something) dejar de hacer algo 3. (not to succeed) fallar; fracasar

failing that phrase en su defecto

failure n fracaso m

fair adj justo or -ta; equitativo or -va ■ n feria f

fair dealing n prácticas fpl comerciales justas

fair price n precio m justo

fair trade n política f comercial de reciprocidad arancelaria

fair trading n prácticas fpl comerciales justas

fair wear and tear n U.K. desgaste m natural

fake n falsificación f; imitación f ■ v falsificar; fingir

faked documents n documentos mpl falsos

fall n caída f; baja f ■ v (go lower) bajar; caer

fall behind v 1. (be in a worse position) quedarse atrás 2. (be late) retrasarse

fall due v vencer

falling adj decreciente; con tendencia a la baja

fall off v disminuir; bajar

fall through v venirse abajo

false adj falso or -sa; falseado or -da

false pretenses npl medios mpl fraudulentos

false weight n peso m escaso

falsification n falsificación f

falsify v falsificar

fame n fama f

family company n empresa f familiar

FAO abbr (for the attention of) a la atención de

fare n billete m; pasaje m

farm out work v mandar trabajo fuera

fast adj rápido or -da ■ adv rápidamente

fast-selling items npl artículos mpl de fácil venta

fault n 1. (blame) culpa f; falta f 2. (mechanical) defecto m; fallo m; tara f

faulty equipment n equipo m defectuoso

favorable adj favorable; propicio or -cia

favorable balance of trade n balanza f comercial favorable

fax n telefax m; fax m ■ v enviar por fax

feasibility n factibilidad f; viabilidad f

feasibility report n informe m de viabilidad (de un proyecto)

fee n 1. (admission) cuota f; derechos mpl 2. (for services) honorarios mpl; emolumentos mpl

feedback n reacción f; respuesta f

ferry n transbordador m; "ferry" m

fiddle n trampa f; timo m ■ v embaucar; falsificar; falsear

field n campo m

field sales manager n jefe m de equipo de ventas

field work n trabajo m de campo; estudios mpl sobre el terreno

FIFO abbr (first in first out) primeras entradas, primeras salidas

figure n cifra f

file n 1. archivo m; fichero m 2. (computer) ficha f de ordenador 3. (documents) expediente m ■ v 1. archivar 2. (register) presentar

file a patent application v solicitar una patente

file documents v archivar documentos

filing cabinet n archivador m

filing card n ficha f de registro

fill a gap v llenar; ocupar un vacío

final adj último or -ma; final

final demand n último requerimiento de pago

final discharge n descargo m final

final dividend n dividendo m final

finalize v finalizar

finance n finanzas fpl ■ v financiar

finance an operation v financiar una operación

finance company n sociedad f financiera

finance director n director m de finanzas

finances npl finanzas fpl

financial adj financiero or -ra

financial asset n activo m financiero

financial crisis n crisis f financiera

financial institution n institución f financiera

financially adj financieramente

financial position n situación f financiera

financial resources n recursos mpl financieros

financial risk n riesgo m financiero

financial settlement n ajuste m financiero

financial year n ejercicio m económico; año m fiscal

financing n financiación f; financiamiento m

find v encontrar

fine adv 1. (very good) muy bien 2. (very small) en trozos pequeños ■ n multa f ■ v multar

fine tuning n ajuste m fino

finished adj acabado or -da; terminado or -da

finished goods n productos mpl acabados

fire n fuego m; incendio m

fire damage n daños mpl causados por incendio

fire-damaged goods npl mercancías fpl dañadas por un incendio

fire insurance n seguro m contra incendios

fire regulations n reglamento m sobre incendios

fire risk n peligro m de incendio

firm adj firme ■ n empresa f; firma f ■ v afirmar

firm price n precio m en firme

first adj primero or -ra

first-class adj de primera clase; excelente

first in first out phrase primeras entradas, primeras salidas

first option n primera opción

first quarter n primer trimestre

fiscal adj fiscal

fiscal measures npl medidas fpl fiscales

fittings npl accesorios mpl

fix v 1. (arrange) fijar 2. (mend) arreglar

fix a meeting for 3 p.m. v fijar una reunión para las 3 de la tarde

fixed adj fijo or -ja

fixed assets npl activo m fijo

fixed costs npl costes mpl fijos

fixed deposit n depósito m a plazo fijo

fixed exchange rate n cambio m fijo

fixed income n renta f fija

fixed interest n interés m fijo

fixed-interest investments npl inversiones fpl de interés fijo

fixed-price agreement n acuerdo m a tanto alzado

fixed scale of charges n lista f de precios fija

fixed-term contract n contrato m de plazo fijo

fixing n fijación f

flat adj 1. (dull) átono or -na 2. (fixed) fijo or -ja; uniforme ■ n piso m; apartamento m

flat rate n tanto m alzado; porcentaje m fijo

flexibility n flexibilidad f

flexible adj flexible

flexible prices n precios mpl flexibles

flexible pricing policy n política f de precios flexibles

flight n 1. vuelo m 2. (of money) fuga f

flight information n información f de vuelos

flight of capital n evasión f de capital(es); fuga f de capital(es)

flip chart n tablero m de hojas sueltas

float n 1. (*money*) fondo m de caja 2. (*of company*) lanzamiento m; flotación f ■ v (*a currency*) (hacer) flotar una divisa

float a company v U.K. fundar una compañía

floating adj flotante

floating exchange rates n tipos mpl de cambio flotantes

floating of a company n U.K. lanzamiento m de una sociedad

flood n inundación f ■ v inundar; desbordar

floor n 1. suelo m 2. (*level*) piso m

floor manager n director m de planta

floor plan n planta f

floor space n superficie f útil

flop n fracaso m ■ v fracasar

flotation n U.K. lanzamiento m de una nueva compañía

flourish v florecer; prosperar

flourishing adj floreciente; próspero or -ra

flourishing trade n comercio m floreciente; próspero

flow n flujo m ■ v fluir; discurrir

flow chart n organigrama m; diagrama m de flujo

flow diagram n diagrama m de flujos; organigrama m

fluctuate v fluctuar; oscilar

fluctuating v fluctuante

fluctuation n fluctuación f; oscilación f

FOB, f.o.b. franco a bordo

follow v seguir

follow up v perseguir; investigar

follow-up letter n carta f de reiteración

forbid v prohibir

forced adj a la fuerza

forced sale n venta f forzosa

force majeure n fuerza f mayor

force prices down v hacer bajar los precios

force prices up v hacer subir los precios

forecast n previsión f; pronóstico m ■ v pronosticar; prever; predecir

forecasting n previsión f

foreign adj extranjero or -ra

foreign currency n moneda f extranjera

foreign exchange n 1. (*changing money*) cambio m de moneda extranjera 2. (*currency*) divisas fpl

foreign exchange broker, dealer n operador m de cambios

foreign exchange market n mercado m de divisas

foreign investments npl inversiones fpl exteriores

foreign money order n giro m postal internacional

foreign trade n comercio m exterior

foresee v prever

forfeit n decomiso m; confiscación f ■ v decomisar; perder el derecho a

forfeit a deposit v perder un depósito

forfeiture n decomiso m; confiscación f

forge v falsificar

forgery n 1. (*action*) falsificación f 2. (*copy*) documento m falso; copia f falsa

fork-lift truck n carretilla f elevadora de horquilla

form n impreso m; formulario m ■ v formar

formal adj formal

formality n formalidad f; trámite m

form of words n fórmulas fpl judiciales

for sale phrase en venta

forward adv a plazo; en fecha futura

forward buying n compra f de futuros

forward contract n contrato m a plazo fijo

forwarding n expedición f; envío m

forwarding address n dirección f de reenvío

forwarding agent n agente mf expedidor or -ra

forwarding instructions npl instrucciones fpl de envío

forward market n mercado m a futuros

forward rate n tipo m de cambio para operaciones a plazo

forward sales n ventas fpl a plazo

fourth quarter n cuarto trimestre

fragile adj frágil

frame n marco m

franc n franco m

franchise n franquicia f; concesión f ■ v franquiciar

franchisee n concesionario or -ria

franchiser n franquiciador or -ra

franchising n franquicia f; concesión f

franco adj franco; libre

frank v franquear

franking machine n máquina f franqueadora

fraud n fraude m; defraudación f; estafa f

fraudulent adj fraudulento or -ta

fraudulently adv fraudulentamente

fraudulent transaction n operación f fraudulenta

free adj 1. libre 2. (no payment) gratuito or -ta; gratis; franco 3. (not occupied) vacante ■ adv (no payment) gratuitamente; gratis ■ v poner en libertad; liberar

free delivery n entrega f gratuita

free gift n regalo m; obsequio m

freelance adj de libre dedicación ■ n **freelancer** trabajador m por libre

free market economy n economía f de libre mercado

free of charge adj gratis

free of duty adj libre de derechos de aduana

free of tax adj libre de impuestos

free on board adj franco a bordo

free on rail adj, adv franco sobre vagón; franco vagón FF.CC.

free port n puerto m franco

free sample n muestra f gratuita

free trade n libre cambio; libre comercio

free trade area n zona f de libre cambio

free trade zone n zona f franca

free trial n prueba f gratuita

freeze n congelación f ■ v (prices) congelar

freeze credits v bloquear los créditos

freeze wages and prices v congelar salarios y precios

free zone n zona f franca

freight n (carriage) flete m; transporte m; porte m

freightage n flete m; fletamento m

freight collect n porte m debido

freight costs npl gastos mpl de transporte

freight depot n estación f de mercancías

freighter n 1. (plane) avión m de carga 2. (ship) buque m de carga

freight forward n porte m debido

freight free adj franco de porte

freightliner n tren m de mercancías de contenedores

freight paid n porte m pagado; franco m a domicilio

freight plane n avión m de carga

freight rates n precio m de transporte; tarifas fpl de flete

freight train n tren m de mercancías

frequent adj frecuente; corriente

frozen adj bloqueado or -da; congelado or -da

frozen account n cuenta f bloqueada

frozen assets npl activo m congelado

frozen credits npl crédito m congelado

fulfill v (carry out) cumplir

fulfill an order v despachar un pedido

fulfillment n cumplimiento m; realización f

full adj lleno or -na

full discharge of a debt n pago m total de una deuda

full payment n pago m íntegro

full price n precio m sin descuento

full refund n reembolso m total

full-scale adj completo or -ta; general

full-time adj a tiempo completo; en plena dedicación

full-time employment n trabajo m a tiempo completo

fund n fondo m ■ v financiar; asignar fondos

fundamental adj fundamental

funding n 1. (of debt) consolidación f de fondos 2. (financing) financiación f; asignación f de fondos

further to phrase con relación a

future delivery n entrega f futura

futures npl futuros mpl

G

gain n 1. (becoming bigger) aumento m 2. (increase in value) ganancia f; beneficio m ■ v 1. (become bigger) aumentar 2. (get) ganar

game n fuego m

gap n hueco m; vacío m

gap in the market n hueco m en el mercado

GDP abbr (gross domestic product) PIB (Producto Interior Bruto)

gear v ajustar

gearing n apalancamiento m

general adj general

general audit n auditoría f general

general average n avería f gruesa

general delivery n U.K. lista f de correos

general insurance n seguro m general

general manager n director m general mf; director m gerente mf

general meeting n junta f general

general office n oficina f general

general post offfice n oficina f central de correos

general strike n huelga f general

gentleman's agreement n acuerdo m entre caballeros

genuine adj genuino or -na

genuine purchaser n comprador m genuino; compradora f genuina

get v recibir; obtener; conseguir

get along v ir haciendo

get around v (a problem) soslayar

get back v (something lost) recuperar

get into debt v endeudarse

get rid of something v deshacerse de algo

get round v U.K. (a problem) soslayar

get the sack v ser despedido

gift n regalo m; obsequio m

gift coupon n cupón m de regalo

gift store n tienda f de regalos

gift voucher n vale m para un regalo

gilt-edged securities n títulos mpl del Estado

gilts npl bonos mpl del Tesoro

giro account n U.K. cuenta f del Girobank

giro account number n U.K. número m de cuenta del Girobank

giro system n U.K. giro m bancario

give v 1. dar 2. (as gift) regalar

give away v regalar

glut n abundancia f ■ v inundar el mercado

GNP *abbr* (*gross national product*) PNB (Producto Nacional Bruto)

go *v* ir

go-ahead *adj* emprendedor *or* -ra; activo *or* -va

going *adj* en marcha

going-out-of-business sale *n* liquidación *f* total por cierre

going rate *n* precio *m* vigente

go into business *v* emprender un negocio

gold card *n* tarjeta *f* oro

good *adj* bueno *or* -na

good buy *n* buena compra

good driver discount *n* descuento *m* por ausencia de siniestralidad

good management *n* buena gestión

good quality *n* buena calidad

goods *npl* mercancías *fpl*; bienes *mpl*

goods depot *n* U.K. depósito *m*; almacén *m* de mercancías

goods in transit *n* mercancías *fpl* en tránsito

goods train *n* tren *m* de mercancías

good value (for money) *n* buen precio

goodwill *n* fondo *m* de comercio

go on strike *v* ir a la huelga

go-slow *n* huelga *f* de celo

government *adj* estatal; del gobierno ■ *n* gobierno *m*

government-backed *adj* con apoyo estatal

government bonds *n* títulos *mpl* del Estado

government contractor *n* contratista *mf* del Estado

government-controlled *adj* controlado por el Estado *or* -da

government-regulated *adj* regulado *or* -da por el Estado

government-sponsored *adj* patrocinado *or* -da por el Estado

government stock *n* títulos *mpl* del Estado

graded hotel *n* U.K. hotel *m* homologado

graded tax *n* U.K. impuesto *m* progresivo

gradual *adj* gradual; progresivo *or* -va

graduated *adj* graduado *or* -da; progresivo *or* -va

graduated income tax *n* impuesto *m* progresivo sobre la renta

graduate trainee *n* licenciado *m* en prácticas

gram, gramme *n* gramo *m*

grand total *n* suma *f* total

grant *n* subvención *f*; beca *f* ■ *v* conceder; otorgar

graph *n* gráfico *m*; gráfica *f*

gratis *adj, adv* gratis

grid *n* cuadrícula *f*

grid structure *n* estructura *f* cuadricular

gross *adj* bruto *or* -ta ■ *v* obtener beneficios brutos

gross *n abbr* (*144*) gruesa *f*

gross domestic product (GDP) *n* Producto Interior Bruto (PIB)

gross earnings *npl* ingresos *mpl* brutos

gross income *n* renta *f* bruta

gross margin *n* margen *m* de beneficio bruto

gross national product (GNP) *n* Producto Nacional Bruto (PNB)

gross profit *n* beneficio *m* bruto

gross salary *n* sueldo *m* bruto

gross tonnage *n* tonelaje *m* bruto

gross weight *n* peso *m* bruto

gross yield *n* rendimiento *m* bruto

group *n* 1. (*of businesses*) grupo *m* 2. (*of people*) grupo *m*; agrupación *f*

growth *n* crecimiento *m*; desarrollo *m*

growth index *n* índice *m* de crecimiento

growth rate *n* tasa *f* de crecimiento

guarantee n garantía f; aval m; fianza f ■ v avalar; garantizar; afianzar

guarantee a debt v avalar una deuda

guaranteed minimum wage n salario m mínimo interprofesional

guarantor n fiador or -ra; garante mf

guideline n directriz f

guild n gremio m; corporación f

H

haggle v regatear

half adj medio or -dia ■ n mitad f

half a dozen, a half-dozen n media docena f

half-price sale n rebajas fpl a mitad de precio

half-year n semestre m

half-yearly accounts npl cuentas fpl semestrales

half-yearly payment n pagos mpl semestrales

half-yearly statement n estado m de cuentas semestral

hand in v presentar; entregar

handle v 1. (deal) manejar; tratar 2. (sell) comerciar en

handling n manejo m; manipulación f

handling charge n gasto m de tramitación

hand luggage n equipaje m de mano

hand over v entregar

handwriting n letra f; escritura f

handwritten adj escrito or -ta a mano

handy adj útil; práctico or -ca

harbor n puerto m

harbor facilities npl instalaciones fpl portuarias

harbor fees, harbor dues npl derechos mpl portuarios

hard adj duro or -ra

hard bargain n negocio m duro

hard bargaining n negocio m duro; trato m difícil

hard copy n copia f impresa

hard currency n moneda f convertible

hard disk n disco m duro

hard selling n venta f agresiva

harmonization n armonización f; concertación f

haulage n acarreo m

haulage contractor n contratista mf de transporte por carretera

haulage costs, haulage rates npl gastos mpl de acarreo

have v tener

head n jefe or -fa

head of department n jefe m de departamento or -fa

head office n oficina f central

headquarters n sede f; domicilio m social

heads of agreement n epígafres mpl de un acuerdo

health n salud f

health insurance n seguro m de enfermedad

healthy profit n beneficio m considerable

heavy adj 1. (important) grande; importante 2. (weight) pesado or -da

heavy costs, heavy expenditure n grandes costes mpl; gran gasto m

heavy equipment n equipo m pesado

heavy goods vehicle n U.K. carnión m de carga pesada

heavy industry n industria f pesada

heavy machinery n maquinaria f pesada

hectare n hectárea f

hedge n **hedging** cobertura f; protección f

help n ayuda f ■ v ayudar

HGV abbr U.K. (heavy goods vehicle) camión m de carga pesada

hidden asset n bien m encubierto

hidden reserves n reservas fpl ocultas

high adj alto or -ta

highest bidder n mejor postor

high interest n interés m elevado

highly-geared company n sociedad f con un gran coeficiente de endeudamiento

highly motivated sales staff n personal m de ventas muy motivado

highly-paid adj muy bien pagado

highly-priced adj muy caro or -ra

highly qualified adj muy cualificado; muy capacitado

high quality n calidad f superior; alta calidad

high-quality goods n productos mpl de primera calidad

high rent n alquiler m elevado

high taxation n imposición f alta

hire v alquilar

hire a car v U.K. alquilar un coche

hire a crane v U.K. alquilar una grúa

hire car n U.K. coche m de alquiler

hire purchase n U.K. compra f a plazos

hire-purchase company n U.K. compañía f que financia la compra a plazos

hire staff v contratar personal

historical figures npl cifras fpl históricas

historic(al) cost n coste m inicial

hive off v descentralizar

hoard v acaparar; acumular

hoarding n 1. U.K. (for posters) valla f publicitaria; cartelera f 2. (of goods) acaparamiento m

hold n (ship) bodega f ■ v 1. (contain) contener; caber 2. (keep) tener; guardar

hold a meeting, hold a discussion v celebrar una reunión; tener una discusión

holder n 1. (person) poseedor or -ra; tenedor or -ra 2. (thing) soporte m

holding company n sociedad f de cartera; "holding"

hold out for v insistir en

hold over v aplazar; posponer

hold the line please, please hold phrase no cuelgue

hold up v (delay) retrasar

hold-up n (delay) retraso m

holiday pay n U.K. paga f de vacaciones

home address n domicilio m particular

home consumption n consumo m doméstico; consumo interior

home market n mercado m interior; mercado m nacional

homeowners insurance n seguro m de la vivienda

home sales n ventas fpl nacionales

homeward freight n flete m de vuelta

homeward journey n viaje m de regreso

homeworker n trabajador m a domicilio

honor a bill v pagar una factura

honorarium n honorarios mpl

honor a signature v aceptar una firma; reconocer una firma

horizontal communication n comunicación f horizontal

horizontal integration n integración f horizontal

hotel n hotel m

hotel accommodations n habitaciones fpl de hotel; capacidad f hotelera

hotel bill n factura f de hotel

hotel manager n director m de hotel

hotel staff n personal m del hotel

hour n hora f

hourly *adj* por hora

hourly-paid workers *n* trabajadores *mpl* pagados por horas

hourly rate *n* tarifa *f* horaria

hourly wage *n* sueldo *m* por hora

house *n* 1. casa *f* 2. (*company*) casa *f* comercial

house insurance *n U.K.* seguro *m* de la vivienda

house magazine *n* boletín *m* interno de una empresa

house-to-house *adj* a domicilio

house-to-house selling *n* venta *f* a domicilio

HP *abbr U.K.* (*hire purchase*) compra *f* a plazos

HQ *abbr* (*headquarters*) sede *f*; domicilio *m* social

hurry up *v* darse prisa

hype *n* bombo *m* publicitario ■ *v* hacer publicidad con mucho bombo

hypermarket *n* hipermercado *m*

I

illegal *adj* ilegal

illegality *n* ilegalidad *f*

illegally *adv* ilegalmente

illicit *adj* ilícito *or* -ta

ILO *abbr* (*International Labour Organization*) OIT (Organización Internacional del Trabajo)

IMF *abbr* (*International Monetary Fund*) FMI (Fondo Monetario Internacional)

imitation *n* imitación *f*

immediate *adj* inmediato *or* -ta

immediately *adv* inmediatamente

imperfect *adj* imperfecto *or* -ta

imperfection *n* defecto *m*; imperfección *f*; tara *f*

implement *n* herramienta *f*; instrumento *m* ■ *v* ejecutar; realizar

implement an agreement *v* poner en práctica un acuerdo

implementation *n* ejecución *f*; puesta *f* en práctica

import *n* importación *f* ■ *v* importar

importance *n* importancia *f*

important *adj* importante

importation *n* importación *f*

import ban *n* prohibición *f* de importar

import duty *n* derechos *mpl* de importación

importer *n* importador *or* -ra

import-export *adj* importación-exportación

importing *adj* importador *or* -ra ■ *n* importación *f*

import levy *n* gravamen *m* sobre las importaciones

import license, import permit *n* licencia *f* de importación

import quota *n* cuota *f* de importación; cupo *m* de importación

import restrictions *n* restricción *f* a las importaciones

imports *npl* importaciones *fpl*

import surcharge *n* sobretasa *f* de importación; recargo *m* de importación

impose *v* imponer; gravar

improvement *n* mejora *f*

impulse *n* impulso *m*

impulse buyer *n* comprador *m* impulsivo

impulse purchase *n* compra *f* impulsiva

incapable *adj* incapaz

incentive *n* incentivo *m*; estímulo *m*

incentive bonus, incentive payment *n* prima *f* de incentivo

incidental expenses *npl* gastos *mpl* menores

include *v* incluir

inclusive *adj* inclusive; inclusivo *or* -va; incluido *or* -da

inclusive charge *n* precio *m* todo incluido

inclusive of tax *n* impuestos *mpl* incluidos

income *n* ingresos *mpl*; renta *f*

income tax *n* impuesto *m* sobre la renta

incoming call *n* llamada *f* de fuera

incoming mail *n* correspondencia *f* recibida; correo *m* entrante

incompetence *n* incompetencia *f*

incompetent *adj* incompetente

incorporate *v* 1. incorporar; incluir 2. (*a company*) constituir en sociedad

incorporation *n* constitución *f* de una sociedad

incorrect *adj* incorrecto *or* -ta

incorrectly *adv* incorrectamente

increase *n* 1. aumento *m*; incremento *m*; subida *f* 2. (*higher salary*) aumento *m* de sueldo ■ *v* aumentar; subir; incrementar

increase in price *v* aumentar de precio; subir de precio

increasing *adj* creciente; en aumento

increasing profits *npl* beneficios *mpl* crecientes

increment *n* incremento *m*; aumento *m*

incremental *adj* incremental

incremental cost *n* coste *m* incremental

incremental scale *n* escala *f* móvil de salarios

incur *v* incurrir en

incur debts *v* contraer deudas

indebted *adj* endeudado *or* -da

indebtedness *n* deuda *f*

indemnification *n* indemnización *f*

indemnify *v* indemnizar; resarcir

indemnify someone for a loss *v* indemnizar a alguien por una pérdida

indemnity *n* indemnidad *f*; indemnización *f*

independent *adj* independiente

independent company *n* compañía *f* independiente

index *n* 1. (*alphabetical*) índice *m*; repertorio *m* 2. (*of prices*) índice *m* ■ *v* catalogar; clasificar

indexation *n* indexación *f*; indiciación *f*

index card *n* ficha *f*

index-linked *adj* ajustado, -a al coste de la vida

index number *n* índice *m*; indicador *m*

indicator *n* indicador *m*

indirect *adj* indirecto *or* -ta

indirect labor costs *npl* costes *mpl* laborales indirectos

indirect tax *n* impuesto *m* indirecto

indirect taxation *n* imposición *f* indirecta

induction *n* iniciación *f*

induction courses, induction training *n* cursos *mpl* de iniciación

industrial *adj* industrial

industrial accident *n* accidente *m* industrial

industrial arbitration tribunal *n* tribunal *m* de arbitraje laboral

industrial capacity *n* capacidad *f* industrial

industrial center *n* centro *m* industrial

industrial design *n* diseño *m* industrial

industrial disputes *npl* conflictos *mpl* colectivos

industrial espionage *n* espionaje *m* industrial

industrial estate *n U.K.* zona *f* industrial

industrial expansion *n* expansión *f* industrial

industrialist *n* industrial *mf*

industrialization *n* industrialización *f*

industrialize *v* industrializar

industrialized societies n sociedades *fpl* industriales

industrial park n zona *f* industrial

industrial processes n procesos *mpl* industriales

industrial relations *npl* relaciones *fpl* laborales

industrial tribunal n magistratura *f* del trabajo

industry n industria *f*

inefficiency n ineficacia *f*; incompetencia *f*

inefficient *adj* ineficaz; incompetente

infer v deducir

inflated currency n moneda *f* inflacionista

inflated prices n precios *mpl* exagerados

inflation n inflación *f*

inflationary *adj* inflacionario *or* -ria; inflacionista

influence n influencia *f* ■ v influir; influenciar

inform v informar

information n información *f*

information bureau n oficina *f* de información

information officer n empleado *m* del servicio de información

infrastructure n infraestructura *f*

infringe v infringir; violar

infringe a patent v violar una patente

infringement of customs regulations n infracción *f* aduanera

infringement of patent n violación *f* de patente

inhabitant n habitante *mf*

in-house *adj* interno *or* -na; de la casa

in-house training n formación *f* en el puesto de trabajo

initial *adj* inicial; primero *or* -ra ■ v poner las iniciales a; rubricar

initial capital n capital *m* inicial

initiate v iniciar

initiate discussions v iniciar conversaciones

initiative n iniciativa *f*

inland *adj* interior

innovate v innovar

innovation n innovación *f*

innovative *adj* innovador *or* -ra

innovator n innovador *or* -ra

input information v introducir datos

input tax n IVA (sobre los bienes y servicios adquiridos por una empresa)

inquire v preguntar; pedir información

inquiry n petición *f* de informes; investigación *f*

insider n iniciado *m*

insider dealing n información *f* privilegiada

insolvency n insolvencia *f*

insolvent *adj* insolvente

inspect v inspeccionar; revisar

inspection n inspección *f*; control *m*

inspector n inspector *or* -ra

installment n plazo *m*

installment plan n compra *f* a plazos

instant *adj* 1. (*current*) del presente mes; de los corrientes 2. (*immediate*) inmediato *or* -ta; instantáneo *or* -nea

instant credit n crédito *m* instantáneo

institute n instituto *m* ■ v instituir

institution n institución *f*

institutional *adj* institucional

institutional investors *npl* inversores *mpl* institucionales

instruction n instrucción *f*

instrument n 1. (*device*) instrumento *m*; aparato *m* 2. (*document*) efecto *m*; documento *m* escrito

insufficiency n insuficiencia *f*

insufficient funds n saldo *m* insuficiente

insurable *adj* asegurable

insurance n seguro *m*

insurance agent n agente *mf* de seguros

insurance broker n corredor m de seguros

insurance claim n declaración f de siniestro

insurance company n compañía f de seguros

insurance contract n contrato m de seguros

insurance coverage n cobertura f del seguro

insurance policy n póliza f de seguros

insurance premium n prima f de seguros

insurance rates n tarifas fpl de seguros

insurance salesman n vendedor m de seguros

insure v asegurar

insurer n asegurador or -ra

intangible adj intangible

intangible assets npl activo m intangible

interest n interés m; rédito m ■ v interesar

interest-bearing deposits npl depósitos mpl con interés

interest charges npl cargos mpl en concepto de interés

interest-free credit n crédito m sin interés

interest rate n tipo m de interés; tasa f de interés

interface n interfaz m ■ v conectar

interim dividend n dividendo m provisional

interim payment n pago m a cuenta

interim report n informe m provisional

intermediary n intermediario or -ria

internal adj 1. (inside a company) interno or -na 2. (inside a country) interior

internal audit n auditoría f interna

internal auditor n auditor m interno

internal telephone n teléfono m interno

international adj internacional

international call n llamada f internacional

international direct dialing n llamadas fpl internacionales directas

International Labour Organization (ILO) n Organización Internacional del Trabajo (OIT)

international law n derecho m internacional

International Monetary Fund (IMF) n Fondo Monetario Internacional (FMI)

international trade n comercio m internacional

Internet n Internet n

interpret v interpretar

interpreter n intérprete mf

interruption n interrupción f

intervention price n precio m de intervención

interview n entrevista f ■ v entrevistar

interviewee n entrevistado or -da

interviewer n entrevistador or -ra

introduce v presentar; introducir

introduction n 1. (bringing into use) presentación f; introducción f 2. (letter) carta f de presentación

introductory offer n oferta f de lanzamiento

invalid adj inválido or -da

invalidate v invalidar

invalidation n invalidación f

invalidity n invalidez f

inventory n 1. (list of contents) inventario m 2. (stock) existencias fpl ■ v inventariar; hacer un inventario

inventory control n control m de existencias

inventory sale n liquidación f de inventario

inventory turnover n rotación f de existencias

inventory valuation n valoración f de existencias

invest v invertir

investigate v investigar

investigation n investigación f
investment n inversión f
investment income n renta f de inversiones
investor n inversor or -ra; inversionista mf
invisible assets npl activo m invisible
invisible earnings npl ingresos mpl invisibles
invisible trade n comercio m invisible
invitation n invitación f
invite v invitar
invoice n factura f ■ v facturar
invoice number n número m de factura
invoice value n precio m facturado
invoicing n facturación f
invoicing department n departamento m de facturación
IOU abbr (I owe you) pagaré m
irrecoverable debt n deuda f incobrable
irredeemable bond n obligación f perpetua
irregular v irregular
irregularities npl irregularidades fpl
irrevocable adj irrevocable
irrevocable acceptance n aceptación f irrevocable
irrevocable letter of credit n carta f de crédito irrevocable
issue n 1. (magazine) número m 2. (of shares) emisión f ■ v (shares) emitir
issue a letter of credit v abrir una carta de crédito
issue instructions v dar instrucciones
issuing bank n banco m emisor
item n 1. (for sale) artículo m 2. (news) noticia f 3. (on agenda) punto m 4. (on balance sheet) partida f
itemize v detallar; especificar
itemized account n cuenta f detallada

itemized invoice n factura f detallada
itinerary n itinerario m

J

job n 1. (employment) empleo m; puesto m de trabajo 2. (piece of work) trabajo m; tarea f
job analysis n análisis m de un puesto de trabajo
job application n solicitud f de empleo
job cuts n reducción f de empleos
job description n descripción f del puesto de trabajo
job satisfaction n satisfacción f laboral
job security n seguridad f en el empleo
job specification n descripción f del puesto de trabajo
job title n cargo m
join v 1. juntar; unir 2. (become part of) ingresar en
joint adj común; conjunto or -ta; colectivo or -va
joint account n cuenta f conjunta; cuenta f en participación
joint discussions npl negociaciones fpl conjuntas
jointly adv conjuntamente; en común
joint management n dirección f conjunta; codirección f
joint managing director n codirector m gerente or -ra
joint owner n co-propietario or -ria
joint ownership n co-propiedad f; condominio m

joint signatory n signatario m colectivo

joint venture n empresa f conjunta

journal n 1. (*accounts book*) libro m diario 2. (*magazine*) revista f; boletín m

journey order n pedido m cursado al representante (comercial)

judge n juez mf ■ v juzgar

judgment, judgement n juicio m; sentencia f

judgment debtor n deudor m judicial

judicial processes n procedimientos mpl judiciales

jump the line v saltarse la cola

junior adj menor; más joven; subalterno or -na

junior clerk n pasante mf; auxiliar mf administrativo or -va

junior executive, junior manager n ejecutivo m auxiliar

junior partner n socio m subalterno; de menor antigüedad

junk bonds npl bonos-basura mpl

junk mail n publicidad f sin interés (por correo)

jurisdiction n jurisdicción f

justify v justificar

K

keen competition n U.K. fuerte competencia f

keen demand n U.K. gran demanda f

keen prices n U.K. precios mpl competitivos

keep a promise v cumplir una promesa

keep back v retener

keep up v sostener; mantener

keep up with the demand v satisfacer la demanda

key adj (*important*) clave ■ n 1. (*on keyboard*) tecla f 2. (*solution*) clave f 3. (*to door*) llave f

keyboard n teclado m ■ v teclear

keyboarder n operador m de teclado

keyboarding n tecleo m; tecleado m

key industry n industria f clave

key money n traspaso m

key personnel, key staff n personal m clave

key post n puesto m clave

kilo, kilogram n kilo m; kilogramo m

knock down v (*price*) rematar

knockdown prices npl precios mpl mínimos; precios mpl de saldo

knock off v 1. (*reduce price*) descontar 2. (*stop work*) terminar de trabajar

knock-on effect n U.K. repercusión f; efecto m secundario

krona n (*currency used in Sweden and Iceland*) corona f

krone n (*currency used in Denmark and Norway*) corona f

L

label n etiqueta f ■ v etiquetar

labeling n etiquetado m

labor n trabajo m

labor costs npl costes mpl laborales

labor disputes npl conflictos mpl laborales

labor force n mano f de obra

labor union n sindicato m

lack of funds n falta f de fondos

land n tierra f ■ v 1. (of plane) aterrizar 2. (passengers) desembarcar

landed costs npl coste m descargado

land goods at a port v descargar mercancías en un puerto

landing card n tarjeta f de desembarque

landing fees npl gastos mpl de descarga

landlady n propietaria f; dueña f

landlord n propietario m; dueño m

lapse v caducar

large adj grande

laser printer n impresora f láser

last adj último or -ma

last in first out n últimos en entrar, primeros en salir

last quarter n último trimestre

late adj atrasado or -da ■ adv tarde; con retraso

late-night opening n abierto por la noche

latest adj último or -ma

late: to be late v retrasarse

launch n lanzamiento m ■ v lanzar

launching n lanzamiento m

launching costs npl costes mpl de lanzamiento

launching date n fecha f de lanzamiento

launder (money) v blanquear (dinero negro)

law n 1. ley f 2. (rule) regla f; norma f 3. (study) derecho m

law courts n tribunales mpl de justicia

lawful adj legal; lícito or -ta

lawful trade n comercio m legal

law of diminishing returns n ley f de rendimientos decrecientes

law of supply and demand n ley f de la oferta y la demanda

lawsuit n pleito m; juicio m; proceso m

lawyer n abogado or -da

lay off workers v despedir por falta de trabajo

LBO abbr (leveraged buyout) compra f apalancada; adquisición f apalancada

L/C abbr (letter of credit) carta f de crédito

lead time n plazo m de espera

leaflet n folleto m; prospecto m

leakage n pérdidas fpl; mermas fpl

lease n arrendamiento m; arriendo m ■ v 1. (of landlord) arrendar (ceder en arriendo) 2. (of tenant) arrendar (tomar en arriendo)

lease back v realizar una operación de cesión-arrendamiento

lease-back n cesión-arrendamiento f

lease equipment v arrendar equipo

leasing n arrendamiento m financiero; "leasing" m

leave n permiso m ■ v 1. (go away) irse; marcharse 2. (resign) abandonar; dejar

leave of absence n excedencia f

ledger n libro m mayor

left adj (not right) izquierdo or -da

left: be left v quedar

left luggage office n U.K. consigna f

legal *adj* 1. (*according to law*) legal; lícito *or* -ta 2. (*referring to law*) jurídico *or* -ca; judicial

legal action *n* acción *f* legal

legal advice *n* asesoramiento *m* jurídico

legal adviser *n* asesor *m* jurídico

legal costs, legal charges *npl* costas *fpl* judiciales

legal currency *n* moneda *f* de curso legal

legal department *n* asesoría *f* jurídica

legal expenses *npl* costas *fpl* judiciales

legal proceedings *n* proceso *m* judicial

legal status *n* condición *f* jurídica; personalidad *f* jurídica

legal tender *n* moneda *f* de curso legal

legislation *n* legislación *f*

lend *v* prestar

lender *n* prestamista *mf*

lending *n* concesión *f* de un préstamo

lending limit *n* límite *m* de crédito

less *adv* menos

lessee *n* arrendatario *or* -ria; inquilino *or* -na

lessor *n* arrendador *or* -ra

let *v* alquilar; arrendar

let an office *v* alquilar una oficina

letter *n* carta *f*

letter of application *n* carta *f* de solicitud

letter of appointment *n* carta *f* de nombramiento

letter of complaint *n* carta *f* de reclamación

letter of credit *n* carta *f* de crédito

letter of intent *n* carta *f* de intención

letter of reference *n* carta *f* de recomendación

letters of administration *n* nombramiento *m* de administrador judicial

letters patent *n* patente *f* de invención

letting agency *n* U.K. agencia *f* de alquiler de viviendas

level *n* nivel *m*

level off, level out *v* nivelarse; estabilizarse

leverage *n* apalancamiento *m* financiero

leveraged buyout *n* compra *f* apalancada; adquisición *f* apalancada

levy *n* recaudación *f* de impuestos ■ *v* recaudar; gravar

liabilities *npl* deudas *fpl*

liability *n* responsabilidad *f*; pasivo *m*

liable for *phrase* responsable de

liable to *phrase* sujeto a *or* -ta

license¹ *n* licencia *f*

license² *v* conceder una licencia; autorizar

licensee *n* persona *f* autorizada; concesionario *or* -ria

licensing *n* licencia *f*

lien *n* gravamen *m*; derecho *m* de retención

life insurance, life assurance *n* seguro *m* de vida

life interest *n* renta *f* vitalicia; usufructo *m* vitalicio

LIFO *abbr* (*last in first out*) últimos en entrar, primeros en salir

lift *n* ascensor *m* ■ *v* levantar; suprimir

lift an embargo *v* levantar un embargo

limit *n* límite *m*; acotación *f* ■ *v* limitar

limitation *n* limitación *f*

limited *adj* limitado *or* -da

limited (liability) company (Ltd) *n* sociedad *f* de responsabilidad limitada (S.R.L.)

limited liability *n* responsabilidad *f* limitada

limited market *n* mercado *m* limitado

limited partnership n sociedad f en comandita

line n línea f; raya f

line management n gestión f lineal

line of credit n línea f de crédito

line organization n organización f lineal

line printer n impresora f de líneas

link n vínculo m; conexión f

liquid assets npl activo m líquido

liquidate a company v liquidar una compañía

liquidate stock v liquidar existencias

liquidation n liquidación f

liquidator n síndico m

liquidity n liquidez f

liquidity crisis n crisis f de liquidez

lira n (currency used in Turkey) lira f

list n 1. lista f; relación f 2. (catalogue) catálogo m; repertorio m ■ v hacer una lista; enumerar

list price n precio m de catálogo

liter n litro m

Lloyd's register n Registro m Marítimo de Lloyd

load n cargamento m ■ v cargar

load a truck, a ship v cargar un camión; cargar un barco

load factor n coeficiente m de ocupación

loading bay n nave f de carga

loading ramp n rampa f de carga

load line n línea f de carga; línea f de flotación

loan n préstamo m ■ v prestar

loan capital n empréstito m

loan stock n obligaciones fpl

local adj local

local call n llamada f local

local government n administración f local

local labor n mano f de obra local

lock n cerradura f ■ v cerrar con llave

lock up a shop, an office v cerrar una tienda; cerrar una oficina

lock up capital n inmovilizar capital

lock-up premises npl local m sin vivienda incorporada

log v anotar; apuntar

log calls v anotar las llamadas recibidas

logo n logotipo m

long adj largo or -ga

long credit n crédito m a largo plazo

long-dated bill n letra f a largo plazo

long-distance flight, long-haul flight n vuelo m de larga distancia

long-range adj a largo plazo

long-standing adj de hace tiempo; de muchos años

long-standing agreement n acuerdo m de muchos años

long-term adj largo plazo

long-term debts npl deudas fpl a largo plazo

long-term forecast n previsión f a largo plazo

long-term liabilities npl pasivo m a largo plazo

long-term loan n préstamo m a largo plazo

long-term objectives npl objetivos mpl a largo plazo

long-term planning n planificación f a largo plazo

loose adj 1. suelto or -ta; a granel 2. (slack) flojo or -ja

lorry n U.K. camión m

lorry driver n U.K. camionero or -ra

lorry-load n U.K. carga f de un camión

lose v perder

lose an order v perder un pedido

lose money v perder dinero

lose value v perder valor

loss n (not a profit) pérdida f

loss adjustment n ajuste m de pérdidas

loss-leader n artículo m de reclamo

loss of an order *n* pérdida *f* de un pedido

loss of customers *n* pérdida *f* de clientela

loss of value *n* pérdida *f* de valor

lot *n* lote *m*

low *adj* bajo *or* -ja ■ *n* mínimo *m*

lower *adj* más bajo *or* -ja; inferior ■ *v* bajar

lowering *n* disminución *f*; reducción *f*

lower prices *v* reducir los precios

low-grade *adj* de baja calidad

low-level *adj* de bajo nivel; de grado inferior

low-quality *adj* de poca calidad; mediocre

low sales *n* ventas *fpl* bajas

Ltd. *abbr* (*limited company*) S.(R.)L. (= sociedad (de responsabilidad) limitada)

luggage *n U.K.* equipaje *m*; maletas *fpl*

lump sum *n* pago *m* único; suma *f* global

luxury goods *npl* artículos *mpl* de lujo

M

machine *n* máquina *f*; aparato *m*

machinery *n* maquinaria *f*

macro-economics *n* macroeconomía *f*

magazine *n* revista *f*

magazine insert *n* encarte *m* publicitario (de una revista)

magazine mailing *n* envío *m* de revistas por correo

magnetic tape, mag tape *n* cinta *f* magnética

mail *n* correo *m*; correspondencia *f* ■ *v* mandar por correo; echar al correo

mailing *n* envío *m* por correo

mailing list *n* lista *f* de destinatarios

mailing piece *n* folleto *m* publicitario enviado por correo

mailing shot *n* envío *m* de publicidad por correo

mail-order *n* pedido *m* por correo

mail-order business, mail-order firm *n* empresa *f* de ventas por correo

mail-order catalog *n* catálogo *m* de ventas por correo

mail shot *n* publicidad *f* por correo

main *adj* principal; mayor

main building *n* edificio *m* principal

main office *n* oficina *f* principal

maintain *v* 1. (*keep at same level*) mantener; conservar 2. (*keep going*) mantener; sostener

maintenance *n* mantenimiento *m*; conservación *f*

maintenance of contacts *n* mantenimiento *m* de relaciones

maintenance of supplies *n* mantenimiento *m* de suministros

major *adj* mayor; importante

majority *n* mayoría *f*

majority stockholder *n* accionista *mf* mayoritario

major stockholder *n* accionista *mf* importante

make *v* hacer; producir

make good *v* (*a defect or loss*) indemnizar; compensar

make money *v* ganar dinero

make out *v* (*invoice*) confeccionar; extender

make provision for *v* tomar medidas

make-ready time *n* tiempo *m* de preparación (de una máquina)

make up for v compensar

maladministration n mala administración f

man n hombre m ■ v asignar personal

manage v dirigir; gestionar; administrar

manageable adj manejable

management n 1. (action) dirección f; gestión f 2. (managers) junta f de directores

management accounts npl cuentas fpl de gestión

management buyout n compra f de una empresa por sus ejecutivos

management consultant n asesor or -ra de empresas

management course n curso m de gestión empresarial

management team n equipo m directivo

management techniques n técnicas fpl de dirección de empresas

management trainee n ejecutivo m en formación

management training n formación f de mandos

manager n 1. (of branch or shop) gerente mf; encargado or -da 2. (of department) director or -ra; jefe or -fa

managerial adj directivo or -va

managerial posts npl órganos mpl de gestión

managerial staff n personal m administrativo

manage to v arreglárselas; conseguir

managing director n director m gerente mf

mandate n mandato m

man-hour n hora-hombre f

manifest adj manifiesto m

manned adj asistido or -da; atendido or -da

manning n dotación f de personal

manning levels npl niveles mpl de dotación de personal

manpower n mano f de obra

manpower forecasting n previsión f de mano de obra

manpower planning n planificación f de la mano de obra

manpower shortage n escasez f de mano de obra

manual adj manual ■ n manual m

manual work n trabajo m manual

manual worker n obrero or -ra

manufacture n fabricación f ■ v manufacturar; fabricar; elaborar

manufactured goods n productos mpl manufacturados

manufacturer n fabricante m

manufacturer's recommended price n precio m de venta recomendado

manufacturing n fabricación f

manufacturing capacity n capacidad f de fabricación

manufacturing costs npl costes mpl de fabricación

manufacturing overhead npl gastos mpl generales de fabricación

margin n (profit) margen m

marginal adj marginal

marginal cost n coste m marginal; coste m incremental

marginal pricing n fijación f de precios marginal

margin of error n margen m de error

marine adj marino or -na

marine insurance n seguro m marítimo

marine underwriter n asegurador or -ra de riesgos marinos

maritime adj marítimo or -ma

maritime law n derecho m marítimo

maritime lawyer n abogado m especializado en derecho marítimo

maritime trade n comercio m marítimo

mark n marca f; señal f ■ v marcar; señalar

mark down v rebajar

marker pen n rotulador m; marcador m

market *n* mercado *m*; plaza *f* ■ *v* vender

marketable *adj* vendible; comerciable

market analysis *n* análisis *m* de mercado

market analyst *n* analista *mf* de mercado

market capitalization *n* capitalización *f* bursátil

market economist *n* economista *mf* de mercado

market forces *npl* fuerzas *fpl* del mercado

market forecast *n* previsión *f* de mercado

marketing *n* mercadotecnia *f*; "marketing" *m*

marketing agreement *n* acuerdo *m* de comercialización

marketing department departamento *m* de 'marketing'

marketing division *n* sección *f* de 'marketing'

marketing manager *n* director *m* de "marketing"

marketing strategy *n* estrategia *f* de 'marketing'

marketing techniques *n* técnicas *fpl* de 'marketing'

market leader *n* líder *m* del mercado

market opportunities *n* oportunidades *fpl* de mercado

market penetration *n* penetración *f* en el mercado

marketplace *n* mercado *m*; plaza *f* del mercado

market price *n* precio *m* de mercado

market rate *n* precio *m* de mercado; tarifa *f* de mercado

market research *n* estudio *m* de mercado; investigación *f* de mercado

market share *n* cuota *f* de mercado

market trends *n* tendencias *fpl* del mercado

market value *n* valor *m* de mercado

mark up *v* recargar

mark-up *n* (*profit margin*) margen *m* de beneficio

mass *n* masa *f*

mass marketing *n* comercialización *f* a gran escala

mass market product *n* producto *m* destinado a un mercado de masas

mass media *n* medios *mpl* de comunicación

mass-produce *v* fabricar en serie

mass-produce cars *v* fabricar coches en serie

mass production *n* producción *f* en serie

Master's degree in Business Administration *n* master *m* en administración de empresas

materials control *n* control *m* de materiales

materials handling *n* manejo *m* de materiales

maternity leave *n* licencia *f* por maternidad

matter *n* cuestión *f*; asunto *m* ■ *v* importar

mature *v* vencer

mature economy *n* economía *f* madura

maturity date *n* fecha *f* de vencimiento

maximization *n* maximización *f*

maximize *v* maximizar

maximum *adj* máximo *or* -ma ■ *n* máximo *m*

maximum price *n* precio *m* máximo

M.B.A. *abbr* (*Master's in Business Administration*) master *m* en administración de empresas

MBO *abbr* (*management buyout*) compra *f* de una empresa por sus ejecutivos

MD *abbr* (*managing director*) director *m* gerente *mf*

mean *adj* medio *or* -dia ■ *n* promedio *m*; media *f*

mean annual increase n aumento m anual medio

means npl (money) recursos mpl; medios mpl ∎ n (ways) medio m; manera f

means test n comprobación f de los recursos económicos

measurement of profitability n evaluación f de la rentabilidad; medición f de la rentabilidad

measurements npl medidas fpl; dimensiones fpl

media coverage n cobertura f periodística

median n mediana f

mediate v mediar

mediation n mediación f

mediator n mediador or -ra; intermediario or -ria

mediocre adj mediocre

medium adj medio or -dia; mediano or -na ∎ n medio m; instrumento m

medium-sized adj mediano or -na

medium-term n plazo m medio

meet v 1. (be satisfactory) cumplir; satisfacer 2. (someone) encontrar; encontrarse (con); reunirse

meet a deadline v cumplir un plazo establecido

meet a demand v satisfacer una demanda; atender una demanda

meet a target v cumplir un objetivo

meet expenses v cubrir gastos

meeting n reunión f; asamblea f

meeting place n lugar m de reunión

member n (of a group) miembro m; socio or -cia

membership n 1. afiliación f; ingreso m 2. (all members) los socios; los miembros

membership card n carnet f

memo, memorandum n memorandum m

memory n (computer) memoria f

mend v arreglar

mention v mencionar

merchandise n mercancías fpl; género m

merchandize v comercializar

merchandize a product v comercializar un producto

merchandizer n comerciante mf

merchandizing n comercialización f; mercadeo m

merchant n comerciante mf ∎ v mercader m

merchant bank n banco m mercantil

merchant marine n marina f mercante

merchant ship, merchant vessel n buque m mercante

merge v fusionar

merger n fusión f

merit n mérito m

merit award, merit bonus n gratificación f por méritos

message n mensaje m; recado m

messenger n mensajero or -ra

microcomputer n microordenador m

micro-economics n microeconomía f

middleman n intermediario or -ria

middle management n mandos mpl intermedios

middle-sized company n empresa f mediana

mid-month accounts npl cuentas fpl de mediados de mes

mid-week adj a mediados de semana

mileage allowance n kilometraje m

million n millón m

millionaire n millonario or -ria

minimum adj mínimo or -ma ∎ n mínimo m

minimum dividend n dividendo m mínimo

minimum payment n pago m mínimo

minimum wage *n* salario *m* mínimo

minority *n* minoría *f*

minority stockholder *n* accionista *m* minoritario

minor stockholders *npl* pequeños accionistas *mpl*

minus *adj* menos

minus factor *n* factor *m* negativo

minute *n* (*time*) minuto *m* ■ *v* tomar nota; levantar acta

minutes *n* (*of meeting*) acta *f* de la reunión

misappropriate *v* malversar

misappropriation *n* malversación *f*

miscalculate *v* calcular mal

miscalculation *n* error *m* de cálculo

miscellaneous *adj* misceláneo *or* -nea; diverso *or* -sa

miscellaneous items *n* artículos *mpl* varios

mismanage *v* administrar mal

mismanagement *n* mala administración

miss *v* **1.** (*not to hit*) errar; fallar **2.** (*not to meet*) no encontrar **3.** (*train, plane*) perder (el tren/avion)

miss an installment *v* saltarse un plazo

miss a target *v* no cumplir un objetivo

missing *adj* desaparecido *or* -da

mistake *n* equivocación *f*; error *m*

misunderstanding *n* malentendido *m*

mixed *adj* mixto *or* -ta; mezclado *or* -da

mixed economy *n* economía *f* mixta

mobile phone *n* *U.K.* teléfono *m* móvil

mobility *n* movilidad *f*

mobilize *v* movilizar

mobilize capital *v* movilizar capital

mock-up *n* maqueta *f*; modelo *m* a escala

mode *n* modo *m*

model *n* **1.** modelo *mf* **2.** (*small copy*) maqueta *f*; modelo *m* a escala ■ *v* (*clothes*) pasar modelos

model agreement *n* prototipo *m* de contrato

modem *n* modem *m*

mode of payment *n* modo *m* de pago

moderate *adj* moderado *or* -da ■ *v* moderar

moderate price *n* precio *m* módico

modern *adj* moderno *or* -na

monetary *adj* monetario *or* -ria

monetary base *n* base *f* monetaria

monetary unit *n* unidad *f* monetaria

money *n* dinero *m*

money changer *n* cambista *mf*

moneylender *n* prestamista *mf*

money-making *adj* lucrativo *or* -va; remunerativo *or* -va

money-making plan *n* plan *m* remunerativo

money markets *npl* mercados *mpl* monetarios

money order *n* giro *m* postal

money rates *n* tipos *mpl* de interés

money supply *n* oferta *f* monetaria

money up front *n* pago *m* por adelantado

monitor *n* (*screen*) pantalla *f* ■ *v* controlar; comprobar

monopolization *n* monopolización *f*

monopolize *v* monopolizar

monopoly *n* monopolio *m*

month *n* mes *m*

month end *n* fin *m* de mes

month-end accounts *npl* cuentas *fpl* de fin de mes

monthly *adj* mensual ■ *adv* mensualmente

monthly payments *npl* pagos *mpl* mensuales

monthly statement n estado m de cuenta mensual

moonlighter n pluriempleado or -da

moonlighting n pluriempleo m

moratorium n moratoria f

more adv más

mortgage n hipoteca f ■ v hipotecar

mortgagee n acreedor m hipotecario

mortgage payments npl pagos mpl de la hipoteca

mortgager, mortgagor n deudor m hipotecario

most-favored nation n nación f más favorecida

motivated adj motivado or -da

motivation n motivación f

motor insurance n seguro m de automóviles

mounting adj creciente

mount up v aumentar; subir

move v trasladar(se); mudar(se)

movement n movimiento m

movements of capital n movimientos mpl de capital

MRP abbr (*manufacturer's recommended price*) precio m de venta recomendado

multicurrency operation n operación f en multiples divisas

multilateral adj multilateral

multilateral agreement n acuerdo m multilateral

multilateral trade n comercio m multilateral

multinational n multinacional f

multiple adj múltiple

multiple entry visa n visado m de entradas múltiples

multiple ownership n propiedad f conjunta

multiple store n U.K. cadena f de grandes almacenes

multiplication n multiplicación f

multiply v multiplicar

multitude n multitud f

mutual adj mutuo or -tua

mutual (insurance) company n mutua f de seguros

mutual fund n fondos mpl mutuos; fondos npl de inversión

N

national adj nacional

national advertising n publicidad f a escala nacional

nationalization n nacionalización f

nationalized industry n industria f nacionalizada

nationwide adj de ámbito nacional

natural resources n recursos mpl naturales

natural wastage n U.K. pérdida f de trabajadores por jubilación

near letter-quality n calidad f de semicorrespondencia

necessary adj necesario or -ria

need n necesidad f ■ v necesitar

negative cash flow n flujo m de caja negativo

neglected business n negocio m descuidado

neglected shares n acciones fpl poco buscadas en la bolsa

negligence n negligencia f

negligent adj descuidado or -da

negligible adj insignificante

negotiable adj negociable

negotiable instrument n instrumento m negociable

negotiate v negociar; gestionar

negotiation n negociación f

negotiator n negociador or -ra

net *adj* neto *or* -ta ■ *v* obtener beneficios netos

net assets, net worth *npl* activo *m* neto; patrimonio *m*

net earnings, net income *n* ganancias *fpl* netas; ingresos *mpl* netos

net income, net salary *n* salario *m* neto; sueldo *m* neto

net loss *n* pérdida *f* neta

net margin *n* margen *m* neto

net price *n* precio *m* neto

net profit *n* beneficio *m* neto

net receipts *npl* ingresos *mpl* netos

net sales *n* ventas *fpl* netas

net weight *n* peso *m* neto

network *n* red *f* ■ *v* difundir a través de la red de emisoras

networking *n* (*making business contracts*) establecimiento de contactos en el mundo de negocios

net worth *n* valor *m* neto

net yield *n* rendimiento *m* neto

news *n* noticia *f*

news agency *n* agencia *f* de prensa

newspaper *n* periódico *m*

niche *n* hueco *m* de un mercado

night *n* noche *f*

night rate *n* tarifa *f* nocturna

night shift *n* turno *m* de noche

nil *n* nada *f*; cero *m*

nil return *n* U.K. declaración *f* de ingresos nulos

NLQ *abbr* (*near letter-quality*) calidad *f* de semicorrespondencia

no-claims bonus *n* U.K. prima *f* por ausencia de siniestralidad

nominal capital *n* capital *m* nominal

nominal ledger *n* libro *m* mayor de resultados

nominal rent *n* renta *f* nominal

nominal value *n* valor *m* nominal

nominee *n* candidato *m* propuesto *or* -a

nominee account *n* cuenta *f* administrada por un apoderado

non-delivery *n* falta *f* de entrega

non-executive director *n* director *m* no ejecutivo

nonfeasance *n* delito *m* por omisión

nonnegotiable instrument *n* documento *m* no negociable

non-payment *n* (*of a debt*) impago *m* de una deuda

non profit-making *adj* sin fines lucrativos

non-recurring items *npl* partidas *fpl* extraordinarias

non-refundable deposit *n* depósito *m* no reembolsable

non-returnable packing *n* envase *m* no retornable

non-stop *adv* sin parar; sin escalas

non-taxable income *n* ingresos *mpl* libres de impuestos

norm *n* norma *f*

normal *adj* normal

no-strike agreement, no-strike clause *n* cláusula *f* que prohibe la huelga

notary public *n* notario *m*

note *n* nota *f* ■ *v* (*details*) apuntar; anotar

note of hand *n* pagaré *m*; letra *f* al propio cargo

nothing *pron* nada

notice *n* 1. (*piece of information*) letrero *m*; anuncio *m*; aviso *m* 2. (*leaving a job*) notificación *f* de despido; de dimisión 3. (*period of time*) plazo *m* 4. (*legal document*) aviso *m*; notificación *f*

notification *n* notificación *f*

notify *v* notificar; avisar

null *adj* nulo *or* -la

number *n* número *m* ■ *v* numerar

numbered account *n* cuenta *f* numerada

numeric, numerical *n* numérico *or* -ca

numeric keypad *n* teclado *m* numérico

O

obey v obedecer; acatar

objective adj objetivo or -va ■ n objetivo m

obligation n 1. (*debt*) deuda f 2. (*duty*) obligación f; compromiso m

obsolescence n obsolescencia f

obsolescent adj obsolescente

obsolete adj obsoleto or -ta

obtain v obtener; conseguir

obtainable adj asequible

occupancy n ocupación f

occupancy rate n índice m de ocupación

occupant n ocupante mf; habitante mf; inquilino or -na

occupation n ocupación f

occupational adj laboral

occupational accident n accidente m laboral

odd adj (*not a pair*) suelto or -ta; desparejado or -da ■ v (*number*) impar

odd numbers npl números mpl impares

off adj 1. (*away from work*) ausente del trabajo 2. (*cancelled*) cancelado or -da; suspendido or -da ■ adv (*reduced by*) con descuento

offer n oferta f ■ v ofrecer

offer for sale n oferta f de venta

offer price n precio m de oferta

office n oficina f; despacho m

office equipment n equipo m de oficina

office furniture n muebles mpl de oficina

office hours npl horario m de oficina

office security n medidas fpl de seguridad (en una oficina)

office space n espacio m para oficinas

office staff n personal m administrativo

office stationery n artículos mpl de papelería para oficina

offices to rent n oficinas fpl de alquiler

official adj oficial ■ n funcionario or -ria

officialese n lenguaje m burocrático

official receiver n administrador or -ra judicial; síndico m

official return n declaración f oficial

offload v descargar; deshacerse de

off-peak adj fuera de horas punta

off-season n temporada f baja

offshore adv en aguas territoriales

off-the-job training n formación f profesional fuera del trabajo

off the record phrase extraoficialmente; fuera de actas

oil n 1. aceite m 2. (*petroleum*) petróleo m

oil-exporting countries npl países mpl exportadores de petróleo

oil price n precio m del crudo; del petróleo

oil-producing countries npl países mpl productores de petróleo

old adj viejo or -ja; antiguo or -gua

old-established adj antiguo or -gua

old-fashioned adj anticuado or -da; pasado or -da de moda

ombudsman n defensor m del pueblo

omission n omisión f

omit v omitir

on account phrase a cuenta

on agreed terms phrase en las condiciones acordadas

on an annual basis phrase anualmente

on an average *phrase* por término medio

on approval *phrase* a prueba

on a short-term basis *phrase* plazo: a corto plazo

on behalf of *phrase* en nombre de

on board *phrase* a bordo

on business *phrase* por asuntos de negocios

on condition that *phrase* a condición de que

on credit *phrase* a crédito

one-off *adj U.K.* único *or* -ca

one-off item *n U.K.* artículo *m* único

one-sided *adj* unilateral

one-sided agreement *n* acuerdo *m* unilateral

one-way fare *n* billete *m* de ida; pasaje *m* sencillo

one-way trade *n* comercio *m* unilateral

on favorable terms *phrase* en condiciones favorables

on line, online *phrase* en línea

on order *adv* pedido *or* -da

on request *phrase* a petición

on sale *phrase* a la venta

on the increase *phrase* en aumento

on-the-job training *n* formación *f* profesional en el trabajo

on time *phrase* a tiempo

OPEC *abbr* (*Organization of Petroleum Exporting Countries*) OPEP (Organización de los Países Exportadores de Petróleo)

open *adj* abierto *or* -ta ■ *v* abrir

open a bank account *v* abrir una cuenta bancaria

open account *n* cuenta *f* abierta

open a line of credit *v* abrir una línea de crédito

open a meeting *v* abrir la sesión

open an account *v* abrir una cuenta

open a new business *v* abrir un negocio

open check *n* cheque *m* abierto; cheque *m* sin cruzar

open credit *n* crédito *m* abierto

open-ended agreement *n* acuerdo *m* modificable

opening *adj* inaugural; inicial ■ *n* apertura *f*; inauguración *f*

opening balance *n* saldo *m* inicial

opening bid *n* oferta *f* inicial

opening hours *npl* horario *m* comercial

opening price *n* precio *m* de apertura; cotización *f* de apertura

opening stock *n U.K.* existencias *fpl* iniciales

opening time *n* hora *f* de apertura

open market *n* mercado *m* libre

open negotiations *v* entablar negociaciones

open-plan office *n* oficina *f* de distribución modificable

open ticket *n* billete *m* abierto

open to offers *phrase* se admiten ofertas

operate *v* 1. operar; manejar 2. (*work*) entrar en vigor

operating *n* funcionamiento *m*; operación *f*

operating budget *n* presupuesto *m* de explotación

operating costs, operating expenses *npl* gastos *mpl* de explotación

operating manual *n* manual *m* de funcionamiento

operating profit *n* beneficio *m* de explotación

operating system *n* sistema *m* operativo

operation *n* operación *f*

operational *adj* operacional

operational budget *n* presupuesto *m* de explotación

operational costs *npl* gastos *mpl* de explotación

operative *adj* operativo *or* -va ■ *n*

operator operario *or* -ria; maquinista *mf*

opinion poll n encuesta f; sondeo m de opinión

opportunity n oportunidad f

optional adj opcional; optativo or -va

optional extras npl extras mpl opcionales

option to purchase n opción f de compra

order n 1. orden m 2. (for goods) pedido m 3. (money) libramiento m; orden f de pago ■ v 1. ordenar 2. (goods) hacer un pedido; encargar

order book n libro m de pedidos

order fulfillment n despacho m de pedidos

order number n número m de pedido

order: on order adv pedido or -da

order picking n selección f de artículos para un pedido

order processing n preparación f de pedidos

ordinary adj ordinario or -ria; corriente

ordinary shares npl acciones fpl ordinarias

ordinary wear and tear n desgaste m natural

organization n 1. organización f 2. (institution) organismo m; asociación f

organizational adj organizativo or -va

organization and methods n organización y métodos

organization chart n organigrama m

Organization of Petroleum Exporting Countries (OPEC) n Organización de los Países Exportadores de Petróleo (OPEP)

organize v organizar; preparar

origin n origen m

original adj original ■ n original m

OS abbr (outsize) talla f muy grande

outbid v pujar más alto; sobrepujar

outgoing adj saliente

outgoing mail n correspondencia f de salida

outgoings npl desembolsos mpl

outlay n desembolso m; gasto m

outlet n mercado m

outline n bosquejo m

out of control phrase fuera de control

out of date adj anticuado or -da; caducado or -da

out-of-pocket expenses npl gastos mpl reemborsables

out of stock adj agotado or -da

out of work adj sin empleo; sin trabajo

output n 1. producción f; rendimiento m 2. (computer) datos mpl de salida ■ v producir

output tax n impuesto m sobre las ventas de bienes o servicios

outright adv en su totalidad

outside adj exterior; externo or -na

outside director n director m externo

outside line n línea f exterior

outside office hours phrase fuera de horas de oficina

outsize n talla f muy grande

outstanding adj 1. (exceptional) notable; destacado or -da; sobresaliente 2. (unpaid) pendiente

outstanding debts npl deudas fpl pendientes

outstanding orders npl pedidos mpl pendientes

overall adv global; en conjunto; general

overall plan n plan m general

overbook v reservar con exceso

overbooking n sobrecontratación m

overcapacity n sobrecapacidad f

overcharge n precio m excesivo; recargo m ■ v cargar en exceso; cobrar de más

overdraft n sobregiro m; descubierto m

overdraft facility n *U.K.* límite m de descubierto bancario

overdraw v girar en descubierto

overdrawn account n cuenta f en descubierto

overdue adj vencido or -da; atrasado or -da

overestimate v sobrevalorar; sobrestimar

overhead npl gastos mpl generales; gastos mpl de producción

overhead budget n presupuesto m de gastos generales

overhead costs, overhead expenses npl gastos mpl generales; gastos mpl de producción

overmanning n exceso m de personal; excedente m laboral

overpayment n pago m en exceso

overproduce v producir en exceso

overproduction n sobreproducción f

overseas adj extranjero or -ra ■ adv en el extranjero ■ n extranjero m

overseas markets npl mercados mpl extranjeros

overseas trade n comercio m exterior

overspend v gastar excesivamente

overspend one's budget v gastar más de lo presupuestado

overstock v acumular en exceso; abarrotar

overstocks npl exceso m de existencias

overtime n horas fpl extraordinarias

overtime ban n prohibición f de hacer horas extras

overtime pay n tarifa f de horas extras

overvalue v sobrevalorar; sobrestimar

overweight: to be overweight adj pesar en exceso

owe v deber

owing adj debido or -da

owing to phrase debido a; a causa de

own v poseer; tener

own brand goods n productos mpl de marca propia

owner n amo m; propietario or -ria; dueño mf or -ña

ownership n propiedad f; posesión f

own label goods n productos mpl de marca propia

P

PA abbr (*personal assistant*) ayudante mf personal

pack n paquete m; envase m ■ v embalar; envasar; empaquetar

package n 1. (*of goods*) paquete m; embalaje m; envase m 2. (*of economic measures*) conjunto m de medidas económicas

package deal n acuerdo m global; transacción f global

packaging n embalaje m; envase m

packaging material n material m de embalaje

packer n embalador or -ra; empaquetador or -ra

packet n paquete m; cajetilla f; bulto m

pack goods into cartons v embalar mercancías en cajas de cartón

packing n embalaje m; envase m

packing case n caja f de embalar

packing charges npl gastos mpl de embalaje

packing list, packing slip n lista f de bultos; de contenidos

pack of envelopes n paquete m de sobres

paid adj pagado or -da

pallet n paleta f

palletize v empaletar

p & p abbr (postage and packing) franqueo y embalaje

panel n panel m; tablero m

panic buying n compra f febril

paper bag n bolsa f de papel

paperclip n sujetapapeles m; clip m

paper feed n alimentador m del papel

paper loss n pérdida f sobre el papel

paper profit n beneficio m ficticio; beneficio m sobre el papel

papers npl papeles mpl; documentos mpl

paperwork n papeleo m

par v par

parcel n paquete m ■ v empaquetar; envolver

parcel post n servicio m de paquetes postales

parent company n sociedad f matriz; casa f matriz

parity n paridad f; igualdad f

part n parte f

part exchange n canje m parcial

partial loss n pérdida f parcial

partial payment n pago m parcial

particulars npl detalles mpl; pormenores mpl

partner n socio or -cia

partnership n sociedad f; asociación f

part owner n copropietario or -ria

part ownership n copropiedad f

part-time adj, adv a tiempo parcial

part-timer n trabajador m a tiempo parcial

part-time work, part-time employment n trabajo m por horas; empleo m a tiempo parcial

party n parte f

par value n valor m a la par

patent n patente f

patent agent n agente mf de patentes y marcas

patent an invention v patentar un invento

patent applied for, patent pending n patente f solicitada; patente f en tramitación

patented adj patentado or -da

pay n paga f ■ v pagar; abonar

pay a bill v pagar una cuenta

payable adj pagadero or -ra

payable at sixty days phrase pagadero a sesenta días

payable in advance phrase pagadero por adelantado

payable on delivery phrase pagadero a la entrega

payable on demand phrase pagadero a la vista

pay a dividend v distribuir un dividendo

pay an invoice v pagar una factura

pay back v devolver; reembolsar

payback clause n cláusula f de reembolso

payback period n periodo m de reembolso

pay by check v pagar con cheque

pay by credit card v pagar con tarjeta de crédito

pay cash v pagar al contado; pagar en efectivo

paycheck n cheque m de sueldo; cheque m de salario

pay desk n caja f

payee n portador or -ra

payer n pagador or -ra

pay in advance v pagar por adelantado

paying adj rentable

paying-in slip n U.K. recibo m (de depósito)

pay in installments v pagar a plazos

pay interest v pagar intereses

payload n carga f útil

payment n pago m; remuneración f

payment by check n pago m mediante cheque

payment by results n pago m a destajo

payment in cash n pago m en metálico; pago m en efectivo

payment in kind n pago m en especie

payment on account n pago m a cuenta

payment order n orden f de pago

pay money down v hacer un depósito; dar una entrada

pay off v 1. (*debt*) redimir; reembolsar 2. (*worker*) despedir

pay out v pagar; desembolsar; abonar

pay phone n teléfono m público

pay raise n aumento m de sueldo

pay slip n hoja f de sueldo; de salario

pay up v pagar una deuda

PC abbr (*personal computer*) ordenador m personal

peak n cumbre f; punto m máximo; cima f ■ v llegar al máximo; alcanzar el punto más alto

peak output n rendimiento m máximo

peak period n horas fpl punta

peg prices v estabilizar los precios

penalize v penalizar; sancionar

penalty n pena f; multa f

penalty clause n cláusula f penal

pending adj pendiente

penetrate a market v penetrar un mercado

pension n pensión f; retiro m

pension fund n fondo m de pensiones

pension plan n plan m de pensiones

per adv per; a; por

per annum adv al año

P/E ratio abbr (*price/earnings ratio*) relación f precio-beneficios

per capita adv, adj per cápita

percent adv por ciento

percentage n porcentaje m; tanto m por ciento

percentage discount n porcentaje m de descuento

percentage increase n porcentaje m de aumento

percentage point n punto m porcentual

per day phrase al día

perform v actuar; ejercer

performance n actuación f; funcionamiento m; rendimiento m

performance rating n valoración f de resultados

per head phrase por persona

per hour phrase por hora

period n periodo m; plazo m

periodic, periodical adj periódico or -ca

periodical n publicación f periódica; revista f

period of notice n periodo m de preaviso

period of validity n periodo m de validez

peripherals npl periféricos mpl

perishable adj perecedero or -ra

perishable goods npl artículos mpl perecederos

perishables n productos mpl perecederos

permanent contract n contrato m permanente

permission n permiso m; licencia f

permit n permiso m; licencia f ■ v permitir

personal adj personal

personal allowances npl deducciones fpl personales

personal assets npl bienes mpl personales

personal assistant n ayudante mf

personal computer n ordenador m personal

personal income n renta f personal

personalized adj con las iniciales

personalized briefcase *n* cartera *f* con las iniciales

personalized checks *n* cheques *mpl* con el nombre impreso

personnel *n* personal *m*

personnel department *n* departamento *m* de personal

personnel management *n* dirección *f* de personal

personnel manager *n* jefe *m* de personal

per week *phrase* por semana

per year *adv* al año

peso *n* (*South American currency*) peso *m*

petty *adj* insignificante

petty cash *n* fondos *mpl*; dinero *m* para gastos menores

petty cash box *n* caja *f* para gastos menores

petty expenses *npl* gastos *mpl* menores

phase *n* fase *f*

phase in *v* introducir gradualmente

phase out *v* reducir gradualmente; retirar gradualmente

phoenix syndrome *n* síndrome del fénix

phone *n* teléfono *m* ■ *v* telefonear; llamar (por teléfono)

phone back *v* volver a telefonear; llamar

phone call *n* llamada *f* telefónica

phone card *n* teletarjeta *f*

phone number *n* número *m* de teléfono

photocopier *n* fotocopiadora *f*

photocopy *n* fotocopia *f* ■ *v* fotocopiar

photocopying *n* fotocopiaje *m*; fotocopia *f*

photocopying service *n* servicio *m* de fotocopias

pick list *n* inventario *m* de posición (en almacén)

piece *n* pieza *f*

piece rate *n* precio *m* a destajo

piecework *n* trabajo *m* a destajo

pie chart *n* gráfico *m* circular; gráfico *m* sectorial

pilferage, pilfering *n* (pequeño) hurto *m*

pilot *adj* piloto ■ *n* (*person*) piloto *mf*

pilot program *n* programa *m* piloto

pioneer *n* pionero *or* -ra ■ *v* iniciar; abrir camino

place *n* 1. lugar *m*; posición *f*; sitio *m* 2. (*job*) puesto *m* ■ *v* colocar; poner; situar

place an order *v* cursar un pedido

place of work *n* lugar *m* de trabajo

plaintiff *n* demandante *mf*; querellante *mf*

plan *n* 1. (*drawing*) plano *m* 2. (*project*) plan *m*; proyecto *m* ■ *v* planear; planificar; proyectar

plane *n* avión *m*

plan investments *v* planificar las inversiones

planner *n* planificador *or* -ra

planning *n* planificación *f*

plant *n* 1. (*factory*) planta *f*; fábrica *f* 2. (*machinery*) maquinaria *f*

plant-hire firm *n* empresa *f* de alquiler de maquinaria

platform *n* (*railway station*) andén *m*

PLC, plc *abbr* (*Public Limited Company*) Sociedad Anónima (S.A.)

plug *n* enchufe *m* ■ *v* 1. (*block*) detener; frenar 2. (*publicize*) dar publicidad

plummet *v* caer

plus *prep* más

plus factor *n* factor *m* positivo

pocket *n* bolsillo *m*; bolsa *f* ■ *v* embolsar

pocket calculator *n* calculadora *f* de bolsillo

pocket diary *n* diario *m* de bolsillo

point *n* punto *m*

point of sale *n* punto *m* de venta

point of sale material n publicidad f en el punto de venta

policy n política f

pool resources v reunir recursos

poor quality n mala calidad f

poor service n servicio m deficiente

popular adj popular

popular prices n precios mpl populares

port n 1. puerto m 2. (computer) conexión f

portable adj portátil

port authority n autoridades fpl portuarias

port charges, port dues/fees npl derechos mpl de dársena; portuarios

portfolio n cartera f (de valores)

portfolio management n gestión f de cartera; administración f de cartera

port of call n puerto m de escala

port of embarkation n puerto m de embarque

port of registry n puerto m de registro

POS, p.o.s. abbr (point of sale) punto m de venta

position n 1. (job) puesto m; cargo m; plaza f 2. (state of affairs) posición f; situación f; postura f

positive adj positivo or -va

positive cash flow n flujo m de caja positivo

POS material n publicidad f en el punto de venta

possess v poseer

possession n posesión f

possibility n posibilidad f

possible adj posible

post n 1. (job) puesto m 2. U.K. (letters) correo m 3. U.K. (system) correos mpl ■ v U.K. enviar; mandar por correo; echar al correo

postage n franqueo m; tarifa f postal

postage and packing n (gastos de) franqueo y embalaje

postage free phrase sin gastos de franqueo

postage paid n franqueo m concertado; porte m pagado

postal adj postal

postal charges, postal rates n gastos mpl de franqueo; tarifas fpl postales

postal order n giro m postal

post an entry v hacer un asiento

postcard n (tarjeta) postal

postcode n U.K. código m postal

postdate v posfechar

poste restante n lista f de correos

post free phrase U.K. sin gastos de franqueo

postpaid adj porte m pagado; franqueo m concertado

postpone v aplazar; posponer

postponed adj aplazado or -da

postponement n aplazamiento m

potential adj potencial ■ n potencial m

potential customers npl clientes mpl eventuales

potential market n mercado m potencial

pound n libra f

pound sterling n libra f esterlina

power n poder m

power of attorney n poder m notarial; poderes mpl

PR abbr (public relations) relaciones fpl públicas

preempt v prevenir

prefer v preferir

preference n preferencia f

preference shares npl acciones fpl preferentes

preferential adj preferente; preferencial

preferential creditor n acreedor m preferente or -ra

preferential duty, preferential tariff n tarifa f preferente; tarifa f preferencial

preferred creditor n acreedor m preferente or -ra

pre-financing n prefinanciación f

premises *npl* local *m*; edificio *m*

premium *n* 1. (*extra charge*) agio *m* 2. (*insurance*) prima *f* de seguros 3. (*on lease*) traspaso *m*

premium offer *n* obsequio *m* publicitario

premium quality *n* alta calidad

prepack, prepackage *v* preempaquetar

prepaid *adj* pagado *or* -da por adelantado

prepare an invoice *v* preparar una factura

prepay *v* pagar por adelantado

prepayment *n* pago *m* por adelantado

prescribe *v* prescribir

present *adj* 1. (*being there*) presente 2. (*now*) actual ■ *n* (*gift*) regalo *m*; obsequio *m* ■ *v* 1. (*give*) regalar; obsequiar 2. (*show a document*) presentar

present a bill for acceptance *v* presentar una letra a la aceptación

present a bill for payment *v* presentar una letra al pago

presentation *n* presentación *f*

present value *n* valor *m* actual

press *n* prensa *f*

press conference *n* conferencia *f* de prensa

press release *n* comunicado *m* de prensa

prestige *n* prestigio *m*

prestige product *n* producto *m* prestigioso

pretax profit *n* beneficio *m* antes de deducir los impuestos

prevent *v* impedir; evitar; prevenir

prevention *n* prevención *f*

preventive *adj* preventivo *or* -va

previous *adj* previo *or* -via; anterior

price *n* precio *m* ■ *v* poner precio a

price ceiling *n* límite *m* de precios

price control *n* control *m* de precios

price differential *n* coeficiente *m* de ajuste de precios

price/earnings ratio (P/E ratio) *n* relación *f* precio-ganancias

price ex quay *n* franco *m* n muelle

price ex warehouse *n* franco *m* en almacén

price ex works *n* precio *m* en fábrica; franco *m* en fábrica

price label *n* etiqueta *f* de precio

price list *n* lista *f* de precios

price range *n* gama *f* de precios

price reductions *n* rebajas *fpl* de precios

price-sensitive product *n* producto *m* sensible a los cambios de precio

price stability *n* estabilidad *f* de los precios

price tag, price ticket *n* etiqueta *f* de precio

price(-cutting) war *n* guerra *f* de precios

pricing *n* fijación *f* de los precios

pricing policy *n* política *f* de precios

primary *adj* primario *or* -ria

primary industry *n* sector *m* primario

prime *adj* principal; primero *or* -ra

prime cost *n* coste *m* de producción

prime rate *n* tipo *m* preferencial de interés bancario

principal *adj* principal ■ *n* 1. (*money*) principal *m* 2. (*person*) mandante *m*

principle *n* principio *m*

printer *n* 1. (*company*) imprenta *f* 2. (*machine*) impresora *f*

print out *v* imprimir

printout *n* impresión *f*

prior *adj* anterior; previo *or* -via

private *adj* privado *or* -da; particular

private enterprise *n* empresa *f* privada

private limited company *n* sociedad *f* limitada (S.L.)

private ownership n propiedad f privada

private property n propiedad f privada

private sector n sector m privado

privatization n privatización f

privatize v privatizar

probation n periodo m de prueba

probationary n de prueba; probatorio or -ria

problem n problema m

problem area n asunto m problemático

problem solver n mediador m de conflictos

problem solving n investigación f de conflictos

procedure n procedimiento m; tramitación f; trámite m

proceed v proceder; seguir; continuar

process n procedimiento m ■ v 1. preparar; elaborar; tramitar 2. (raw materials) elaborar

process figures v elaborar cifras

produce n productos mpl ■ v 1. producir; fabricar 2. (bring out) presentar 3. (yield) producir; dar

producer n productor or -ra; fabricante m

product n producto m

product advertising n anuncio m del producto

product cycle n ciclo m del producto

product design n diseño m de productos

product development n desarrollo m de productos

product engineer n ingeniero m de producto

production n 1. producción f 2. (showing) presentación f

production cost n coste m de producción

production department n departamento m de producción

production line n cadena f de montaje

production manager n director m de producción

production standards npl normas fpl de producción

production target n objetivo m de producción

production unit n unidad f de producción

productive adj productivo or -va

productive discussions npl conversaciones fpl fructíferas

productivity n productividad f

productivity agreement n acuerdo m de productividad

productivity bonus n prima f de productividad

product line n gama f de productos; línea f de productos

product mix n gama f de productos de una compañía

professional adj (expert) profesional ■ n (expert) profesional mf

professional qualifications n títulos mpl profesionales

profit n ganancia f; beneficio m

profitability n 1. (making a profit) rentabilidad f 2. (ratio of profit to cost) coeficiente m de rentabilidad

profitable adj rentable; productivo or -va; lucrativo or -va

profit after tax n beneficio m neto de impuestos

profit and loss account n cuenta f de pérdidas y ganancias

profit before tax n beneficio m antes de deducir los impuestos

profit center n centro m de beneficios

profit-making adj rentable; lucrativo or -va

profit margin n margen m de beneficio

profit-oriented company n empresa f con fines de lucro

profit-sharing n participación f en los beneficios

pro forma (invoice) n factura f pro forma

program n programa m

program a computer v programar un ordenador

programming language n lenguaje m de programación

progress n progreso m; marcha f; avance m ■ v progresar; avanzar

progress chaser n responsable mf del progreso de un trabajo

progressive adj progresivo or -va

progressive taxation n tributación f progresiva

progress payments npl pagos mpl a cuenta

progress report n informe m sobre la marcha de un trabajo

prohibitive adj prohibitivo or -va

project n proyecto m; plan m ■ v proyectar

project analysis n análisis m de proyectos

projected adj proyectado or -da; previsto or -ta

projected sales n ventas fpl previstas

project manager n director m de proyecto

promise n promesa f; compromiso m ■ v prometer

promissory note n pagaré m; letra f al propio cargo

promote v 1. (advertise) promocionar 2. (give better job) ascender

promote a corporate image v promocionar la imagen pública de una empresa

promote a new product v promocionar un nuevo producto

promotion n 1. (publicity) promoción f 2. (to better job) ascenso m

promotional adj de promoción; en promoción

promotion(al) budget n presupuesto m de promoción

promotion of a product n promoción f de un producto

prompt adj pronto or -ta; rápido or -da; inmediato or -ta

prompt payment n pronto pago m

prompt service n servicio m rápido

proof n prueba f

property n propiedad f

proportion n parte f; proporción f

proportional adj proporcional

proposal n proposición f; propuesta f

propose v (a motion) proponer

propose to v (do something) proponer(se)

proposition n propuesta f; proposición f

proprietary company n sociedad f de cartera

proprietor n propietario m; dueño mf or -ña

proprietress n propietaria f; dueña f

pro rata adv, adj prorrata

prosecute v procesar; enjuiciar

prosecution n 1. (legal action) procesamiento m 2. (party in legal action) parte f acusadora; acusación f

prosecution counsel n fiscal m

prospective adj eventual

prospective buyer n posible comprador or -ra

prospects npl perspectivas fpl

prospectus n prospecto m; folleto m

prosperous adj próspero

protect v proteger

protection n protección f

protectionist n proteccionista

protective adj protector or -ra; proteccionista

protective tariff n arancel m proteccionista

protest n 1. protesta f 2. (official document) protesto m ■ v protestar contra algo

protest a bill v protestar una letra

protest strike n huelga f de protesta

provide v proveer

provided that, providing phrase a condición de que

provide for v prever

provision n 1. (*condition*) disposición f; estipulación f 2. (*money put aside*) provisión f de fondos; reserva f

provisional adj provisional

provisional budget n presupuesto m provisional

provisional forecast of sales n previsión f provisional de ventas

proviso n condición f; salvedad f

proxy n 1. (*deed*) procuración f; poder m 2. (*person*) poderhabiente mf; apoderado or -da

proxy vote n voto m por poderes

public adj público or -ca

public finance n finanzas fpl públicas

public funds n fondos mpl públicos

public holiday n fiesta f nacional

public image n imagen f pública

publicity n publicidad f

publicity budget n presupuesto m publicitario

publicity campaign n campaña f publicitaria

publicity department n departamento m de publicidad

publicity expenditure n gastos mpl de publicidad

publicity manager n director m de publicidad

publicize v dar publicidad; divulgar

Public Limited Company (Plc) n sociedad f anónima (S.A.)

public opinion n opinión f pública

public relations n relaciones fpl públicas

public relations department n departamento m de relaciones públicas

public relations man n persona f dedicada a las relaciones públicas

public relations officer n responsable mf de relaciones públicas

public sector n sector m público

public transportation n transporte m público

purchase n compra f ■ v comprar

purchase ledger n libro m mayor de compras

purchase order n orden f de compra

purchase price n precio m de compra

purchaser n comprador or -ra

purchase tax n impuesto m de venta

purchasing n compra f

purchasing department n departamento m de compras; sección f de compras

purchasing manager n jefe m de compras

purchasing power n poder m adquisitivo

put v (*place*) poner

put back v (*later*) aplazar

put in order v ordenar

put in writing v poner por escrito

put money down v dar una entrada

Q

qty. abbr (*quantity*) cantidad f

qualified adj 1. cualificado or -da; capacitado or -da 2. (*with reservations*) con reservas; condicionado or -da

qualify v capacitar

qualify as v obtener el título de; sacar el título de

quality n calidad f

quality control n control m de calidad

quality controller n inspector m de calidad

quality label n signo m de calidad

quango n organismo m paraestatal

quantity n cantidad f

quantity discount n descuento m por cantidad

quarter n 1. (*25%*) cuarto m; cuarta parte f 2. (*three months*) trimestre m

quarter day n día m de ajuste

quarterly adj trimestral ■ adv trimestralmente; cada tres meses

quay n muelle m

question n pregunta f; cuestión f ■ v preguntar; cuestionar

questionnaire n cuestionario m; encuesta f

quorum n quórum m

quota n cupo m; cuota f

quotation n **quote** cotización f; presupuesto m

quote v 1. (*estimate costs*) cotizar; ofrecer un precio 2. (*reference*) citar; indicar

quoted company n sociedad f cotizada en bolsa

quoted shares n acciones fpl que se cotizan en bolsa

R

racketeer n estafador or -ra; timador or -ra

racketeering n negocio m ilícito

rail n ferrocarril m

railroad n ferrocarril m

rail transportation n transporte m por ferrocarril

railway n U.K. ferrocarril m

railway station n estación f de ferrocarril

raise v 1. aumentar; subir 2. (*a question*) plantear 3. (*obtain money*) conseguir ■ n (*salary*) aumento m de salario; aumento m de sueldo

raise an invoice v U.K. preparar una factura

rally n recuperación f ■ v recuperarse

R&D abbr (*research and development*) investigación y desarrollo (I+D)

random adj al azar; aleatorio or -ria

random check n chequeo m al azar

random error n error m aleatorio

random sample n muestra f aleatoria

random sampling n muestreo m aleatorio

range n 1. (*series of items*) gama f; surtido m 2. (*variation*) escala f ■ v oscilar

rapid adj rápido or -da

rate n 1. (*amount*) tasa f; coeficiente m 2. (*price*) precio m; tarifa f

rate of exchange n tipo m de cambio

rate of inflation n tasa f de inflación

rate of interest n rédito m; tipo m de interés

rate of production n ritmo m de producción

rate of return n tasa f de rendimiento

ratification n ratificación f

ratify v ratificar

rating n clasificación f

ratio n razón f; relación f

rationalization n racionalización f

rationalize v racionalizar

raw materials npl materias fpl primas

reach v llegar; alcanzar

reach a decision v tomar una decisión

reach an agreement v llegar a un acuerdo

readjust v reajustar

readjustment n reajuste m

ready adj listo or -ta; preparado or -da

ready cash n efectivo m

real adj real; verdadero or -ra

real estate n bienes mpl raíces; propiedad f inmobiliaria

real income, real wages n renta f real

realizable assets npl activo m realizable

realization n realización f

realization of assets n liquidación f de activo

realize v 1. realizar 2. (understand) darse cuenta

realize a project, a plan v realizar un proyecto; realizar un plan

realize property, assets v liquidar propiedades; realizar activos

real-time system n sistema m de ordenador a tiempo real

reapplication n segunda solicitud f

reapply v volver a presentarse

reappoint v volver a nombrar

reappointment n nuevo nombramiento m

reason n razón f

reassess v revaluar

reassessment n revaluación f

rebate n 1. (money back) reembolso m 2. (price reduction) rebaja f; descuento m

receipt n 1. (paper) recibo m; resguardo m 2. (receiving) recepción f

receipt book n talonario m de recibos

receipts npl ingresos mpl; entradas fpl

receivable adj a cobrar; por cobrar

receivables npl efectos mpl a cobrar

receive v recibir

receiver n (liquidator) síndico m

receiver (who receives) n destinatario or -ria; receptor m

reception n recepción f; acogida f

reception clerk n recepcionista mf

reception desk n recepción f

receptionist n recepcionista mf

recession n recesión f

reciprocal adj recíproco or -ca; bilateral

reciprocal agreement n acuerdo m recíproco; acuerdo m bilateral

reciprocal trade n comercio m recíproco

reciprocity n reciprocidad f

recognition n reconocimiento m

recognize a union v reconocer a un sindicato

recommend v recomendar; aconsejar

recommendation n recomendación f

reconcile v cuadrar; ajustar

reconciliation n reconciliación f; concertación f

reconciliation of accounts n conciliación f de cuentas

record n 1. récord m 2. (for personnel) historial m; expediente m 3. (of what has happened) acta f; registro m; informe m ■ v registrar; anotar

record-breaking adj récord

recorded delivery n U.K. entrega f con acuse de recibo

records npl archivos mpl

recoup one's losses v resarcirse de las pérdidas

recover v 1. (get better) recuperarse; mejorar 2. (get something back) recuperar; recobrar

recoverable adj recuperable

recovery n 1. (getting better) reactivación f 2. (getting something back) recuperación f; rescate m

rectification n rectificación f

rectify v corregir; rectificar

recurrent adj que se repite; constante

recycle v reciclar

recycled paper n papel m reciclado

redeem v amortizar; redimir

redeemable adj rescatable; amortizable

redeem a bond v vender un bono; amortizar una obligación

redeem a debt v pagar una deuda

redeem a pledge v rescatar una prenda

redemption n (of a loan) amortización f; rescate m

redemption date n fecha f de amortización; fecha f de rescate

redevelop v renovar

redevelopment n renovación f urbana

redistribute v redistribuir

red tape n burocracia f; papeleo m

reduce (a price) v rebajar un precio; reducir un precio

reduced rate n precio m reducido; tarifa f reducida

reduce expenditure v reducir gastos

reduction n reducción f; rebaja f

redundancy n U.K. excedente m de plantilla; despido m

redundant adj redundante

re-elect v reelegir

reelection n reelección f

re-employ v emplear de nuevo

reemployment n reempleo m

re-export n reexportación f ■ v reexportar

refer v 1. (pass to someone) remitir 2. (to item) referirse; mencionar

reference n referencia f

reference number n número m de referencia

refinancing of a loan n refinanciación f de un préstamo

refresher course n curso m de reciclaje; curso m de actualización

refund n devolución f; reembolso m ■ v reembolsar; devolver

refundable adj reembolsable

refundable deposit n depósito m reembolsable

refunding of a loan n conversión f de un préstamo

refusal n negativa f; rechazo m

refuse v rehusar; negar(se); rechazar

regarding prep relativo a; en cuanto a

regardless of prep sin tener en cuenta

region n región f

regional adj regional

register n 1. (large book) libro m de registro 2. (official list) registro m ■ v 1. (at hotel) registrarse; inscribirse 2. (in official list) registrar; inscribir (en un registro) 3. (letter) certificar

register a company v inscribir una compañía en un registro

register a property v registrar una propiedad

register a trademark v registrar una marca comercial

registered adj registrado or -da; certificado or -da

registered design n diseño m registrado

registered letter n carta f certificada

registered office n domicilio m social

registered trademark n marca f registrada

register of directors n relación f de directivos de una empresa

register of stockholders n libro m registro de accionistas

registrar n registrador or -ra; secretario m general

Registrar of Companies n Registro m Mercantil

registration n registro m; inscripción f; matrícula f

registration fee n cuota f de inscripción; matrícula f

registration form n boletín m de inscripción

registration number n número m de registro; número m de matrícula

registry n registro m

registry office n oficina f del registro civil

regular v (always at same time) regular ■ adj (ordinary) normal; ordinario or -ria; corriente

regular customer n cliente mf habitual

regular income n ingreso m fijo

regular route n ruta f habitual

regular size n tamaño m normal

regular staff n personal m fijo

regulate v 1. (adjust) regular 2. (by law) reglamentar

regulation n regulación f; reglamentación f

regulations npl normas fpl; reglamento m

reimbursement n reembolso m; reintegro m

reimbursement of expenses n reembolso m de gastos

reimport n reimportación f ■ v reimportar

reimportation n reimportación f

reinsurance n reaseguro m

reinsure v reasegurar

reinsurer n reasegurador or -ra

reinvest v reinvertir

reinvestment n reinversión f

reject n producto m defectuoso ■ v rechazar

rejection n rechazo m

relating to phrase referente; relativo a

relation n relación f

relations n relaciones fpl

release n liberación f ■ v 1. (free) liberar 2. (make public) divulgar; publicar 3. (put on the market) poner a la venta; lanzar al mercado

release dues v despachar pedidos atrasados

relevant adj apropiado or -da; pertinente

reliability n fiabilidad f

reliable adj fiable; de confianza; cumplidor or -ra

remain v 1. (be left) quedar; sobrar 2. (stay) quedarse

remainder n (things left) resto m

remember v recordar; acordarse (de)

remind v recordar

reminder n recordatorio m; advertencia f

remit v remitir

remit by check v remitir por cheque

remittance n envío m; giro m

remote control n mando m a distancia

removal n 1. mudanza f; traslado m 2. (sacking someone) destitución f; despido m

remove v 1. quitar; destituir; suprimir 2. (to new house) trasladar; mudar

remunerate v remunerar

remuneration n remuneración f

render an account v presentar una cuenta; presentar una factura

renew v renovar; prorrogar

renewal n renovación f; prórroga f

renew a lease v prorrogar un arrendamiento

renewal notice n notificación f de renovación

renewal premium n prima f de renovación

renew a subscription v renovar una suscripción; renovar un abono

rent n alquiler m; renta f ■ v (pay money for) alquilar; arrendar

rent a car v alquilar un coche

rent a crane v alquilar una grúa

rental n alquiler m

rental agency n agencia f de alquiler de viviendas

rental car n coche m de alquiler

rental income n ingresos mpl por alquiler; renta f por alquiler

rent collector n cobrador m de alquileres

rent control n control m de rentas; control m de alquileres

rent-free adj exento de alquiler

rent tribunal n tribunal m de rentas

renunciation n renuncia f

reorder n nuevo pedido m ■ v renovar un pedido

reorganization n reorganización f

reorganize v reorganizar

rep abbr (representative) representante mf

repair n reparación f ■ v reparar; componer

repay v pagar; reembolsar; resarcir

repayable adj reembolsable

repayment n reembolso m; pago m

repeat v repetir

repeat an order v renovar un pedido

repeat order n pedido m suplementario

replace v reemplazar; sustituir; reponer

replacement n 1. (item) reemplazo m; repuesto m 2. (person) sustituto or -ta

replacement value n valor m de reposición

reply n respuesta f; contestación f ■ v responder; contestar

reply coupon n boletín m de respuesta

report n informe m; memoria f ■ v 1. informar 2. (go to a place) presentarse

report v, on progress v informar sobre la marcha

report a loss v anunciar un déficit

report for an interview v presentarse a una entrevista

report to someone v rendir cuentas a alguien

repossess v recuperar; recobrar

represent v representar

representative adj representativo or -va ■ n representante mf

repudiate v repudiar

repudiate an agreement v negarse a cumplir un acuerdo

reputation n reputación f

request n ruego m; petición f; solicitud f ■ v pedir; solicitar

request: on request phrase petición: a petición

require v 1. requerir 2. (demand) exigir

requirements npl requisitos mpl

resale n reventa f

resale price n precio m de reventa

rescind v rescindir; anular

research n investigación f ■ v investigar

research and development n investigación y desarrollo (I+D)

research program n programa m de investigación

research worker, researcher n investigador or -ra

reservation n reserva f

reserve n 1. reserva f 2. (supplies) reservas fpl ■ v reservar

reserve currency n divisas fpl de reserva

reserve price n precio m mínimo aceptable

reserves npl reservas fpl

residence n residencia f

residence permit n permiso m de residencia

resident adj residente ■ n residente mf; habitante mf

resign v resignar; dimitir

resignation n dimisión f; renuncia f

resolution n resolución f

resolve v resolver; decidir

resources npl recursos mpl

respect v respetar; acatar

respond v responder

response n respuesta f; reacción f

responsibilities npl responsabilidades fpl; obligaciones fpl

responsibility n responsabilidad f

responsible (for) adj responsable

responsible to someone v ser responsable ante alguien

rest n 1. descanso m 2. (*remainder*) resto m

restock v renovar existencias; repostar

restocking n renovación f de existencias

restraint n restricción f

restraint of trade n restricción f comercial

restrict v restringir; limitar

restrict credit v limitar el crédito

restriction n restricción f; limitación f

restrictive adj restrictivo or -va

restrictive practices n prácticas fpl restrictivas

restructure v reestructurar

restructuring n reestructuración f

restructuring of a loan n consolidación f de un préstamo

restructuring of the company n reestructuración f de la compañía

result n (*general*) resultado m

result from v resultar de; derivar de

result in v resultar; dar por resultado

results npl (*company's profit or loss*) resultados mpl

resume v reanudar

résumé n curriculum (vitae) m

resume negotiations v reanudar las negociaciones

retail n venta f al por menor; venta f detalle ■ v vender; venderse al por menor

retail dealer n comerciante mf al por menor; minorista mf

retailer n detallista mf; minorista mf

retail goods v vender al por menor

retailing n comercio m al por menor

retail outlets n tiendas fpl al detall

retail price n precio m al por menor

retail price index n índice m de precios al consumo

retire v (*from one's job*) jubilarse; retirarse

retirement n jubilación f; retiro m

retirement age n edad f de jubilación

retiring adj saliente

retrain v reciclar

retraining n reciclaje m profesional

retrenchment n reducción f de gastos

retrieval n recuperación f; rescate m

retrieval system n sistema m de recuperación

retrieve v recuperar; rescatar

retroactive adj retroactivo or -va

retroactive pay raise n aumento m retroactivo de salarios

return n 1. vuelta f; regreso m 2. (*profit*) ganancia f; rendimiento m 3. (*sending back*) devolución f ■ v (*send back*) devolver

returnable adj retornable

return address n remite m

return a letter to sender v devolver una carta al remitente

returned empties npl envases mpl devueltos

return on investment n rendimiento m de la inversión

returns npl (*profits*) beneficios mpl ■ n (*unsold goods*) productos mpl devueltos sin vender

revaluation n reevaluación f

revalue v revaluar

revenue n ingreso m

revenue accounts npl contabilidad f de ingresos

revenue from advertising n ingresos mpl por publicidad

reversal n inversión f; revocación f

reverse adj revertido or -da ■ v revocar

reverse charge call *n U.K.* llamada *f* a cobro revertido

reverse takeover *n* contra OPA *f*

reverse the charges *v U.K.* llamar a cobro revertido

revise *v* revisar; corregir

revoke *v* revocar

revolving credit *n* crédito *m* renovable

rider *n* cláusula *f* adicional

right *adj* **1.** (*not left*) derecho *or* -a **2.** (*not wrong*) correcto *or* -ta ■ *n* (*legal title*) derecho *m*

rightful *adj* legítimo *or* -ma

rightful claimant *n* derechohabiente *m*

rightful owner *n* propietario legítimo *or* propietaria legítima

right-hand man *n* brazo *m* derecho; hombre *m* de confianza

right of veto *n* derecho *m* de veto

right of way *n* derecho *m* de paso

rights issue *n* emisión *f* de derechos

rise *n* **1.** (*increase*) alza *f*; subida *f*; aumento *m* **2.** *U.K.* (*salary*) aumento *m* de salario; aumento *m* de sueldo ■ *v* subir

risk *n* riesgo *m* ■ *v* (*money*) arriesgar

risk capital *n* capital-riesgo *m*

risk-free investment *n* inversión *f* sin riesgo

risk premium *n* prima *f* de riesgo

risky *adj* arriesgado *or* -da

rival company *n* empresa *f* competidora

road *n* carretera *f*

road haulage *n* transporte *m* por carretera

road hauler *n* transportista *mf*

road tax *n* impuesto *m* de circulación

road transportation *n* transporte *m* por carretera

rock-bottom prices *n* precios *mpl* reventados

ROI *abbr* (*return on investment*) rendimiento *m* de la inversión

rolling plan *n* plan *m* periódicamente actualizado

roll on/roll off ferry *n* ferry roll-on roll-off

rollout *n* (*of product*) lanzamiento *m*

roll over credit, a debt *v* refinanciar un crédito; refinanciar una deuda

room *n* **1.** (*general*) sala *f* **2.** (*hotel*) habitación *f* **3.** (*space*) espacio *m*

room reservations *npl* departamento *m* de reservas

room service *n* servicio *m* de habitaciones de un hotel

rough *adj* (*estimate*) aproximado *or* -da

rough calculation *n* cálculo *m* aproximado

rough draft *n* borrador *m*; bosquejo *m*

rough estimate *n* cálculo *m* aproximado

round down *v* redondear por defecto

round up *v* redondear por exceso

routine *adj* rutinario *or* -ria; habitual ■ *n* rutina *f*; costumbre *f*

routine call *n* llamada *f* rutinaria

routine work *n* trabajo *m* rutinario

royalty *n* canon *m*; derechos *mpl* de autor

rubber check *n* cheque *m* sin fondos

rule *n* norma *f*; regla *f* ■ *v* **1.** (*be in force*) regir **2.** (*give decision*) decretar

ruling *adj* vigente ■ *n* decisión *f*; fallo *m*

run *n* **1.** (*regular route*) ruta *f* habitual **2.** (*rush to buy*) demanda *f* excesiva **3.** (*work routine*) ciclo *m* de trabajo ■ *v* **1.** (*be in force*) ser válido; regir **2.** (*buses, trains*) circular *v* **3.** (*manage*) dirigir; llevar **4.** (*work machine*) utilizar; hacer funcionar

run a risk *v* correr un riesgo

run into debt *v* endeudarse; adeudarse

running n (of machine) funcionamiento m

running costs, running expenses npl gastos mpl corrientes; gastos de mantenimiento

running total n total m acumulado

run out v agotar las existencias

run to v ascender a

rush n prisa f ■ v precipitarse

rush hour n horas fpl punta

rush job n trabajo m urgente

rush order n pedido m urgente

S

sack v **someone** v despedir a alguien

safe adj seguro or -ra ■ n caja f fuerte; caja f de caudales

safe deposit n caja f de seguridad

safeguard v proteger

safe investment n inversión f segura

safety n seguridad f

safety measures npl medidas fpl de seguridad

safety precautions npl precauciones fpl; medidas fpl de precaución

safety regulations npl normas fpl de seguridad

salability n facilidad f de venta

salable adj vendible

salaried adj asalariado or -da

salary n salario m; sueldo m

salary check n cheque m de sueldo

salary review n revisión f de sueldos

sale n 1. (at a low price) liquidación f; saldo m; rebajas fpl 2. (selling) venta f

sale by auction n venta f en subasta

sale on approval n venta f a prueba

sale or return n venta f a prueba; venta f en depósito

sales npl ventas fpl

sales analysis n análisis m de ventas

sales book n libro m de ventas

sales budget n presupuesto m de ventas

sales campaign n campaña f de ventas

sales chart n gráfico m de ventas

sales clerk n vendedor or -ra

sales conference n reunión f de ventas

sales curve n curva f de ventas

sales department n sección f de ventas

sales drive n campaña f de ventas; promoción f de ventas

sales executive n ejecutivo m de ventas

sales figures npl cifras fpl de ventas

sales force n personal m de ventas

sales forecast n previsión f de ventas

sales ledger n libro m mayor de ventas

sales ledger clerk n encargado m del libro de ventas

sales literature n información f publicitaria

salesman n 1. (in shop) dependiente mf or -ta; vendedor m 2. (representative) representante mf

sales manager n director m comercial

sales people n personal m de ventas

sales pitch n rollo m publicitario

sales promotion n promoción f de ventas

sales receipt n comprobante m de caja

sales representative n representante mf

sales revenue n ingresos mpl de ventas; facturación f

sales target n objetivo m de ventas

sales tax n impuesto m sobre la venta

sales team n equipo m de ventas

sales volume n volumen m de ventas

salvage n 1. (action) salvamento m; rescate m 2. (things saved) objetos mpl salvados ■ v salvar

salvage vessel n buque m de salvamento

sample n (group) muestra f; muestreo m ■ v 1. (ask questions) hacer un muestreo 2. (test) probar

sampling n (statistics) muestreo m por áreas

satisfaction n satisfacción f

satisfy v (customer) satisfacer

satisfy a demand v satisfacer una demanda

saturate v saturar

saturate the market v saturar el mercado

saturation n saturación f

save v 1. ahorrar; economizar; guardar 2. (on computer) archivar; guardar

save on v ahorrar; economizar

save up v ahorrar

savings npl ahorros mpl

savings account n cuenta f de ahorro

savings and loan association n sociedad f hipotecaria; sociedad f de crédito hipotecario

scale n (system) escala f

scale down v reducir a escala

scale of charges n lista f de precios

scale up v aumentar a escala

scarcity value n valor m de escasez

scheduled flight n vuelo m regular

scheduling n programación f

screen n pantalla f

screen candidates v seleccionar candidatos or -tas; pasar por la criba

scrip n certificado m provisional de acciones

scrip issue n emisión f de acciones gratuitas

seal n precinto m ■ v 1. (attach a seal) sellar; precintar 2. (envelope) cerrar

sealed envelope n sobre m cerrado

sealed tenders npl ofertas fpl lacradas

season n 1. (time for something) temporada f 2. (time of year) estación f

seasonal adj estacional

seasonal adjustments n ajustes mpl estacionales

seasonal demand n demanda f estacional

seasonally adjusted figures npl cifras fpl ajustadas estacionalmente

seasonal variations n variaciones fpl estacionales

season ticket n abono m; billete m de abono

second adj segundo or -da ■ v (member of staff) trasladar temporalmente

secondary adj secundario or -ria

secondary industry n industria f secundaria

second-class adv de segunda clase; de segunda categoría

secondhand n usado or -da; de segunda mano

second quarter n segundo trimestre

seconds npl artículos mpl con desperfectos

secret adj secreto or -ta ■ n secreto m

secretarial college *n* escuela *f* de secretariado

secretary *n* **1.** secretario *or* -ria **2.** (*government minister*) ministro *m* del gobierno

section *n* sección *f*; departamento *m*

sector *n* sector *m*

secured creditor *n* acreedor *m* con garantía *or* -ora

secured debts *npl* deudas *fpl* garantizadas

secured loan *n* préstamo *m* garantizado

secure funds *v* conseguir fondos

secure investment *n* inversión *f* segura

secure job *n* empleo *m* seguro

securities *npl* títulos *mpl*; valores *mpl*

security *n* **1.** (*being safe*) seguridad *f* **2.** (*guarantee*) fianza *f*; garantía *f*

security guard *n* guardia *m* de seguridad; vigilante *m*

security of employment *n* seguridad *f* de empleo

security of tenure *n* derecho *m* de ocupación

see-safe *n* *U.K.* venta *f* a prueba; venta *f* en depósito

seize *v* embargar; confiscar; incautar; secuestrar

seizure *n* embargo *m*; incautación *f*; secuestro *m*

selection *n* selección *f*; surtido *m*

selection procedure *n* procedimiento *m* de selección

self-employed *adj* autónomo *or* -ma

self-financing *adj* autofinanciado *or* -da ■ *n* autofinanciación *f*

self-regulation *n* autorregulación *f*

self-regulatory *adj* autorregulado *or* -da

sell *v* vender

sell-by date *n* fecha *f* de caducidad

seller *n* vendedor *or* -ra

seller's market *n* mercado *m* de vendedores

sell forward *v* vender con entrega aplazada; vender a futuros

selling *n* venta *f*

selling price *n* precio *m* de venta

sell off *v* liquidar

sell out *v* **1.** (*all stock*) agotar las existencias **2.** (*sell one's business*) vender un negocio

semi-annual *adj* semestre *m*

semi-finished products *n* productos *mpl* semiacabados

semi-skilled workers *npl* obreros *mpl* semicualificados

send *v* enviar

send an invoice by mail *v* enviar una factura por correo

send a package by airmail *v* enviar un paquete por correo aéreo

send a package by surface mail *v* enviar un paquete por vía terrestre o marítima

send a shipment by sea *v* enviar una carga por vía marítima

sender *n* remitente *mf*

senior *adj* mayor; más antiguo; superior

senior manager, senior executive *n* director *m* principal

senior partner *n* socio *m* principal

sentence *n* sentencia *f*

separate *adj* separado *or* -da ■ *v* separar; dividir

separate: under separate cover *adj* por separado

sequester, sequestrate *v* secuestrar; embargar

sequestration *n* embargo *m*

sequestrator *n* embargador *or* -ra

serial number *n* número *m* de serie

serve *v* servir; atender

serve a customer *v* atender a un cliente

service *n* **1.** servicio *m* **2.** (*of machine*) revisión *f* ■ *v* (*a machine*) revisar

service a debt *v* pagar los intereses de una deuda

service center *n* centro *m* de reparaciones

service charge *n* suplemento *m* por el servicio

service department *n* servicio *m* de mantenimiento

service industry *n* industria *f* de servicios

service manual *n* manual *m* de mantenimiento

set *adj* fijo *or* -ja ■ *n* juego *m* ■ *v* establecer; fijar

set against *v* compensar; deducir

setback *n* revés *m*

set price *n* precio *m* fijo

set targets *v* fijar objetivos

settle *v* 1. (*an invoice*) saldar una factura; pagar una factura 2. (*arrange things*) establecerse

settle a claim *v* pagar una reclamación

settle an account *v* liquidar una cuenta; saldar una cuenta

settlement *n* 1. (*agreement*) acuerdo *m* 2. (*payment*) finiquito *m*; pago *m*

setup *n* 1. (*company*) empresa *f* 2. (*organization*) sistema *m*

set up a company *v* crear; fundar una compañía

set up in business *v* poner un negocio; establecerse

share *n* 1. participación *f* 2. (*in a company*) acción *f* ■ *v* 1. (*divide among*) dividir; repartir 2. (*use with someone*) compartir

share an office *v* compartir una oficina

share capital *n* capital *m* en acciones

share certificate *n* U.K. título *m*; certificado *m* de una acción

shareholder *n* U.K. accionista *mf*

shareholding *n* tenencia *f* de acciones

share issue *n* U.K. emisión *f* de acciones

sharp practice *n* negocio *m* deshonesto (pero no ilegal)

sheet of paper *n* hoja *f* de papel

shelf *n* estantería *f*; anaquel *m*

shelf filler *n* empleado *m* para mantener llenos los estantes

shelf life of a product *n* periodo *m* de conservación de un producto

shell company *n* sociedad *f* ficticia (para la compra de acciones)

shelter *n* refugio *m*

shelve *v* dar carpetazo; arrinconar

shelving *n* (*shelves*) estantería *f*

shift *n* 1. (*change*) cambio *m* 2. (*team of workers*) turno *m*

shift key *n* tecla *f* de mayúsculas

shift work *n* trabajo *m* por turnos

ship *n* barco *m*; buque *m* ■ *v* expedir

ship broker *n* agente *mf* marítimo *or* -a

shipment *n* envío *m*; carga *f*

shipper *n* expedidor *or* -ra; transportista *mf*

shipping *n* envío *m*; expedición *f*

shipping agent *n* agente *mf* marítimo *or* -a; agencia *f* de transportes

shipping charges, shipping costs *npl* costes *mpl* de envío

shipping clerk *n* agente *mf* expedidor *or* -ra

shipping company *n* compañía *f* naviera; compañía *f* marítima

shipping instructions *npl* instrucciones *fpl* de envío

shipping line *n* compañía *f* naviera

shipping note *n* nota *f* de envío; nota *f* de expedición

shop *n* U.K. tienda *f*

shop around *v* comparar precios

shop assistant *n* U.K. dependiente *mf or* -ta

shoplifter *n* ratero *m* de tiendas; mechera *f*

shoplifting *n* hurto *m* en las tiendas

shopper *n* comprador *or* -ra

shopping n 1. (action) ir de compras; ir de tiendas 2. (goods bought) compras fpl

shopping arcade n galería f comercial

shopping center n centro m comercial

shopping mall n galería f comercial

shopping precinct n zona f comercial peatonal

shop-soiled adj deteriorado or -da

shop window n escaparate m

shortage n escasez f; falta f

short credit n crédito m a corto plazo

short-dated bills npl letras fpl a corto vencimiento

shortfall n déficit m; insuficiencia f

shortlist n preselección f; terna f ■ v preseleccionar

short of phrase menos de lo necesario; escaso or -sa

short-term adj a corto plazo

short-term contract n contrato m de corta duración

short-term credit n crédito m a corto plazo

short-term debts npl deudas fpl a corto plazo

short-term loan n préstamo m a corto plazo

show n (exhibition) exposición f; feria f ■ v mostrar; indicar; enseñar

show a profit v mostrar un beneficio

showcase n vitrina f

showroom n sala f de exposición

shrinkage n contracción f; encogimiento m; reducción f

shrink-wrapped adj envasado or -da al vacío

shrink-wrapping n envase m al vacío

shut adj cerrado or -da ■ v cerrar

side n lado m

sideline n negocio m suplementario

sight n vista f

sight draft n giro m a la vista

sign n señal f; letrero m; rótulo m ■ v firmar

sign a check v firmar un cheque

sign a contract v firmar un contrato

signatory n signatario or -ria; firmante mf

signature n firma f

silent partner n socio m comanditario; socio m en comandita

simple interest n interés m simple

single adj único or -ca; sencillo or -lla

Single European Market n Mercado Unico Europeo

sink v hundirse

sister company n compañía f asociada

sister ship n buque m gemelo (de la misma flota)

sit-down protest n sentada f

sit-down strike n huelga f de brazos caídos

site n sitio m; lugar m; solar m

site engineer n ingeniero m de obra

sitting tenant n inquilino m en posesión

situated adj situado or -da

situation n situación f

situations vacant n ofertas fpl de trabajo

size n tamaño m; dimensiones fpl

skeleton staff n personal m reducido al mínimo

skill n habilidad f; técnica f; destreza f

skilled adj cualificado or -da; especializado or -da

skilled labor n mano f de obra cualificada

skilled workers npl obreros mpl cualificados

slack adj flojo or -ja; débil

slash prices, credit terms v reducir drásticamente (los precios o las condiciones)

sleeping partner n U.K. socio m comanditario; socio m en comandita

slip n 1. (*mistake*) error m 2. (*piece of paper*) resguardo m

slow adj lento or -ta; atrasado or -da

slow down v desacelerar; reducir

slowdown n desaceleración f; reducción f

slow payer n moroso or -sa

slump n 1. (*depression*) depresión f; crisis f económica 2. (*rapid fall*) baja f repentina; caída f repentina ■ v caer en picado; hundirse

slump in sales n caída f de las ventas

small adj pequeño or -ña

small ads npl anuncios mpl breves

small businesses npl pequeñas fpl empresas

small businessman n pequeño m empresario

small change n moneda f suelta

small-scale adj a pequeña escala

small-scale enterprise n empresa f a pequeña escala

smart card n tarjeta f inteligente

SME (small and medium-sized businesses) PYME (pequeñas y medianas empresas)

soar v dispararse; remontarse

social adj social

social costs npl costes mpl sociales

social security n seguridad f social

society n sociedad f; club m

socio-economic groups npl grupos mpl socioeconómicos

soft currency n moneda f débil

soft loan n préstamo m sin interés; crédito m blando

soft sell n venta f sin presionar al cliente

software n programa m informático; "software" m

sole adj único or -ca; exclusivo or -va

sole agency n representación f exclusiva

sole agent n representante m exclusivo

sole owner n propietario único or propietaria única

sole right n exclusiva f

sole trader n comerciante m exclusivo

solicitor n abogado or -da

solicit orders v solicitar pedidos

solution n solución f

solve a problem v resolver un problema; solucionar un problema

solvency n solvencia f

solvent adj solvente

soon adv pronto

source of income n fuente f de ingresos

space n espacio m

spare part n pieza f de recambio; de repuesto

spare time n tiempo m libre

special adj especial

special drawing rights (SDRs) n derechos mpl especiales de giro (DEG)

specialist n especialista mf

specialization n especialización f

specialize v especializar

special offer n oferta f especial

specification n especificación f

specify v especificar; precisar; indicar

speech of thanks n palabras fpl de agradecimiento

spend v 1. (*money*) gastar 2. (*time*) pasar

spending money n dinero m para gastos personales

spending power n poder m adquisitivo

spinoff n efecto m indirecto

spoil v estropear

sponsor n patrocinador or -ra; padrino m ■ v patrocinar

sponsorship n patrocinio m

spot n (place) lugar m

spot cash n pago m al contado; dinero m en mano

spot price n precio m de entrega inmediata

spot purchase n compra f al contado

spread a risk v repartir un riesgo

spreadsheet n hoja f de cálculo

square n plaza f del mercado

stability n estabilidad f

stabilization n estabilización f

stabilize v estabilizar(se)

stable adj estable

stable currency n moneda f estable

stable economy n economía f estable

stable exchange rate n tipo m de cambio estable

stable prices n precios mpl estables

staff n personal m; plantilla f ■ v contratar personal

staff appointment n empleo m fijo

staff meeting n reunión f de personal; asamblea f de personal

stage n fase m; etapa f ■ v (organize) presentar

stage a recovery v experimentar una recuperación

staged payments npl pagos mpl por etapas

stagger v escalonar

stagnant adj estancado or -da

stagnation n estancamiento m

stamp n 1. sello m 2. (on document) estampilla f; timbre m ■ v 1. (letter) franquear; poner el sello 2. (mark) sellar; timbrar

stamp duty n impuesto m del timbre

stand n local m de exposición; "stand" m

standard adj normal; estándar ■ n norma f; modelo m; patrón m

standardization n normalización f; estandarización f

standardize v normalizar; estandarizar

standard letter n carta f tipo; carta f estándar

standard rate (of tax) n tasa f de impuestos normal

standby arrangements npl planes mpl de contingencia

standby credit n crédito m de apoyo; crédito m "stand by"

standby ticket n billete m en lista de espera

stand down v retirarse (de una elección)

standing n reputación f

standing order n domiciliación f bancaria

stand security for v avalar a

stand surety for someone v avalar; afianzar

staple n grapa f ■ v grapar

staple industry n industria f principal

staple papers together v grapar papeles

staple product n producto m principal

stapler n grapadora f

start n comienzo m; principio m; inicio m ■ v comenzar; empezar

starting adj inicial

starting date n fecha f inicial

starting point n punto m de partida

starting salary n salario m inicial

start-up n puesta f en marcha (de un negocio)

start-up costs npl costes mpl; gastos mpl iniciales

state n estado m ■ v declarar; afirmar

statement n declaración f; informe m

statement of account n estado m de cuentas

statement of expenses n relación f de gastos

state-of-the-art adj muy moderno

station n (train) estación f

statistical adj estadístico or -ca

statistical analysis n análisis m estadístico

statistician n estadístico or -ca

statistics npl estadísticas fpl

status n status m; posición f

status inquiry n petición f de informes sobre crédito

status symbol n símbolo m de prestigio

statute of limitations n ley f de prescripción

statutory adj statutario or -ria; reglamentario or -ria; legal

statutory holiday n U.K. fiesta f oficial; vacaciones fpl reglamentarias

stay n (time) estancia f; permanencia f ■ v permanecer; quedarse; alojarse

stay of execution n aplazamiento m de una sentencia

steadiness n estabilidad f

sterling n libra f esterlina

stevedore n estibador m

stiff competition n competencia f dura

stimulate the economy v estimular la economía

stimulus n estímulo m

stipulate v estipular

stipulation n estipulación f

stock n (goods) existencias fpl ■ v (goods) almacenar; tener existencias

stockbroker n corredor or -ra; agente mf de bolsa

stockbroking n correduría f de bolsa

stock certificate n U.K. certificado m de una acción

stock code n código m de almacenamiento

stock control n control m de existencias

stock controller n jefe m de almacén

stock exchange n bolsa f

stockholder n accionista mf

stock issue n emisión f de acciones

stockist n distribuidor or -ra

stock level n nivel m de existencias

stock list n inventario m; lista f de existencias

stock market n mercado m de valores; bolsa f

stock market valuation n tasación f de acciones

stock movements npl movimientos mpl de existencias

stock of raw materials n reservas fpl de materias primas

stockpile n reservas fpl ■ v acumular

stockroom n almacén m; depósito m

stock size adj talla f; tamaño m corriente

stocktaking n U.K. inventario m

stocktaking sale n U.K. liquidación f de inventario

stock turnover n U.K. rotación f de existencias

stock up v acumular

stock valuation n U.K. valoración f de existencias

stop n parada f; alto m ■ v parar; frenar; detener; contener

stoppage n suspensión f; paro m

stoppage of payments n suspensión f de pagos

stop payment on a check v detener el pago de un cheque

stop payments v suspender pagos

storage n 1. almacenaje m 2. (cost) coste m de almacenaje 3. (in warehouse) depósito m; almacenamiento m

storage capacity n capacidad f de almacenaje

storage facilities *npl* instalaciones *fpl* de almacenaje

storage unit *n* unidad *f* de almacenaje

store *n* 1. tienda *f* 2. almacén *m*; depósito *m* 3. (*items kept*) reserva *f* 4. (*large shop*) grandes almacenes *mpl* ■ *v* almacenar; guardar

storekeeper *n* tendero *or* -ra; comerciante *mf*

storeroom *n* almacén *m*; depósito *m*

storm damage *n* daños *mpl* por tormenta

straight line depreciation *n* amortización *f* anual uniforme; lineal

strategic *adj* estratégico *or* -ca

strategic planning *n* planificación *f* estratégica

strategy *n* estrategia *f*

street directory *n* guía *f* urbana; callejero *m*

strength *n* fuerza *f*; vitalidad *f*

strike *n* huelga *f* ■ *v* ir a la huelga; declararse en huelga

striker *n* huelguista *mf*

strong *adj* fuerte; vigoroso *or* -sa; firme

strong currency *n* moneda *f* fuerte

structural *adj* estructural

structural adjustment *n* ajuste *m* estructural

structural unemployment *n* paro *m* estructural

structure *n* estructura *f* ■ *v* (*arrange*) estructurar

study *n* estudio *m* ■ *v* estudiar

subcontract *n* subcontrato *m* ■ *v* subcontratar

subcontractor *n* subcontratista *mf*

subject *n* asunto *m*; tema *f*

subject to *phrase* sujeto a *or* -ta

sub judice *adj* sub judice; en manos de los tribunales

sublease *n* subarriendo *m* ■ *v* subarrendar

sublessee *n* subarrendatario *or* -ria

sublessor *n* subarrendador *or* -ra

sublet *v* subarrendar

subsidiary *adj* subsidiario *or* -ria; secundario *or* -ria ■ *n* filial *f*

subsidiary company *n* compañía *f* filial; compañía *f* subsidiaria

subsidize *v* subvencionar

subsidy *n* subsidio *m*; subvención *f*

subtotal *n* total *m* parcial

subvention *n* subvención *f*

succeed *v* 1. (*do well*) tener éxito; prosperar 2. (*follow someone*) suceder

succeed in *v* conseguir hacer algo

success *n* éxito *m*

successful *adj* afortunado *or* -da; próspero *or* -ra

successful bidder *n* adjudicatario *or* -ria

sue *v* demandar

suffer damage *v* sufrir daños

sufficient *adj* suficiente

sum *n* suma *f*; total *m*

summons *npl* citación *f* judicial; emplazamiento *m*

sundries, sundry items *n* artículos *mpl* varios

superior *adj* (*better quality*) superior

supermarket *n* supermercado *m*

superstore *n* hipermercado *m*

supervise *v* supervisar

supervision *n* supervisión *f*

supervisor *n* supervisor *or* -ra

supervisory *n* de supervisión; de control

supplement *n* suplemento *m*

supplementary *adj* suplementario *or* -ria

supplier *n* suministrador *or* -ra; proveedor *or* -ra; abastecedor *or* -ra

supply *n* 1. (*action*) oferta *f*; abastecimiento *m*; suministro *m* 2. (*stock of goods*) reserva *f*; provisión *f* ■ *v* suministrar; abastecer; proveer

supply and demand *n* oferta *f* y demanda

supply price *n* precio *m* de oferta

supply side economics *n* economía *f* de oferta

support *v* respaldar; apoyar

support price *n* precio *m* de sub-vención

surcharge *n* sobretasa *f*; recargo *m*

surety *n* **1.** (*person*) garante *mf*; fi-ador *or* -ra **2.** (*security*) fianza *f*; ga-rantía *f*

surface *n* superficie *f*

surface mail *n* correo *m* por via terrestre o marítima

surface transportation *n* trans-porte *m* por carretera o por via marítima

surplus *n* excedente *m*; exceso *m*; superávit *m*

surplus dividend *n* dividendo *m* por superávit

surrender *n* (*insurance policy*) res-cate *m*

surrender a policy *v* rescatar una póliza

surrender value *n* valor *m* de res-cate

survey *n* **1.** (*examination*) inspec-ción *f* **2.** (*general report*) estudio *m*; informe *m* ■ *v* (*inspect*) inspeccion-ar

surveyor *n* inspector *m* de obra

suspend *v* suspender

suspension *n* suspensión *f*

suspension of deliveries *n* sus-pensión *f* de entregas

suspension of payments *n* sus-pensión *f* de pagos

swap *n* intercambio *m* ■ *v* cambi-ar; intercambiar

swatch *n* muestra *f* pequeña

switch *v* (*change*) cambiar

switchboard *n* centralita *f*

switch over to *v* cambiarse a; pasarse a

swop *n* intercambio *m* ■ *v* inter-cambiar

symbol *n* símbolo *m*

sympathy strike *n* huelga *f* de solidaridad

synergy *n* sinergia *f*

system *n* sistema *m*

systems analysis *n* análisis *m* de sistemas

systems analyst *n* analista *mf* de sistemas

T

tabulate *v* tabular

tabulation *n* tabulación *f*

tabulator *n* tabulador *or* -ra

tachograph *n* tacógrafo *m*

tacit agreement *n* acuerdo *m* tácito

tacit approval *n* aprobación *f* táci-ta

take *n* (*money received*) ingresos *mpl*; recaudación *f* ■ *v* **1.** tomar **2.** (*need*) llevar; hacer falta **3.** (*receive money*) ingresar en caja; recibir

take a call *v* recibir una llamada

take action *v* tomar medidas

take a risk *v* arriesgarse

take legal action *v* entablar un pleito

take legal advice *v* consultar a un abogado

take note *v* tomar nota

take off *v* **1.** (*deduct*) rebajar; qui-tar **2.** (*plane*) despegar

take on freight *v* fletar

take on more staff *v* emplear más personal

take out a policy *v* hacerse un se-guro

take over v tomar posesión; hacerse cargo; sustituir

takeover n adquisición f

takeover bid n oferta f pública de adquisición (OPA)

takeover target n objeto m de una OPA

take place v tener lugar

take someone to court v llevar a alguien ante los tribunales

take stock v hacer un inventario

take the initiative v tomar la iniciativa

take the soft option v decidirse por la opción más fácil

take time off work v tomarse tiempo libre (durante el trabajo)

take up an option v suscribir una opción

takings npl ingresos mpl de un negocio; recaudación f (de un negocio)

tangible adj tangible

tangible assets npl activo m tangible

tanker n buque m cisterna; petrolero m

tare n tara f

target n objetivo m; meta f ■ v tener como objetivo

target market n mercado m previsto

tariff n (price) tarifa f; precio m

tariff barriers n barreras fpl arancelarias

task n tarea f

tax n impuesto m ■ v gravar con un impuesto

taxable adj sujeto a impuesto; imponible

taxable income n renta f imponible

tax adjustment n ajuste m impositivo

tax allowance n desgravación f fiscal

tax assessment n cálculo m de la base impositiva

taxation n imposición f; impuesto m

tax avoidance n evasión f de impuestos; elusión f de impuestos

tax code n código m impositivo; código m fiscal

tax collection n recaudación f de impuestos

tax collector n recaudador m de impuestos or -ra

tax concession n desgravación f fiscal; privilegio m fiscal

tax consultant n asesor or -ra fiscal

tax credit n crédito m por impuestos pagados

tax deducted at source n impuestos mpl retenidos en el origen

tax-deductible adj desgravable

tax deductions n retención f fiscal; deducción f de impuestos

tax evasion n evasión f de impuestos; fraude m fiscal

tax-exempt adj exento de impuestos or -ta

tax exemption n exención f fiscal

tax form n formulario m de declaración de la renta

tax-free adj libre de impuestos

tax haven n paraíso m fiscal

tax inspector n inspector m de Hacienda

tax loophole n laguna f fiscal

tax offense n infracción f fiscal

tax paid n impuesto m pagado

taxpayer n contribuyente mf

tax rate n tipo m impositivo; tipo m de gravamen

tax reductions n reducción f de los impuestos

tax relief n desgravación f fiscal

tax return, tax declaration n declaración f de renta

tax shelter n amparo m fiscal

tax system n sistema m tributario

tax year n año m fiscal; ejercicio m fiscal

teach v enseñar

technique n técnica f

telephone n teléfono m ■ v telefonear; llamar

telephone book n guía f telefónica

telephone call n llamada f telefónica

telephone directory n guía f telefónica

telephone exchange n central f telefónica

telephone line n línea f telefónica

telephone number n número m de teléfono

telephone operator n telefonista mf

telephone subscriber n abonado m telefónico

telephone switchboard n centralita f telefónica

telephonist n U.K. telefonista mf

telesales n ventas fpl por teléfono

teleworking n teletrabajo m

telex n télex m ■ v enviar por télex

teller n cajero m de un banco or -ra

temp n secretario m eventual; interino or -ina ■ v hacer trabajo eventual

temp agency n agencia f de trabajo temporal

temporary employment n ocupación f temporal; empleo m eventual

temporary staff n personal m eventual

tenancy n 1. (*agreement*) contrato m de arrendamiento m 2. (*period*) periodo m de arrendamiento m

tenant n inquilino or -na; arrendatario or -ria

tender n (*offer to work*) oferta f

tenderer n postor m; licitador m

tender for a contract v licitar para un contrato

tendering n oferta f

tenure n 1. (*right*) tenencia f; ocupación f; posesión f 2. (*time*) mandato m

term n 1. (*part of academic year*) trimestre m 2. (*time of validity*) plazo m; término m

terminal adj terminal

terminal bonus n bonificación f recibida al concluir un seguro

terminate v terminar

terminate an agreement v poner término a un acuerdo

termination n terminación f

termination clause n cláusula f resolutoria

term insurance n seguro m temporal

term loan n préstamo m a plazo fijo

terms npl condiciones fpl; términos mpl

terms of employment n condiciones fpl de servicio

terms of payment n condiciones fpl de pago

terms of reference npl mandato m; campo m de aplicación

terms of sale n condiciones fpl de venta

territory n territorio m

tertiary industry n industria f terciaria; industria f de los servicios

tertiary sector n sector m terciario; sector m de los servicios

test n examen m; ensayo m; prueba f ■ v probar; someter a prueba

text n texto m

theft n robo m

third party n tercero m

third-party insurance n seguro m contra terceros

third quarter n tercer trimestre m

threshold n umbral m

threshold price n precio m umbral

throughput n rendimiento m

ticket n billete m; entrada f

ticket clerk n taquillero or -ra

ticket office n taquilla f; despacho m de billetes

tie-up n (*link*) enlace m; conexión f

tighten up on v intensificar (el control)

tight money n dinero m escaso

till n caja f

time and motion study n estudio m de desplazamientos y tiempos

time deposit n depósito m a plazo; imposición f a plazo

time limit n plazo m; término m

time limitation n plazo m de tiempo límite

time: on time phrase tiempo: a tiempo

time rate n tarifa f horaria; tarifa f por horas

time scale n calendario m

timetable n horario m; calendario m ■ v preparar un horario

timing n medida f de tiempo

tip n 1. (advice) confidencia f 2. (money) propina f ■ v 1. (give money) dar una propina 2. (say what might happen) pronosticar; prever

TIR abbr (Transports Internationaux Routiers) Transporte Internacional por Carretera

token n símbolo m

token charge n precio m simbólico

token payment n pago m simbólico

toll n peaje m

toll free adj a cobro revertido

toll free number n número m de llamada gratuita

ton n tonelada f

tonnage n tonelaje m

tonne n tonelada f métrica

tool n herramienta f

tool up v instalar la maquinaria en una fábrica

top adj superior; principal ■ n 1. (highest point) cima f; cumbre f 2. (upper surface) parte f superior ■ v (go higher than) superar

top management n alta dirección f

top quality n alta calidad f; calidad f superior

top-selling adj más vendido or -da

total adj total ■ n total m; totalidad f ■ v totalizar; sumar

total amount n cantidad f total

total assets npl activos mpl totales

total cost n coste m total

total expenditure n gastos mpl totales

total income n renta f total

total invoice value n valor m total de factura

total output n producción f total

total revenue n ingreso m total

track record n antecedentes mpl

tractor-trailer n camión m con remolque; camión m articulado

trade n (business) comercio m ■ v comerciar (en)

trade agreement n acuerdo m comercial; tratado m comercial

trade association n agrupación f sectorial

trade cycle n ciclo m económico

trade deficit, trade gap n déficit m comercial

trade description n descripción f comercial

trade directory n guía f comercial

trade discount n descuento m para comerciantes del sector

trade fair n feria f comercial

trade in v (buy and sell) comerciar (en)

trade-in n canje m parcial

trade-in price n precio m con entrega de artículo usado

trade journal, trade magazine n revista f profesional especializada

trademark, trade name n marca f comercial; nombre m comercial

trade mission n misión f comercial

trade price n precio m al detallista

trader n comerciante mf

trade terms npl descuento m para comerciantes del sector

trade union n U.K. sindicato m

trade unionist n sindicalista mf

trading n comercio m

trading company *n* sociedad *f* comercial

trading loss *n* pérdida *f* de ejercicio

trading partner *n* empresa *f* que comercia con otra

trading profit *n* beneficios *mpl* de explotación

train *n* tren *m* ■ *v* 1. (*learn*) prepararse; formarse; aprender 2. (*teach*) preparar; capacitar; formar

trainee *n* aprendiz *or* -za

traineeship *n* aprendizaje *m*

training *n* aprendizaje *m*; capacitación *f*; formación *f*

training levy *n* U.K. impuesto *m* para financiar la formación profesional

training officer *n* responsable *mf* de la capacitación

transact business *v* hacer negocios

transaction *n* transacción *f*; operación *f*

transfer *n* 1. traslado *m*; transferencia *f* 2. (*travel*) transbordo *m* ■ *v* (*move to new place*) trasladar; transferir

transferable *adj* transferible

transfer fee *n* traspaso *m*

transfer of funds *n* transferencia *f* de fondos

transferred charge call *n* U.K. llamada *f* a cobro revertido

transit *n* tránsito *m*

transit lounge *n* sala *f* de tránsito

transit visa *n* visado *m* de tránsito

translate *v* traducir

translation *n* traducción *f*

translation bureau *n* agencia *f* de traducciones

translator *n* traductor *or* -ra

transport *n* transporte *m* ■ *v* transportar; llevar

transportation facilities *npl* medios *mpl* de transporte

treasury *n* Tesoro *m*; Hacienda *f* Pública

treble *v* triplicar

trend *n* tendencia *f*

trial *n* 1. (*court case*) proceso *m*; juicio *m* 2. (*test of product*) prueba *f*; ensayo *m*

trial and error *n* tanteo *m*

trial balance *n* balance *m* de comprobación

trial period *n* periodo *m* de prueba

trial sample *n* muestra *f*

triple *adj* triple ■ *v* triplicar

triplicate: in triplicate *phrase* por triplicado

troubleshooter *n* mediador *m* de conflictos *or* -ra

troubleshooting *n* investigación *f* de conflictos

truck *n* 1. (*lorry*) camión *m* 2. (*railway wagon*) vagón *m* (de ferrocarril)

trucker *n* camionero *or* -ra

trucking *n* acarreo *m*; transporte *m* por carretera

truckload *n* carga *f* de un camión

true *adj* verdadero *or* -ra

true copy *n* compulsa *f*; copia *f* exacta

trust company *n* compañía *f* fiduciaria

turnaround *n* 1. (*goods sold*) rotación *f* de existencias 2. (*making profitable*) reactivación *f* 3. (*of plane*) descarga *f* y carga de un avión

turn down *v* rechazar

turnkey operation *n* operación *f* llaves en mano

turnkey operator *n* agente *mf* de operaciones llaves en mano

turn over *v* (*make sales*) girar (volumen de ventas)

turnover *n* 1. (*of staff*) rotación *f* de personal 2. (*of stock*) rotación *f* (de mercancías) 3. (*sales*) volumen *m* de ventas; cifra *f* de negocios

turnover tax *n* impuesto *m* sobre el volumen de ventas

U

unaccounted for *adj* inexplicado *or* -da; desaparecido *or* -da; sin figurar

unaudited *adj* no verificado *or* -da

unaudited accounts *npl* cuentas *fpl* sin verificar

unauthorized expenditure *n* gastos *mpl* no autorizados

unavailability *adj* indisponibilidad *f*

unavailable *adj* inasequible

unchanged *adj* inalterado *or* -da; invariable

unchecked figures *npl* cifras *fpl* sin comprobar

unclaimed baggage *n* equipaje *m* no reclamado

unconditional *adj* incondicional; sin condiciones

unconfirmed *adj* sin confirmar

undated *adj* sin fecha

undelivered *adj* no entregado *or* -da

under *prep* 1. (*according to*) conforme a; según 2. (*down*) abajo 3. (*less than*) por debajo de; menos de

undercharge *v* cobrar de menos

under construction *phrase* en construcción

under contract *phrase* bajo contrato

under control *phrase* bajo control

undercut a competitor *v* vender a precio más bajo que un rival

underdeveloped countries *npl* países *mpl* subdesarrollados

underequipped *adj* mal equipado *or* -da

under new management *n* cambio *m* de dirección

underpaid *adj* mal pagado *or* -da

undersell *v* vender más barato

undersigned *n* abajo firmante *mf*

underspend *v* gastar menos

understand *v* entender; comprender

understanding *n* acuerdo *m*

undertake *v* emprender; encargarse de; comprometerse

undertaking *n* 1. (*company*) empresa *f* 2. (*promise*) compromiso *m*; promesa *f*

underwrite *v* 1. (*guarantee*) avalar 2. (*pay costs*) garantizar el pago

underwriting syndicate *n* consorcio *m* asegurador; emisor

undischarged bankrupt *n* quebrado *m* no rehabilitado

uneconomic rent *n* renta *f* que no llega a cubrir los costes

unemployed *adj* parado *or* -da; desempleado *or* -da

unemployment *n* paro *m*; desempleo *m*

unemployment pay *n* subsidio *m* de paro

unexplained *adj* inexplicado *or* -da

unfair *adj* injusto *or* -ta

unfair competition *n* competencia *f* desleal

unfair dismissal *n* despido *m* injusto

unfavorable *adj* desfavorable; adverso *or* -sa

unfavorable exchange rate *n* tipo *m* de cambio desfavorable

unfulfilled order *n* pedido *m* no servido; pedido *m* por servir

unilateral *adj* unilateral

union *n* sindicato *m*

union recognition *n* reconocimiento *m* de un sindicato

unique selling point, unique selling proposition *n* argumento *m* de venta

unit n 1. unidad f 2. (in unit trust) título m

unit cost n coste m unitario; coste m por unidad

unite v unir

unit price n precio m por unidad

unit trust n U.K. fondos mpl mutuos; fondos npl de inversión

unlimited liability n responsabilidad f ilimitada

unlisted adj que no figura en la guía telefónica

unload v 1. descargar 2. (get rid of) deshacerse de

unobtainable adj inalcanzable; imposible de conseguir

unofficial adj extraoficial; no oficial; oficioso or -sa

unpaid adj impagado or -da; sin pagar

unpaid invoices npl facturas fpl impagadas

unsealed envelope n sobre m abierto

unsecured creditor n acreedor m común or -ra; acreedor m sin garantía

unskilled adj no cualificado or -da

unsold adj no vendido or -da; sin vender

unsubsidized adj no subvencionado or -da

unsuccessful adj fracasado or -da; sin éxito

update n actualización f ■ v actualizar; poner al día

updating n actualización f; puesta f al día

up front adj por adelantado

up-market adj de primera calidad

upset price n precio m inicial

up to phrase hasta

up to date adj actual; moderno or -na; al día

upturn n mejora f; reactivación f

upward trend n tendencia f alcista

urgent adj urgente

use n uso m ■ v emplear; usar; utilizar

useful adj útil

user n usuario or -ria

user-friendly adj de fácil uso; de fácil manejo

use up spare capacity v utilizar capacidad ociosa

USP abbr (unique selling point or unique selling proposition) argumento m de venta

usual adj normal; usual; habitual

utilization n utilización f; uso m

V

vacancy n (for job) plaza f; vacante f

vacant adj vacante; libre; disponible

vacate v desocupar

vacation pay n paga f de vacaciones

valid adj válido or -da; valedero or -ra

validity n validez f

valuation n valoración f; evaluación f; tasación f

value n valor m ■ v valorar; tasar; evaluar

value added tax (VAT) n impuesto m sobre el valor añadido (IVA)

valuer n tasador or -ra

van n camioneta f

variable costs npl costes mpl variables

variance n variación f; discrepancia f

variation n variación f

VAT *abbr U.K. (value added tax)* IVA (impuesto sobre el valor añadido)

vehicle *n* vehículo *m*

vendor *n* vendedor *or* -ra

venture *n (business)* empresa *f* ■ *v (risk)* arriesgar

venture capital *n* capital-riesgo *m*

venue *n* lugar *m*; punto *m* de reunión

verbal *adj* verbal

verbal agreement *n* acuerdo *m* verbal

verification *n* verificación *f*

verify *v* verificar

vertical communication *n* comunicación *f* vertical

vertical integration *n* integración *f* vertical

vested interest *n* interés *m* personal; intereses *mpl* creados

veto a decision *v* vetar una decisión

via *prep* por; vía

viable *adj* viable

videoconference *n* videoconferencia *f*

violate *v* violar

VIP lounge *n* salón *m* VIP (salón de personalidades)

visa *n* visado *m*

visible imports *npl* importaciones *fpl* visibles

visible trade *n* comercio *m* de visibles

visit *n* visita *f* ■ *v* visitar

voicemail *n* audiomensajería *f*

void *adj (not valid)* nulo *or* -la; inválido *or* -da ■ *v* invalidar

volume *n* volumen *m*

volume discount *n* descuento *m* por volumen

volume of sales *n* volumen *m* de ventas

volume of trade, volume of business *n* volumen *m* comercial; volumen *m* de negocios

voluntary liquidation *n* liquidación *f* voluntaria

voluntary redundancy *n* baja *f* incentivada; voluntaria

vote of thanks *n* voto *m* de gracias

voucher *n* **1.** bono *m*; vale *m* **2.** *(document from an auditor)* comprobante *m*

W-Z

wage *n* sueldo *m*; salario *m*

wage claim *n* reivindicación *f* salarial

wage freeze *n* congelación *f* de salarios

wage levels *npl* niveles *mpl* de salarios

wage negotiations *npl* negociaciones *fpl* salariales

wage scale *n* escala *f* salarial; escala *f* de salarios

waive a payment *v* renunciar a un pago

waiver *n (of right)* renuncia *f*

waiver clause *n* cláusula *f* de renuncia

warehouse *n* almacén *m* ■ *v* almacenar

warehouseman *n* almacenista *mf*

warehousing *n* almacenaje *m*

warn *v* avisar

warning *n* aviso *m*; advertencia *f*

warrant *n (document)* autorización *f*; orden *f* ■ *v* **1.** *(guarantee)* garantizar **2.** *(justify)* justificar

warranty *n* garantía *f*

wastage *n* pérdida *f*; desperdicio *m*

waste n desperdicio m; desecho m; residuos mpl ■ v (use too much) desperdiciar; malgastar

waybill n carta f de porte

weak adj débil; flojo or -ja

weak market n mercado m débil

wear and tear n desgaste m natural; desgaste m normal

website n sitio m web; website f

web n: **the web** n la Web; la Red

week n semana f

weekly adj semanalmente

weigh v pesar

weighbridge n báscula f puente; puente-báscula m

weight n peso m

weighted average n promedio m ponderado; media f ponderada

weighted index n índice m ponderado

weighting n ponderación f

weight limit n peso m máximo

welcome n acogida f

welfare n bienestar m

well-paid job n trabajo m bien remunerado

wharf n muelle m; embarcadero m

white knight n rescatador m de empresas

whole-life insurance n seguro m corriente de vida

wholesale adv al por mayor

wholesale dealer n mayorista mf; comerciante mf al por mayor

wholesale discount n descuento m al por mayor

wholesale price n precio m al por mayor

wholesale price index n índice m de precios al por mayor

wholesaler n mayorista mf; comerciante mf al por mayor

wide adj amplio or -plia

wildcat strike n huelga f salvaje

win a contract v conseguir un contrato

winding up n liquidación f

window n ventana f

window display n escaparate m

wind up v 1. (a company) liquidar una sociedad 2. (a meeting) terminar; concluir

withdraw v retirar (una oferta); sacar (dinero)

withdrawal n (of money) retirada f; retiro m; reintegro m

withdraw a takeover bid v retirar una oferta de adquisición

withholding tax n retención f de impuestos en origen

witness n testimonio m; testigo mf ■ v (a document) firmar como testigo

witness an agreement v actuar de testigo

wording n texto m

word-processing n tratamiento m de textos

work n trabajo m ■ v trabajar

worker n trabajador or -ra; obrero or -ra; operario or -ria

worker director n U.K. delegado m del personal or -da

work force n mano f de obra

working capital n capital m operativo; capital m circulante

working conditions npl condiciones fpl de trabajo

working party n grupo m de trabajo

work in progress n trabajo m en curso

workman n obrero m

work permit n permiso m de trabajo

workshop n taller m

workstation n (at computer) estación f; puesto m de trabajo

work-to-rule n huelga f de celo; paro m técnico

world n mundo m

world market n mercado m mundial

worldwide adj mundial; global ■ adv mundialmente

World Wide Web n Telaraña f mundial

worry n inquietud f; preocupación f

worth n (*value*) valor m
worth: be worth v valer
worthless *adj* sin valor
wrapper, wrapping n envoltorio m
wrapping paper n papel m de envolver
wrap up v (*goods*) envolver
wreck n 1. (*company*) empresa f en ruinas 2. (*ship*) naufragio m ■ v (*ruin*) naufragar; fracasar
writ n orden f; mandato m
write v escribir
write (out) a check v extender un cheque
write down v (*assets*) depreciar el valor de un activo
writedown n (*of asset*) depreciación f de un activo
write off v (*debt*) anular; cancelar
write-off n (*loss*) deuda f incobrable; pérdida f total
write out v copiar; escribir sin abreviar

writing n escrito m; escritura f; letra f
written agreement n acuerdo m por escrito
wrong *adj* erróneo *or* -nea; equivocado *or* -da
wrongful dismissal n despido m injusto
year n año m
year end n cierre m del ejercicio
yearly payment n pago m anual
yellow pages n páginas *fpl* amarillas
yield n (*on investment*) rendimiento m; producción f; renta f ■ v (*interest*) rendir; devengar
young *adj* joven
younger *adj* más joven; menor
zero n cero m
zero-rated *adj* con un IVA del 0%
zip code n código m postal

Español-Inglés
Spanish-English

A

a *adv* per

abajo 1. down 2. under 3. below

abajo firmante *mf* undersigned

abandonar 1. to leave 2. to abandon

abandono *m* **de responsabilidad** disclaimer

abarrotar to overstock

abastecedor supplier

abastecer 1. to supply 2. to cater to

abastecimiento *m* supply

abierto *adj* open

abierto por la noche late-night opening

abogado 1. lawyer 2. solicitor 3. counsel

abogado *m* **defensor** defense counsel

abogado *m* **especializado en derecho marítimo** maritime lawyer

abonado *m* **telefónico** telephone subscriber

abonar 1. to pay 2. to pay out 3. (*acreditar*) to credit

abono *m* 1. (*crédito*) season ticket 2. (*billete*) credit entry

abordar (*embarcarse*) to board

a bordo on board

abrir to open

abrir camino to pioneer

abrir la sesión to open a meeting

abrir una carta de crédito to issue a letter of credit

abrir una cuenta to open an account

abrir una cuenta bancaria to open a bank account

abrir una línea de crédito to open a line of credit

abrir un negocio to open a new business

abundancia *f* 1. abundance 2. glut

acabado *adj* finished

acabar to complete

acaparamiento *m* hoarding

acaparar 1. (*acumular*) to hoard 2. (*capturar*) to capture

acaparar el mercado to corner the market

a cargo de *adj* chargeable (to)

acarreo *m* 1. haulage 2. (*transporte*) trucking

acatar 1. to respect 2. to obey

a causa de owing to

accesible *adj* accessible

acceso *m* 1. access 2. (*mercado*) entry

accesorios *mpl* fittings

accidente *m* **industrial** industrial accident

accidente *m* **laboral** occupational accident

acción *f* 1. action 2. (*finanzas*) share

acción *f* **de primera categoría** blue chip

acciones *fpl* **ordinarias** 1. ordinary shares 2. equities

acciones *fpl* **poco buscadas en la bolsa** neglected shares

acciones *fpl* **preferentes** preference shares

acciones *fpl* **que se cotizan en bolsa** quoted shares

accionista *mf* 1. stockholder 2. *U.K.* shareholder

accionista *mf* **importante** major stockholder

accionista *mf* **mayoritario** majority stockholder

accionista *m* **minoritario** minority stockholder

acción *f* **legal** 1. legal action 2. action

acción _f_ **preferente acumulativa** cumulative preference share

aceite _m_ oil

aceptable _adj_ acceptable

aceptación _f_ acceptance

aceptación _f_ **de una oferta** acceptance of an offer

aceptación _f_ **irrevocable** irrevocable acceptance

aceptar 1. to accept 2. to allow 3. to agree

aceptar hacer algo to agree to do something

aceptar la entrega de mercancías to accept delivery of a shipment

aceptar la responsabilidad de algo to accept liability for something

aceptar una firma to honor a signature

aceptar una letra to accept a bill

aclaración _f_ explanation

aclarar 1. to clear 2. to clarify

a cobrar _adj_ receivable

a cobro revertido _adj_ toll free

acogida _f_ 1. reception 2. welcome

acomodamiento _m_ composition

acomodar to arrange

acomodo _m_ (_acuerdo_) arrangement

a condición de que 1. on condition that 2. provided that _o_ providing

aconsejar 1. to advise 2. to recommend

acordado _adj_ agreed

acordar to agree

acordarse (de) to remember

a corto plazo _adj_ short-term

acotación _f_ (_límite_) limit

acreditar to credit

a crédito on credit

acreedor creditor

acreedor _m_ **común** unsecured creditor

acreedor _m_ **con garantía** secured creditor

acreedor _m_ **diferido** deferred creditor

acreedor _m_ **hipotecario** mortgagee

acreedor _m_ **preferente** 1. preferential creditor 2. preferred creditor

acreedor _m_ **sin garantía** unsecured creditor

acta _f_ (_registro_) record

acta _f_ **de la reunión** minutes

acta _f_ **notarial** affidavit

actividad _f_ activity

activo _adj_ 1. active 2. go-ahead ■ asset

activo _m_ **circulante** current assets

activo _m_ **congelado** frozen assets

activo _m_ **fijo** fixed assets

activo _m_ **financiero** financial asset

activo _m_ **intangible** intangible assets

activo _m_ **invisible** invisible assets

activo _m_ **líquido** liquid assets

activo _m_ **neto** net assets _o_ net worth

activo _m_ **realizable** realizable assets

activos _mpl_ **totales** total assets

activo _m_ **tangible** tangible assets

activo _m_ **y pasivo** _m_ assets and liabilities

acto _m_ **de marcar** dialing

actuación _f_ performance

actual _adj_ 1. present 2. current 3. (_moderno_) up to date

actualización _f_ 1. update 2. updating

actualizar to update

actuar 1. to act 2. to perform

actuar de testigo to witness an agreement

actuario actuary

a cuenta on account

acuerdo *m* 1. agreement 2. compromise 3. (*arreglo*) arrangement 4. (*arreglo*) understanding 5. (*conformidad*) compliance 6. (*después de un conflicto*) settlement

acuerdo *m* **a tanto alzado** fixed-price agreement

acuerdo *m* **bilateral** reciprocal agreement

acuerdo *m* **comercial** trade agreement

acuerdo *m* **de comercialización** marketing agreement

acuerdo *m* **de doble imposición** double taxation agreement

acuerdo *m* **de muchos años** long-standing agreement

acuerdo *m* **de productividad** productivity agreement

acuerdo *m* **entre caballeros** gentleman's agreement

acuerdo *m* **global** package deal

acuerdo *m* **modificable** open-ended agreement

acuerdo *m* **multilateral** multilateral agreement

acuerdo *m* **por escrito** written agreement

acuerdo *m* **recíproco** reciprocal agreement

acuerdo *m* **tácito** tacit agreement

acuerdo *m* **unilateral** one-sided agreement

acuerdo *m* **verbal** verbal agreement

acumulación *f* accrual

acumulación *f* **de interés** accrual of interest

acumulación *f* **de trabajo atrasado** backlog

acumular 1. to accumulate 2. to hoard 3. (*existencias*) to stockpile 4. (*existencias*) to stock up

acumular en exceso to overstock

acumularse 1. to accumulate 2. to accrue

acumulativo *adj* cumulative

acusación *f* 1. accusation 2. charge 3. (*parte acusadora*) prosecution

acusado defendant

acusar 1. to accuse 2. to charge

acusar recibo de una carta to acknowledge receipt of a letter

acuse *m* **de recibo** acknowledgement

adecuado *adj* adequate

adelantado *adj* advanced

adeudar to debit an account

adeudarse to run into debt

adeudo debit entry

adición *f* addition

adicional *adj* additional

adjudicación *f* adjudication

adjudicar to award

adjudicar un contrato a alguien to award a contract to someone

adjudicar un derecho a alguien to assign a right to someone

adjudicatario successful bidder

adjuntar 1. to attach 2. to enclose

adjunto *m* 1. attachment 2. deputy

administración *f* administration

administración *f* **de cartera** portfolio management

administración *f* **local** local government

administrador official receiver

administrar to manage

administrar mal to mismanage

administrativo *adj* administrative

admisible *adj* acceptable

admitir to admit

a domicilio *adj* 1. house-to-house 2. door-to-door

adquirir 1. to acquire 2. to buy

adquisición *f* 1. acquisition 2. takeover

adquisición *f* **apalancada** leveraged buyout; LBO

aduana *f* customs

Aduanas y Arbitrios Customs and Excise

aduanero customs officer *o* customs official

ad valorem *adj, adv* ad valorem

adverso *adj* unfavorable

advertencia *f* **1.** reminder **2.** warning

aerograma *m* air letter

aeropuerto *m* airport

afianzar 1. to guarantee **2.** to stand surety for someone

afiliación *f* **1.** affiliation **2.** membership

afiliado *adj* **1.** affiliated **2.** associate

afirmar 1. to firm **2.** (*declarar*) to state

afirmativo *adj* affirmative

afortunado *adj* successful

agencia *f* agency

agencia *f* **de alquiler de viviendas 1.** rental agency **2.** *U.K.* letting agency

agencia *f* **de cambio** *U.K.* bureau de change

agencia *f* **de cobro de morosos** debt collection agency

agencia *f* **de informes comerciales** credit agency

agencia *f* **de prensa** news agency

agencia *f* **de publicidad** advertising agency

agencia *f* **de trabajo temporal** temp agency

agencia *f* **de traducciones** translation bureau

agencia *f* **de transportes** shipping agent

agencia *f* **exclusiva** concession

agenda *f* **1.** appointments book **2.** calendar **3.** *U.K.* diary

agenda *f* **de mesa (de despacho)** desk diary

agente *mf* **1.** agent **2.** broker

agente *mf* **de aduanas** customs broker

agente *mf* **de bolsa** stockbroker

agente *mf* **del credere** del credere agent

agente *mf* **de operaciones llaves en mano** turnkey operator

agente *mf* **de patentes y marcas** patent agent

agente *mf* **de seguros** insurance agent

agente *mf* **expedidor 1.** forwarding agent **2.** shipping clerk

agente *mf* **marítimo 1.** ship broker **2.** shipping agent

agio *m* (*especulación*) premium

agotado *adj* out of stock

agotar las existencias 1. to sell out **2.** to run out

a granel *adj* loose

agrario *adj* agricultural

agregado commercial attaché

agrícola *adj* agricultural

agropecuario *adj* agricultural

agrupación *f* **1.** group **2.** consolidation

agrupación *f* **sectorial** trade association

agrupar 1. to batch **2.** to bracket together **3.** to consolidate

ahorrar 1. to save **2.** to save up **3.** to save on

ahorros *mpl* savings

aire *m* air

ajustado, -a al coste de la vida *adj* index-linked

ajustar 1. to adjust **2.** to gear **3.** (*cuadrar*) to reconcile

ajuste *m* adjustment

ajuste *m* **de pérdidas** loss adjustment

ajuste *m* **estructural** structural adjustment

ajuste *m* **financiero** financial settlement

ajuste *m* **fino** fine tuning

ajuste *m* **impositivo** tax adjustment

ajustes *mpl* **estacionales** seasonal adjustments

a la atención de *abbr* (*for the attention of*) FAO

a la fuerza *adj* forced

al año *adv* 1. per annum 2. per year

a la orden *adj* custom-built *o* custom-made

a largo plazo *adj* long-range

a la venta on sale

al azar *adj* random

albarán *m* delivery note

alcanzar to reach

alcanzar el punto más alto to peak

al cierre *adj* closing

alcista *mf* (*bolsa*) bull

al contado *adv* cash

al día per day ■ *adj* up to date

aleatorio *adj* random

alegar to claim

alimentación *f* **continua** continuous feed

alimentador *m* **del papel** paper feed

almacén *m* 1. warehouse 2. store 3. storeroom 4. (*depósito*) depository 5. (*depósito*) stockroom

almacenaje *m* 1. storage 2. warehousing

almacenaje *m* **frigorífico** cold storage

almacenamiento *m* storage

almacenar 1. to store 2. to warehouse 3. (*tener existencias*) to stock

almacén *m* **central** depot

almacén *m* **de mercancías** *U.K.* goods depot

almacén *m* **frigorífico** cold store

almacenista *mf* warehouseman

almuerzo *m* **de negocios** business lunch

alojarse to stay

al por mayor *adv* wholesale

alquilar 1. to rent 2. to let 3. to hire 4. (*fletar*) to charter

alquilar una grúa 1. to rent a crane 2. *U.K.* to hire a crane

alquilar una oficina to let an office

alquilar un coche 1. to rent a car 2. *U.K.* to hire a car

alquiler *m* 1. rental 2. rent 3. (*medio de transporte*) charter

alquiler *m* **elevado** high rent

alta calidad 1. high quality 2. premium quality 3. top quality

alta dirección *f* top management

alternativa *f* alternative

alternativo *adj* alternative

alto *adj* high ■ (*freno*) stop

alza *f* rise

amarradero *m* berth

a mediados de semana *adj* mid-week

americano American ■ *adj* American

amo *m* 1. owner 2. *informal* (*jefe*) boss

amortizable *adj* redeemable

amortización *f* 1. amortization 2. depreciation 3. (*rescate*) redemption

amortización *f* **acelerada** accelerated depreciation

amortización *f* **anual uniforme** straight line depreciation

amortizar 1. to amortize 2. to depreciate 3. (*redimir*) to redeem

amortizar una obligación to redeem a bond

amparo *m* **fiscal** tax shelter

ampliación *f* 1. expansion 2. extension

ampliar 1. to expand 2. to extend

amplio *adj* wide

añadir to add

añadir el 10% por el servicio to add on 10% for service

análisis *m* analysis

análisis *m* **coste-beneficio** cost-benefit analysis

análisis *m* **de costes** cost analysis

análisis *m* **de mercado** market analysis

análisis *m* **de proyectos** project analysis

análisis *m* **de sistemas** systems analysis

análisis _m_ **de un puesto de trabajo** job analysis

análisis _m_ **de ventas** sales analysis

análisis _m_ **estadístico** statistical analysis

analista _mf_ **de mercado** market analyst

analista _mf_ **de sistemas** systems analyst

analizar to _o_ to analyze

analizar las posibilidades del mercado to analyze the market potential

anaquel _m_ shelf

andén _m_ platform

anexo _m_ annex

año _m_ year

año _m_ **base** base year

año _m_ **civil** calendar year

año _m_ **fiscal** 1. financial year 2. tax year

anotación _f_ entry

anotar 1. to log 2. to note 3. (_registrar_) to record

anotar las llamadas recibidas to log calls

anotar una contrapartida to contra an entry

anotar un contraasiento to contra an entry

antecedentes _mpl_ track record

antedatar 1. to backdate 2. to antedate

anteproyecto _m_ draft plan _o_ draft project

anterior _adj_ 1. prior 2. previous

anticipado _adj_ advanced

anticipar 1. to advance 2. (_prever_) to anticipate

anticipo _m_ advance

anticipo _m_ **a cuenta** advance on account

anticipo _m_ **de caja a cuenta** cash advance

anticuado _adj_ 1. dated 2. out of date 3. old-fashioned

antiguo _adj_ 1. old 2. old-established

anual _adj_ annual

anualmente _adv_ annually ■ on an annual basis

anulación _f_ cancellation

anular 1. to cancel 2. to rescind 3. (_deuda_) to write off

anular un acuerdo to call off a deal

anular un cheque to cancel a check

anular un contrato to cancel a contract

anunciante _mf_ advertiser

anunciar 1. to announce 2. to advertise

anunciar una vacante to advertise a vacancy

anunciar un déficit to report a loss

anunciar un nuevo producto to advertise a new product

anuncio _m_ 1. (_aviso_) announcement 2. (_aviso_) notice 3. (_publicitario_) advertisement 4. (_publicitario_) commercial

anuncio _m_ **del producto** product advertising

anuncios _mpl_ **breves** small ads

anuncios _mpl_ **por palabras** classified ads _o_ advertisements

apalancamiento _m_ gearing

apalancamiento _m_ **financiero** leverage

aparato _m_ 1. device 2. instrument 3. machine

apartamento _m_ 1. apartment 2. flat

apelación _f_ appeal

apelar to appeal

apéndice _m_ appendix

a pequeña escala _adj_ small-scale

apertura _f_ opening

a petición on request

aplazado _adj_ 1. deferred 2. postponed

aplazamiento _m_ 1. deferment 2. postponement

aplazamiento *m* **de pago** deferment of payment

aplazamiento *m* **de una sentencia** stay of execution

aplazar 1. to defer **2.** to postpone **3.** to adjourn **4.** to put back **5.** to hold over

aplazar una reunión to adjourn a meeting

a plazo *adv* forward

aplicación *f* application

aplicar to apply

apoderado 1. attorney **2.** proxy

apoyar 1. to back up **2.** to support

apoyo *m* **financiero** backing

apreciación *f* appreciation

apreciar to appreciate

aprecio *m* appreciation

a precio reducido *adj* cut-price

apremiar to chase

aprender to train

aprendiz 1. apprentice **2.** trainee

aprendizaje *m* **1.** training **2.** traineeship

aprobación *f* approval

aprobación *f* **tácita** tacit approval

aprobar to carry

aprobar los términos de un contrato to approve the terms of a contract

apropiación *f* **indebida de fondos** conversion of funds

apropiado *adj* **1.** appropriate **2.** relevant

aprovechar 1. to capitalize on **2.** to exploit

aproximadamente *adv* approximately

aproximado *adj* **1.** approximate **2.** (*cálculo*) rough

a prueba on approval

aptitud *f* capacity

apuntar 1. to note **2.** to log

arancel *m* duty

arancel *m* **aduanero** customs tariff

arancel *m* **proteccionista** protective tariff

arbitraje *m* arbitration

arbitrar to arbitrate

arbitrar un litigio to adjudicate in a dispute

arbitrar un litigio to arbitrate in a dispute

árbitro *mf* **1.** arbitrator **2.** adjudicator

archivador *m* filing cabinet

archivar 1. to save **2.** to back up **3.** to file

archivar documentos to file documents

archivo *m* **1.** file **2.** computer file

archivos *mpl* records

área *f* area

argumento *m* argument

argumento *m* **de venta** unique selling point *o* unique selling proposition; USP

armonización *f* harmonization

arreglar 1. to fix **2.** to mend

arreglárselas 1. to cope **2.** to manage to

arreglo *m* arrangement

arrendador lessor

arrendamiento *m* lease

arrendamiento *m* **financiero** leasing

arrendar 1. to rent **2.** to let

arrendar (ceder en arriendo) to lease

arrendar (tomar en arriendo) to lease

arrendar equipo to lease equipment

arrendatario 1. lessee **2.** tenant

arriendo *m* lease

arriesgado *adj* risky

arriesgar 1. to risk **2.** to venture

arriesgarse to take a risk

arrinconar to shelve

arruinado *adj informal* broke

arruinar to bankrupt

artículo *m* **1.** article **2.** item

artículo *m* **de reclamo** loss-leader

artículos *mpl* **con desperfectos** seconds

artículos *mpl* **de fácil venta** fast-selling items

artículos *mpl* **de lujo** luxury goods

artículos *mpl* **de papelería para oficina** office stationery

artículos *mpl* **perecederos** perishable goods

artículos *mpl* **varios 1.** sundries *o* sundry items **2.** miscellaneous items

artículo *m* **único** *U.K.* one-off item

asalariado *adj* salaried

asamblea *f* **1.** assembly **2.** meeting **3.** conference

asamblea *f* **de personal** staff meeting

ascender (*promoción*) to promote

ascender a 1. (*total*) to run to **2.** (*total*) to amount to

ascenso *m* promotion

ascensor *m* lift

asegurable *adj* insurable

asegurador 1. insurer **2.** marine underwriter

asegurar to insure

asegurar la vida de alguien *U.K.* to assure someone's life

asequible *adj* **1.** available **2.** obtainable

asesor 1. adviser *o* advisor **2.** consultant **3.** management consultant **4.** tax consultant

asesoramiento *m* **jurídico** legal advice

asesoría *f* **1.** consultancy **2.** consulting firm *o* consultancy firm

asesoría *f* **jurídica** legal department

asesor *m* **jurídico** legal adviser

asiento *m* entry

asiento *m* **de débito** debit entry

asignación *f* assignment

asignación *f* **de fondos** funding

asignar 1. to allocate **2.** to assign **3.** (*fondos*) to appropriate

asignar fondos to fund

asignar fondos a un proyecto 1. to commit funds to a project **2.** to earmark funds for a project

asignar personal to man

asistencia *f* (*ayuda*) assistance

asistido *adj* **1.** (*atendido*) attended **2.** (*atendido*) manned

asistido por ordenador assisted: computer-assisted

asistir 1. (*ayudar*) to assist **2.** (*reunión*) to attend

asociación *f* **1.** association **2.** partnership **3.** organization

asociado *adj* associate

aspirante *mf* candidate

aspirar a to aim

asunto *m* **1.** matter **2.** subject **3.** (*de negocios*) business

asunto *m* **problemático** problem area

atacar to attack

atasco *m* bottleneck

atención *f* attention

atender to serve

atender a un cliente to serve a customer

atender una demanda to meet a demand

atendido *adj* manned

aterrizar to land

a tiempo on time

a tiempo completo *adj* full-time

a tiempo parcial *adj, adv* part-time

átono *adj* **1.** dull **2.** flat

atracar 1. to berth **2.** to dock

atractivo *m* **1.** appeal **2.** attraction

atractivo *m* **para los clientes** customer appeal

atraer 1. to attract **2.** to appeal to

atrasado *adj* **1.** slow **2.** (*pago*) late **3.** (*pago*) overdue

atrasos *mpl* arrears

audiomensajería *f* voicemail

auditar to audit

auditor *m* auditor

auditor *m* **externo** external auditor

auditoría *f* **1.** audit **2.** auditing

auditoría *f* **externa** external audit

auditoría *f* **general** general audit

auditoría *f* **interna** internal audit

auditor *m* **interno** internal auditor

auge *m* boom

aumentar 1. (*subir*) to raise 2. (*subir*) to increase 3. (*subir*) to climb 4. (*subir*) to mount up 5. (*ganar*) to gain 6. (*prosperar*) to boom

aumentar a escala to scale up

aumentar de precio to increase in price

aumento *m* 1. increase 2. increment 3. gain 4. rise 5. (*valor*) appreciation

aumento *m* **anual medio** mean annual increase

aumento *m* **de salario** 1. raise 2. *U.K.* rise

aumento *m* **de sueldo** 1. pay raise 2. raise 3. increase 4. *U.K.* rise

aumento *m* **de sueldo por coste de vida** cost-of-living increase

aumento *m* **retroactivo de salarios** retroactive pay raise

ausencia *f* absence

ausente *adj* absent

ausente del trabajo *adj* off

autentificar to authenticate

autobús *m* bus

autobús *m* **del aeropuerto** airport bus

autoedición *f* desk-top publishing; DTP

autofinanciación *f* self-financing

autofinanciado *adj* self-financing

autónomo *adj* (*trabajador*) self-employed

autoridad *f* authority

autoridades *fpl* **portuarias** port authority

autorización *f* 1. authorization 2. warrant

autorizado *adj* authorized

autorizar 1. to authorize 2. to entitle 3. (*licencia*) to license

autorizar el pago to authorize payment

autorregulación *f* self-regulation

autorregulado *adj* self-regulatory

autoservicio *m* **mayorista** cash-and-carry

auxiliar *mf* assistant

auxiliar *mf* **administrativo** junior clerk

aval *m* guarantee

avalar 1. to guarantee 2. to underwrite 3. to stand surety for someone

avalar a to stand security for

avalar una deuda to guarantee a debt

avance *m* 1. advance 2. progress

avanzar 1. to advance 2. to progress

avería *f* 1. (*máquina*) breakdown 2. (*seguro*) average

avería *f* **gruesa** general average

averiarse to break down

avión *m* plane

avión *m* **chárter** charter plane

avión *m* **de carga** 1. freighter 2. freight plane

avisar 1. to notify 2. to warn

aviso *m* 1. notice 2. warning

ayuda *f* 1. assistance 2. help

ayudante *mf* assistant

ayudante *mf* **personal** personal assistant; PA

ayudar 1. to assist 2. to help

B

baja *f* 1. decline 2. fall 3. drop
bajada *f* **de precio** decrease in price
baja *f* **incentivada** voluntary redundancy
bajar 1. to lower 2. to drop 3. (*disminuir*) to decline 4. (*disminuir*) to fall 5. (*disminuir*) to fall off
baja *f* **repentina** slump
bajista *mf* bear
bajo *adj* low
bajo contrato under contract
bajo control under control
balance *m* balance
balance *m* **de comprobación** trial balance
balance *m* **general** balance sheet
balanza *f* **comercial** balance of trade
balanza *f* **comercial favorable** favorable balance of trade
balanza *f* **de pagos** balance of payments
banca *f* banking
bancarrota *f* bankruptcy
banco *m* bank
banco *m* **central** central bank
banco *m* **comercial** clearing bank
banco *m* **de crédito** credit bank
banco *m* **de descuento** 1. discount house 2. discounter
banco *m* **emisor** issuing bank
Banco Europeo de Inversiones (BEI) European Investment Bank (EIB)
banco *m* **mercantil** merchant bank

banquero banker
barato *adj* cheap
barco *m* ship
barco *m* **de carga** cargo ship
barrera *f* barrier
barreras *fpl* **arancelarias** 1. customs barriers 2. tariff barriers
basar to base
báscula *f* **puente** weighbridge
base *f* 1. base 2. basis
base *f* **de datos** database
base *f* **monetaria** monetary base
básico *adj* basic
beca *f* grant
beneficiario beneficiary
beneficiarse de to benefit from
beneficio *m* 1. benefit 2. profit 3. gain
beneficio *m* **antes de deducir los impuestos** 1. pretax profit 2. profit before tax
beneficio *m* **bruto** gross profit
beneficio *m* **considerable** healthy profit
beneficio *m* **de explotación** operating profit
beneficio *m* **ficticio** paper profit
beneficio *m* **neto** net profit
beneficio *m* **neto de impuestos** profit after tax
beneficios *mpl* 1. returns 2. earnings 3. (*participación*) equity
beneficios *mpl* **crecientes** increasing profits
beneficios *mpl* **de explotación** trading profit
beneficios *mpl* **de la empresa** corporate profits
beneficios *mpl* **distribuibles** distributable profit
beneficios *mpl* **extraordinarios** excess profits
beneficios *mpl* **netos de impuestos** after-tax profit
beneficio *m* **sobre el papel** paper profit
bien *m* **encubierto** hidden asset
bienes *mpl* goods

bienes *mpl* **de capital 1.** (*activo fijo*) capital assets **2.** (*equipo*) capital goods

bienes *mpl* **de consumo 1.** consumer goods **2.** consumables

bienes *mpl* **de consumo duraderos** consumer durables

bienes *mpl* **de equipo** capital equipment

bienes *mpl* **duraderos** durables

bienes *mpl* **personales** personal assets

bienes *mpl* **raíces** real estate

bienestar *m* welfare

bilateral *adj* **1.** bilateral **2.** reciprocal

billete *m* **1.** bill **2.** banknote **3.** (*pasaje*) fare **4.** (*pasaje*) ticket

billete *m* **abierto** open ticket

billete *m* **de abono** season ticket

billete *m* **de banco 1.** bank bill **2.** bill **3.** banknote **4.** currency note

billete *m* **de ida** one-way fare

billete *m* **en lista de espera** standby ticket

blanco *m* blank

blanquear (dinero negro) to launder (money)

bloqueado *adj* frozen

bloquear to block

bloquear los créditos to freeze credits

bodega *f* (*buque*) hold

boicot *m* boycott

boicotear to boycott

boletín *m* **1.** bulletin **2.** journal

boletín *m* **de inscripción** registration form

boletín *m* **de respuesta** reply coupon

boletín *m* **interno de una empresa** house magazine

bolsa *f* **1.** stock exchange **2.** stock market **3.** (*bolsillo*) pocket **4.** (*saco*) bag

bolsa *f* **de contratación 1.** commodity market **2.** commodity exchange

bolsa *f* **de papel** paper bag

bolsillo *m* pocket

bombo *m* **publicitario** hype

bonificación *f* bonus

bonificación *f* **recibida al concluir un seguro** terminal bonus

bono *m* **1.** bond **2.** debenture **3.** (*vale*) voucher

bonos-basura *mpl* junk bonds

bonos *mpl* **del Tesoro** gilts

"boom" *m* boom

borrador *m* **1.** draft **2.** rough draft

bosquejo *m* **1.** rough draft **2.** outline

brazo *m* **derecho** right-hand man

británico *adj* British

bruto *adj* gross

buena calidad good quality

buena compra good buy

buena gestión good management

bueno *adj* good

buen precio good value (for money)

bulto *m* packet

buque *m* ship

buque *m* **cisterna** tanker

buque *m* **de carga** freighter

buque *m* **de contenedores** container ship

buque *m* **de salvamento** salvage vessel

buque *m* **gemelo (de la misma flota)** sister ship

buque *m* **mercante** merchant ship *o* merchant vessel

burocracia *f* **1.** bureaucracy **2.** red tape

búsqueda *f* **de clientes** canvassing

C

caber to hold
cada tres meses *adv* quarterly
cadena *f* chain
cadena *f* **de grandes almacenes** *U.K.* multiple store
cadena *f* **de montaje** 1. assembly line 2. production line
caducado *adj* out of date
caducar 1. (*expirar*) to expire 2. (*prescribir*) to lapse
caducidad *f* (*expiración*) expiry
caer 1. to fall 2. to plummet 3. to drop
caer en picado to slump
caída *f* 1. drop 2. fall
caída *f* **de las ventas** 1. drop in sales 2. slump in sales
caída *f* **repentina** slump
caja *f* 1. case 2. (*taquilla*) till 3. (*taquilla*) pay desk 4. (*taquilla*) cash desk 5. (*supermercado*) checkout
caja *f* **de artículos sueltos para la venta** dump bin
caja *f* **de cartón** 1. carton 2. cardboard box
caja *f* **de caudales** safe
caja *f* **de embalar** packing case
caja *f* **de seguridad** safe deposit
caja *f* **fuerte** safe
caja *f* **para gastos menores** petty cash box
caja *f* **registradora** cash register
cajero *m* cashier
cajero *m* **automático** 1. ATM 2. *U.K.* cash dispenser
cajero *m* **de un banco** teller
cajetilla *f* packet
cajón *m* crate
calculadora *f* calculator

calculadora *f* **de bolsillo** pocket calculator
calcular 1. to calculate 2. to count 3. to evaluate 4. (*estimar*) to estimate
calcular el promedio to average
calcular mal to miscalculate
cálculo *m* 1. calculation 2. estimate
cálculo *m* **aproximado** 1. rough estimate 2. rough calculation
cálculo *m* **de costos** costing
cálculo *m* **de la base impositiva** tax assessment
calendario *m* 1. time scale 2. timetable
calidad *f* quality
calidad *f* **de semicorrespondencia** near letter-quality; NLQ
calidad *f* **superior** 1. high quality 2. top quality
callejero *m* street directory
Cámara *f* **de Comercio** Chamber of Commerce
cambiable *adj* exchangeable
cambiar 1. to change 2. to switch 3. to swap
cambiar de dueño to change hands
cambiar divisas to exchange
cambiarse a to switch over to
cambio *m* 1. change 2. (*divisas*) exchange 3. (*movimiento*) shift
cambio *m* **de dirección** under new management
cambio *m* **de moneda extranjera** foreign exchange
cambio *m* **en especie** bartering
cambio *m* **fijo** fixed exchange rate
cambista *mf* money changer
camión *m* 1. *U.K.* lorry 2. truck
camión *m* **articulado** 1. tractor-trailer 2. *U.K.* articulated lorry *o* articulated vehicle
camión *m* **con remolque** 1. tractor-trailer 2. *U.K.* articulated lorry *o* articulated vehicle

camión *m* **de carga pesada** *U.K.* heavy goods vehicle; HGV

camionero 1. trucker **2.** *U.K.* lorry driver

camioneta *f* van

campaña *f* campaign

campaña *f* **de ventas 1.** sales campaign **2.** sales drive

campaña *f* **publicitaria 1.** advertising campaign **2.** publicity campaign

campo *m* **1.** area **2.** field **3.** (*rural*) country

campo *m* **de aplicación** terms of reference

canal *m* channel

canales *mpl* **de distribución 1.** channels of distribution **2.** distribution channels

cancelación *f* cancellation

cancelación *f* **de una cita** cancellation

cancelado *adj* **1.** off **2.** canceled

cancelar 1. to cancel **2.** to write off

candidato candidate

candidato *m* **a un puesto de trabajo** applicant for a job

candidato *m* **propuesto** nominee

canjear to exchange

canje *m* **parcial 1.** part exchange **2.** trade-in

canon *m* royalty

cantidad *f* **1.** quantity **2.** amount ■ *abbr* qty.

cantidad *f* **total** total amount

capacidad *f* capacity

capacidad *f* **de almacenaje** storage capacity

capacidad *f* **de endeudamiento** borrowing power

capacidad *f* **de fabricación** manufacturing capacity

capacidad *f* **hotelera** hotel accommodations

capacidad *f* **industrial** industrial capacity

capacitación *f* training

capacitado *adj* qualified

capacitar 1. to train **2.** to qualify

capaz *adj* capable

capaz de *adj* capable of

capital *m adj* capital

capital *m* **circulante** working capital

capital *m* **disponible** available capital

capital *m* **en acciones 1.** equity capital **2.** share capital

capital *m* **inicial** initial capital

capitalista *mf* capitalist

capitalización *f* capitalization

capitalización *f* **bursátil** market capitalization

capitalización *f* **de las reservas** capitalization of reserves

capitalizar to capitalize

capital *m* **nominal** nominal capital

capital *m* **operativo** working capital

capital-riesgo *m* **1.** risk capital **2.** venture capital

carga *f* **1.** cargo **2.** shipment

carga *f* **aérea** air freight

carga *f* **de un camión 1.** truckload **2.** *U.K.* lorry-load

carga *f* **en cubierta** deck cargo

cargamento *m* load

carga *f* **por peso muerto** deadweight cargo

cargar 1. to load **2.** to charge

cargar en cuenta to debit an account

cargar en exceso to overcharge

cargar una compra en cuenta to charge a purchase

cargar un barco to load a truck *o* to a ship

cargar un camión to load a truck *o* to a ship

carga *f* **útil** payload

cargo *m* **1.** charge **2.** (*acusación*) charge **3.** (*puesto*) job title **4.** (*puesto*) position

cargos *mpl* **adicionales** additional charges

cargos *mpl* **en concepto de interés** interest charges

carnet *m* **1.** (*documento*) carnet **2.** (*socio*) membership card

caro *adj* **1.** *U.K.* dear **2.** expensive

carretera *f* road

carretilla *f* **elevadora de horquilla** fork-lift truck

carta *f* letter

carta *f* **adjunta 1.** covering letter **2.** covering note

carta *f* **certificada** registered letter

carta *f* **comercial** business letter

carta *f* **de crédito** letter of credit; L/C

carta *f* **de crédito general** circular letter of credit

carta *f* **de crédito irrevocable** irrevocable letter of credit

carta *f* **de intención** letter of intent

carta *f* **de nombramiento** letter of appointment

carta *f* **de porte** waybill

carta *f* **de presentación** introduction

carta *f* **de reclamación** letter of complaint

carta *f* **de recomendación** letter of reference

carta *f* **de reiteración** follow-up letter

carta *f* **de solicitud** letter of application

carta *f* **estándar** standard letter

carta *f* **explicatoria 1.** covering letter **2.** covering note

carta *f* **tipo** standard letter

carta *f* **urgente** express letter

cartel *m* cartel

cartelera *f* **1.** billboard **2.** *U.K.* hoarding

cartera *f* (*maletín*) briefcase

cartera *f* (*de valores*) portfolio

cartera *f* **con las iniciales** personalized briefcase

cartón *m* **1.** cardboard **2.** carton

cartulina *f* card

casa *f* house

casa *f* **comercial** house

casa *f* **matriz** parent company

"cash flow" *m* cash flow

cash flow actualizado discounted cash flow; DCF

catalogar to index

catálogo *m* **1.** catalog **2.** list

catálogo *m* **de ventas por correo** mail-order catalog

categoría *f* **1.** category **2.** (*clase*) class **3.** (*clase*) bracket

causa *f* (*proceso*) court case

cedente *mf* assignor

celebrar una reunión to hold a meeting *o* to hold a discussion

censor auditor

censor jurado de cuentas 1. certified public accountant **2.** *U.K.* certified accountant

central *adj* central

centralita *f* switchboard

centralita *f* **telefónica** telephone switchboard

centralización *f* centralization

centralización *f* **de las compras** central purchasing

centralizar to centralize

central *f* **telefónica** telephone exchange

centro *m* center

centro *m* **comercial 1.** business center **2.** shopping center

centro *m* **de beneficios** profit center

centro *m* **de costes** cost center

centro *m* **de la ciudad 1.** downtown **2.** city center

centro *m* **de reparaciones** service center

centro *m* **de transporte** depot

centro *m* **industrial** industrial center

cercano *adj* close to

cero *m* **1.** zero **2.** nil

cerrado *adj* **1.** closed **2.** shut

cerradura *f* lock

cerrar 1. to close **2.** to shut **3.** to close down **4.** (*sobre*) to seal

cerrar con llave to lock

cerrar una cuenta to close an account

cerrar una cuenta bancaria to close a bank account

cerrar una oficina to lock up a shop *o* to an office

cerrar una tienda to lock up a shop *o* to an office

cerrar un trato to clinch

certificada certified copy

certificado *m* certificate ■ *adj* registered

certificado *m* **de aduana** clearance certificate

certificado *m* **de aprobación** certificate of approval

certificado *m* **de depósito** certificate of deposit

certificado *m* **de garantía** certificate of guarantee

certificado *m* **de origen** certificate of origin

certificado *m* **de registro** certificate of registration

certificado *m* **de una acción** *U.K.* 1. stock certificate 2. share certificate

certificado *m* **provisional de acciones** scrip

certificar 1. to certify 2. to register

cesión *f* cession

cesionario assignee

cesión-arrendamiento *f* leaseback

cheque *m* 1. *U.K.* cheque 2. check

cheque *m* **abierto** open check

cheque *m* **al portador** check to bearer

cheque *m* **conformado** certified check

cheque *m* **cruzado** *U.K.* crossed check

cheque *m* **de administración** cashier's check

cheque *m* **de salario** paycheck

cheque *m* **de sueldo** 1. salary check 2. paycheck

cheque *m* **en blanco** blank check

cheque *m* **en pago de dividendos** dividend warrant

chequeo *m* **al azar** random check

cheques *mpl* **con el nombre impreso** personalized checks

cheque *m* **sin cruzar** open check

cheque *m* **sin fondos** rubber check

chocar to crash

chófer *m* driver

choque *m* crash

cíclico *adj* cyclical

ciclo *m* cycle

ciclo *m* **del producto** product cycle

ciclo *m* **de trabajo** run

ciclo *m* **económico** 1. economic cycle 2. trade cycle

cierre *m* 1. closing 2. closure 3. close

cierre *m* **del ejercicio** year end

cif *abbr* (*cost, insurance and freight*) c.i.f.

cifra *f* figure

cifra *f* **de negocios** turnover

cifras *fpl* **ajustadas estacionalmente** seasonally adjusted figures

cifras *fpl* **de ventas** sales figures

cifras *fpl* **estimadas** estimated figures

cifras *fpl* **históricas** historical figures

cifras *fpl* **reales** actuals

cifras *fpl* **sin comprobar** unchecked figures

cima *f* 1. top 2. peak

cinta *f* **magnética** magnetic tape *o* mag tape

circuito cerrado closed circuit TV

circulación *f* circulation

circular *f* 1. circular letter 2. to run

cita *f* appointment

citación *f* **judicial** summons
citar to quote
clarificar 1. to clear **2.** to clarify
claro *adj* clear
clase *f* **1.** (*categoría*) class **2.** (*categoría*) bracket
clase *f* **económica** economy class
clase *f* **preferente (en aviones)** business class
clase *f* **turista** economy class
clasificación *f* **1.** classification **2.** rating
clasificación *f* **crediticia** credit rating
clasificar 1. to classify **2.** to index
cláusula *f* **1.** clause **2.** article
cláusula *f* **adicional** rider
cláusula *f* **de excepción** escape clause
cláusula *f* **de exclusión** exclusion clause
cláusula *f* **de reembolso** payback clause
cláusula *f* **de renuncia** waiver clause
cláusula *f* **de rescisión** cancellation clause
cláusula *f* **penal** penalty clause
cláusula *f* **que prohibe la huelga** no-strike agreement *o* no-strike clause
cláusula *f* **resolutoria** termination clause
clausura *f* closure
clausurar to close a meeting
clave key ■ *adj* (*importante*) key
cliente *mf* **1.** client **2.** customer
cliente *mf* **habitual** regular customer
clientela *f* **1.** clientele **2.** custom
clientes *mpl* **eventuales** potential customers
clip *m* paperclip
club *m* society
coacreedor co-creditor
coaseguro *m* co-insurance
cobertura *f* **1.** cover **2.** hedging

cobertura *f* **del dividendo** dividend cover
cobertura *f* **del seguro** insurance coverage
cobertura *f* **periodística** media coverage
cobrable *adj* cashable
cobrador collector
cobrador *m* **de alquileres** rent collector
cobrador *m* **de morosos** debt collector
cobrar 1. to charge **2.** to collect **3.** *U.K.* to encash
cobrar de más to overcharge
cobrar de menos to undercharge
cobrar una deuda to collect a debt
cobrar un cheque to cash a check
cobro *m* collection
cobro *m* **a la entrega** cash on delivery; COD *o* c.o.d.
cobro *m* **de morosos** debt collection
cobro *m* **en metálico** *U.K.* encashment
cobro *m* **por recogida** collection charges *o* collection rates
coche *m* **de alquiler 1.** rental car **2.** *U.K.* hire car
coche *m* **en gran demanda** best-selling car
codificación *f* coding
código *m* code
código *m* **de almacenamiento** stock code
código *m* **de barras** bar code
código *m* **fiscal** tax code
código *m* **impositivo** tax code
código *m* **postal 1.** zip code **2.** *U.K.* postcode **3.** *U.K.* area code
códigos *mpl* **legibles por ordenador** computer-readable codes
código *m* **territorial** *U.K.* area code
codirección *f* joint management

codirector co-director

codirector *m* **gerente** joint managing director

coeficiente *m* rate

coeficiente *m* **de ajuste de precios** price differential

coeficiente *m* **de amortización** depreciation rate

coeficiente *m* **de errores** error rate

coeficiente *m* **de ocupación** load factor

coeficiente *m* **de rentabilidad** profitability

coincidir to agree

coincidir con to agree with

colaboración *f* 1. collaboration 2. contribution

colaborar to collaborate

colateral *adj* collateral

colectivo *adj* 1. collective 2. joint

colisión *f* crash

colocar to place

columna *f* **del debe** debit column

columna *f* **del haber** credit column

comenzar 1. to begin 2. to start

comerciable *adj* marketable

comercial *adj* commercial

comercialización *f* 1. commercialization 2. merchandizing

comercialización *f* **a gran escala** mass marketing

comercializar 1. to commercialize 2. to merchandize

comercializar un producto to merchandize a product

comerciante *mf* 1. dealer 2. merchant 3. trader 4. merchandizer 5. storekeeper

comerciante *mf* **al por mayor** 1. wholesaler 2. wholesale dealer

comerciante *mf* **al por menor** retail dealer

comerciante *m* **exclusivo** sole trader

comerciar (en) 1. to deal in 2. to trade in 3. to trade

comerciar con to do business with

comerciar con alguien to deal with someone

comerciar en to handle

comercio *m* 1. commerce 2. trade 3. trading

comercio *m* **al por menor** retailing

comercio *m* **de exportación** export trade

comercio *m* **de visibles** visible trade

comercio *m* **electrónico** e-commerce

comercio *m* **exterior** 1. external trade 2. foreign trade 3. overseas trade

comercio *m* **floreciente** flourishing trade

comercio *m* **interior** domestic trade

comercio *m* **internacional** international trade

comercio *m* **invisible** invisible trade

comercio *m* **legal** lawful trade

comercio *m* **marítimo** maritime trade

comercio *m* **multilateral** multilateral trade

comercio *m* **recíproco** reciprocal trade

comercio *m* **unilateral** one-way trade

cometer to commit

comienzo *m* 1. beginning 2. start

comisión *f* 1. commission 2. (*corretaje*) commission 3. (*corretaje*) broker's commission *o* brokerage

comisión *f* **de arbitraje** arbitration board *o* arbitration tribunal

comisionista *mf* commission agent

comisionista *mf* **al por mayor** factor

comité *m* commission

cómodo *adj* convenient

compañía *f* company

compañía f **afiliada** associate company

compañía f **asociada** sister company

compañía f **de seguros** 1. insurance company 2. *U.K.* assurance company

compañía f **fiduciaria** trust company

compañía f **filial** subsidiary company

compañía f **independiente** independent company

compañía f **marítima** shipping company

compañía f **naviera** 1. shipping line 2. shipping company

compañía f **que financia la compra a plazos** *U.K.* hire-purchase company

compañía f **subsidiaria** subsidiary company

comparable *adj* comparable

comparación f comparison

comparar to compare

comparar con to compare with

comparar precios to shop around

compartir to share

compartir una oficina to share an office

compensación f compensation

compensar 1. (*indemnizar*) to compensate 2. (*indemnizar*) to make up for 3. (*indemnizar*) to make good 4. (*deducir*) to set against

competencia f 1. competition 2. (*pericia*) expertise

competencia f **desleal** unfair competition

competencia f **dura** stiff competition

competencia f **encarnizada** cut-throat competition

competente *adj* 1. competent 2. capable

competidor competitor

competir (con) to compete (with)

competitividad f competitiveness

competitivo *adj* 1. competitive 2. competing

complementario *adj* complementary

completamente nuevo *adj* brand new

completar to complete

completo *adj* 1. complete 2. comprehensive 3. full-scale

componer to repair

compra f 1. purchase 2. purchasing 3. buying

compra f **a granel** bulk buying

compra f **al contado** 1. cash purchase 2. spot purchase

compra f **apalancada** leveraged buyout; LBO

compra f **a plazos** 1. installment plan 2. *U.K.* hire purchase; HP

compra f **de futuros** forward buying

compra f **de una empresa por sus ejecutivos** management buyout; MBO

comprador 1. buyer 2. purchaser 3. shopper

compradora f **genuina** genuine purchaser

comprador m **genuino** genuine purchaser

comprador m **impulsivo** impulse buyer

compra f **febril** panic buying

compra f **impulsiva** impulse purchase

comprar 1. to buy 2. to purchase

comprar a futuros to buy forward

comprar al contado to buy for cash

comprar en efectivo to buy for cash

compras *fpl* shopping

comprender to understand

comprobación f check

comprobación f **de los recursos económicos** means test comprobante *m* voucher

comprobante *m* de caja sales receipt

comprobar 1. to check 2. to monitor

comprometerse to undertake

compromiso *m* 1. compromise 2. (*cita*) appointment 3. (*obligación*) obligation 4. (*obligación*) commitment 5. (*promesa*) undertaking 6. promise

compromisos *mpl* commitments

compulsa *f* 1. certified copy 2. true copy

común *adj* 1. common 2. joint

comunicación *f* communication

comunicaciones *fpl* communications

comunicación *f* horizontal horizontal communication

comunicación *f* vertical vertical communication

comunicado *m* communication

comunicado *m* de prensa press release

comunicar 1. to communicate 2. to announce

comunicarse to communicate

comunidad *f* community

con apoyo estatal *adj* government-backed

conceder 1. to grant 2. to extend 3. (*adjudicar*) to award 4. (*dar*) to allow

conceder una licencia to license

concernir to concern

concertación *f* 1. harmonization 2. reconciliation

concesión *f* 1. concession 2. franchise 3. franchising

concesionario 1. concessionaire 2. franchisee 3. licensee 4. dealer

concesión *f* de un préstamo lending

conciliación *f* conciliation

conciliación *f* de cuentas reconciliation of accounts

concluir 1. to conclude 2. to wind up

conclusión *f* conclusion

con cupón de interés cum coupon

con descuento *adv* off

condición *f* 1. condition 2. (*salvedad*) proviso

condicionado *adj* qualified

condicional *adj* conditional

condiciones *fpl* terms

condiciones *fpl* de empleo conditions of employment

condiciones *fpl* de pago terms of payment

condiciones *fpl* de servicio terms of employment

condiciones *fpl* de trabajo working conditions

condiciones *fpl* de venta 1. conditions of sale 2. terms of sale

condición *f* jurídica legal status

con dividendo *adv* cum dividend

condominio *m* joint ownership

conducir to drive

conductor *m* driver

conectar 1. to connect 2. to interface

con excepción de excluding

conexión *f* 1. connection 2. tie-up 3. link 4. (*informática*) port

confeccionar to make out

con fecha de *adj* dated

conferencia *f* conference

conferencia *f* de prensa press conference

confesar 1. to confess 2. to declare

confianza *f* confidence

confiar to entrust

confidencia *f* tip

confidencial *adj* confidential

confidencialidad *f* confidentiality

confirmación *f* confirmation

confirmar to confirm

confirmar a alguien en su puesto de trabajo to confirm someone in a job

confirmar una reserva to confirm a reservation

confiscación *f* 1. forfeiture 2. forfeit

confiscar to seize

conflicto *m* **de intereses** conflict of interest

conflictos *mpl* **colectivos** industrial disputes

conflictos *mpl* **laborales** labor disputes

conforme a (*según*) under

conformidad *f* (*acuerdo*) compliance

congelación *f* freeze

congelación *f* **de créditos** credit freeze

congelación *f* **de salarios** wage freeze

congelado *adj* frozen

congelar to freeze

congelar salarios y precios to freeze wages and prices

conglomerado *m* conglomerate

congreso *m* 1. congress 2. conference

conjuntamente *adv* jointly

conjunto *adj* joint

conjunto *m* **de medidas económicas** package

con las iniciales *adj* personalized

conmutar to commute

conocimiento *m* **de embarque** bill of lading

con precio competitivo *adj* competitively priced

con relación a further to

con reservas *adj* qualified

con retraso *adv* late

conseguir 1. to get 2. to manage to 3. to obtain 4. to raise

conseguir fondos to secure funds

conseguir hacer algo to succeed in

conseguir un contrato to win a contract

consejero 1. consultant 2. adviser *o* advisor 3. (*director*) director

consejo *m* **(de administración)** board

conservación *f* maintenance

conservar to maintain

considerar to consider

consigna *f* 1. baggage check 2. *U.K.* left luggage office

consignación *f* consignment

consignador consignor

consignar 1. to consign 2. to dispatch 3. (*asignar*) to appropriate

consignatario consignee

consolidación *f* **de fondos** funding

consolidación *f* **de un préstamo** restructuring of a loan

consolidado to consolidated

consolidar 1. to consolidate 2. to establish

consorcio *m* consortium

consorcio *m* **asegurador** underwriting syndicate

constante constant ■ *adj* recurrent

constar de to consist of

constitución *f* **de una sociedad** incorporation

constituir en sociedad to incorporate

constituirse parte civil to bring a civil action

construir 1. to build 2. to develop

consultar to consult

consultar a un abogado to take legal advice

consultoría *f* consulting firm *o* consultancy firm

consumidor consumer

consumo *m* consumption

consumo *m* **doméstico** home consumption

consumo interior home consumption

contabilidad *f* 1. accounting 2. bookkeeping

contabilidad *f* **de costes** cost accounting

contabilidad f **de costes actuales** current cost accounting

contabilidad f **de ingresos** revenue accounts

contable mf 1. accountant 2. bookkeeper

contable mf **de costes** cost accountant

contable mf **jefe** controller

contactar to contact

contacto m contact

contar to count

con tendencia a la baja adj falling

contenedor m container

contener 1. to contain 2. to hold 3. (parar) to check 4. (frenar) to stop

contenerización f containerization

contenido m contents

contestación f 1. answer 2. reply

contestador m **automático** answering machine

contestar 1. to answer 2. to reply

contestar el teléfono to answer the telephone

contestar una carta to answer a letter

contingencia f contingency

continuación f continuation

continuamente adv continually

continuar 1. to continue 2. to proceed

continuo constant ■ adj 1. continual 2. continuous

contraasiento m adv contra entry

contracción f shrinkage

contractual adj contractual

contraer deudas to incur debts

contraoferta f counter-offer o counterbid

contra OPA f reverse takeover

contrapartida f adv contra entry

contra reembolso cash on delivery; COD o c.o.d.

contrario adj contrary

contraste m contrast

contratar to contract

contratar personal 1. to hire staff 2. to staff

contratista mf contractor

contratista mf **del Estado** government contractor

contratista mf **de transporte por carretera** haulage contractor

contrato m 1. contract 2. agreement

contrato m **a plazo fijo** forward contract

contrato m **de arrendamiento** m tenancy

contrato m **de Bolsa** contract note

contrato m **de corta duración** short-term contract

contrato m **de empleo** contract of employment

contrato m **de plazo fijo** fixed-term contract

contrato m **de seguros** insurance contract

contrato m **de venta** bill of sale

contrato m **en exclusiva** exclusive agreement

contrato m **permanente** permanent contract

contribución f contribution

contribución f **de capital** contribution of capital

contribuir to contribute

contribuyente mf 1. contributor 2. taxpayer

control m 1. control 2. check 3. inspection

controlado por el Estado adj government-controlled

controlar 1. to control 2. to monitor

controlar un negocio to control a business

control m **de alquileres** rent control

control m **de calidad** quality control

control m **de crédito** credit control

control m **de divisas** exchange control

control *m* **de existencias 1.** inventory control **2.** stock control

control *m* **de materiales** materials control

control *m* **de precios** price control

control *m* **de rentas** rent control

control *m* **presupuestario** budgetary control

con un IVA del 0% *adj* zero-rated

convenido *adj* agreed

conveniente *adj* convenient

convenio *m* **1.** agreement **2.** covenant

convenio *m* **salarial colectivo** collective wage agreement

conversaciones *fpl* **fructíferas** productive discussions

conversión *f* conversion

conversión *f* **de divisas** currency conversion

conversión *f* **de un préstamo** refunding of a loan

convertibilidad *f* convertibility

convertir to convert

convocar to convene

convocar (una reunión) to call

cooperación *f* co-operation

cooperar to co-operate

cooperativa *f* co-operative

cooperativo *adj* co-operative

coparticipación *f* copartnership

copia *f* **1.** copy **2.** duplicate

copia *f* **auténtica** certified copy

copia *f* **carbón** carbon copy

copia *f* **de reserva** backup copy

copia *f* **exacta** true copy

copia *f* **falsa** forgery

copia *f* **impresa** hard copy

copia *f* **impresa (de ordenador)** computer printout

copiar 1. to copy **2.** to duplicate **3.** (*escribir*) to write out

copiar una factura to duplicate an invoice

copropiedad *f* **1.** co-ownership **2.** part ownership

co-propiedad *f* joint ownership

copropietario 1. co-owner **2.** part owner

co-propietario joint owner

corona *f* **1.** krone **2.** krona

corporación *f* **1.** corporation **2.** guild

corrección *f* correction

correcto *adj* **1.** correct **2.** right **3.** accurate

corredor stockbroker

corredor *m* **de seguros** insurance broker

correduría *f* **de bolsa** stockbroking

corregir 1. to correct **2.** to rectify **3.** to revise

correo *m* **1.** mail **2.** *U.K.* post

correo *m* **aéreo** airmail

correo *m* **electrónico 1.** electronic mail **2.** email

correo *m* **entrante** incoming mail

correo *m* **por vía terrestre o marítima** surface mail

correos *mpl U.K.* post

correr un riesgo to run a risk

correspondencia *f* **1.** correspondence **2.** mail

correspondencia *f* **de salida** outgoing mail

correspondencia *f* **recibida** incoming mail

corresponder 1. to agree with **2.** to agree

corresponder a algo to correspond with something

correspondiente *mf* correspondent

corresponsal *mf* correspondent

corretaje *m* broker's commission *o* brokerage

corriente *adj* **1.** common **2.** frequent **3.** (*actual*) current **4.** (*ordinario*) ordinary **5.** (*ordinario*) regular

costar to cost

costas *fpl* costs

costas *fpl* **judiciales 1.** legal costs *o* legal charges **2.** legal expenses

coste *m* **1.** charge **2.** cost

coste, seguro y flete cost, insurance and freight

costear los gastos de alguien to defray someone's expenses

coste *m* **de almacenaje** storage

coste *m* **de la gestión de deudas** factoring charges

coste *m* **de producción 1.** production cost **2.** prime cost

coste *m* **descargado** landed costs

coste *m* **de ventas** cost of sales

coste *m* **de vida** cost of living

coste *m* **directo** direct cost

coste *m* **incremental 1.** incremental cost **2.** marginal cost

coste *m* **inicial** historic(al) cost

coste *m* **marginal** marginal cost

coste *m* **por unidad** unit cost

costes *mpl* start-up costs

costes *mpl* **de distribución** distribution costs

costes *mpl* **de envío** shipping charges *o* shipping costs

costes *mpl* **de fabricación** manufacturing costs

costes *mpl* **de lanzamiento** launching costs

costes *mpl* **excesivos** excessive costs

costes *mpl* **fijos** fixed costs

costes *mpl* **laborales** labor costs

costes *mpl* **laborales indirectos** indirect labor costs

costes *mpl* **sociales** social costs

costes *mpl* **variables** variable costs

coste *m* **total** total cost

coste *m* **unitario** unit cost

costo *m* cost

costo *m* **más honorarios** cost plus

costoso *adj* **1.** costly **2.** expensive

costumbre *f* routine

cotejar 1. to check **2.** to compare

cotidiano *adj* day-to-day

cotización *f* quote

cotización *f* **de apertura** opening price

cotizar 1. (*calcular*) to quote **2.** (*contribuir*) to contribute

"crack" *m* crash

crear to set up a company

creciente *adj* **1.** increasing **2.** mounting

crecimiento *m* growth

crecimiento *m* **económico** economic growth

crédito *m* credit

crédito *m* **abierto** open credit

crédito *m* **a corto plazo 1.** short-term credit **2.** short credit

crédito: a crédito credit: on credit

crédito *m* **a largo plazo 1.** long credit **2.** extended credit

crédito *m* **al consumidor** consumer credit

crédito *m* **bancario** bank credit

crédito *m* **barato** cheap money

crédito *m* **blando** soft loan

crédito *m* **congelado** frozen credits

crédito *m* **de apoyo** standby credit

crédito *m* **instantáneo** instant credit

crédito *m* **por impuestos pagados** tax credit

crédito *m* **renovable** revolving credit

crédito *m* **sin interés** interest-free credit

crédito *m* **"stand by"** standby credit

crisis *f* **del dólar** dollar crisis

crisis *f* **de liquidez** liquidity crisis

crisis *f* **económica 1.** slump **2.** depression

crisis *f* **financiera** financial crisis

crónico *adj* chronic

cruzar un cheque *U.K.* to cross a check

cuadrar 1. (*ajustar*) to reconcile 2. (*saldar*) to balance

cuadrícula *f* grid

cualificado *adj* 1. skilled 2. qualified

cuarta parte *f* quarter

cuarto *m* quarter

cuarto trimestre fourth quarter

cúbico *adj* cubic

cubierta *f* 1. deck 2. (*funda*) cover

(precio del) cubierto *m* cover charge

cubrir to cover

cubrir gastos 1. to break even 2. to cover costs 3. to meet expenses

cubrir un riesgo to cover a risk

cuenta 1. account 2. (*restaurante*) check 3. *U.K.* (*restaurante*) bill

cuenta *f* **abierta** 1. open account 2. charge account

cuenta *f* **acreedora** account in credit

cuenta: a cuenta account: on account

cuenta *f* **administrada por un apoderado** nominee account

cuenta *f* **a plazo** deposit account

cuenta *f* **bancaria** bank account

cuenta *f* **bloqueada** 1. frozen account 2. account on stop

cuenta *f* **compensada** contra account

cuenta *f* **conjunta** joint account

cuenta *f* **con saldo positivo** account in credit

cuenta *f* **corriente** 1. checking account 2. check account 3. drawing account 4. *U.K.* current account

cuenta *f* **de ahorro** savings account

cuenta *f* **de caja** cash account

cuenta *f* **de capital** capital account

cuenta *f* **de crédito** 1. charge account 2. credit account

cuenta *f* **de depósito** deposit account

cuenta *f* **de garantía bloqueada** escrow account

cuenta *f* **de gastos de representación** expense account

cuenta *f* **del Girobank** *U.K.* giro account

cuenta *f* **de no residente** external account

cuenta *f* **de pérdidas y ganancias** profit and loss account

cuenta *f* **detallada** 1. itemized account 2. detailed account

cuenta *f* **en descubierto** overdrawn account

cuenta *f* **en participación** joint account

cuenta *f* **inactiva** dead account

cuenta *f* **numerada** numbered account

cuenta *f* **presupuestaria** budget account

cuentas *fpl* **a cobrar** accounts receivable

cuentas *fpl* **anuales** annual accounts

cuentas *fpl* **a pagar** accounts payable

cuentas *fpl* **de fin de mes** month-end accounts

cuentas *fpl* **de gestión** management accounts

cuentas *fpl* **de mediados de mes** mid-month accounts

cuentas *fpl* **por cobrar** accounts receivable

cuentas *fpl* **semestrales** half-yearly accounts

cuentas *fpl* **sin verificar** unaudited accounts

cuestión *f* 1. matter 2. question

cuestionar to question

cuestionario *m* questionnaire

culpa *f* 1. (*falta*) fault 2. (*falta*) blame

culpar to blame

cumbre *f* 1. peak 2. top

cumplidor *adj* reliable

cumplimiento *m* 1. (*realización*) fulfillment 2. (*ejecución*) execution

cumplir 1. to carry out 2. to fulfill 3. (*satisfacer*) to meet 4. (*ejecutar*) to execute

cumplir una promesa to keep a promise

cumplir un objetivo to meet a target

cumplir un plazo establecido to meet a deadline

cuota *f* 1. quota 2. fee

cuota *f* **de depreciación** allowance for depreciation

cuota *f* **de importación** import quota

cuota *f* **de inscripción** registration fee

cuota *f* **de mercado** market share

cupo *m* quota

cupo *m* **de importación** import quota

cupón *m* coupon

cupón *m* **de anuncio** coupon ad

cupón *m* **de regalo** gift coupon

curriculum (vitae) *m* 1. résumé 2. *U.K.* curriculum vitae; CV

cursar un pedido to place an order

curso *m* **comercial** commercial course

curso *m* **de actualización** refresher course

curso *m* **de gestión empresarial** management course

curso *m* **de reciclaje** refresher course

cursos *mpl* **de iniciación** induction courses *o* induction training

curva *f* curve

curva *f* **de ventas** sales curve

D

dañado *adj* damaged

dañar to damage

daño *m* damage

daños *mpl* **causados por incendio** fire damage

daños *mpl* **materiales** damage to property

daños *mpl* **por tormenta** storm damage

daños *mpl* **y perjuicios** damages

dar 1. to give 2. (*conceder*) to allow 3. (*producir*) to produce

dar carpetazo to shelve

dar empleo to employ

dar instrucciones 1. to brief 2. to issue instructions

dar por resultado to result in

dar publicidad 1. to publicize 2. to plug

darse cuenta to realize

darse prisa to hurry up

dar una entrada 1. to pay money down 2. to put money down

dar una propina to tip

datos *mpl* data

datos *mpl* **de salida** output

de aduanas customs clearance

de ámbito nacional *adj* nationwide

de baja calidad *adj* low-grade

de bajo nivel *adj* low-level

debate *m* 1. debate 2. discussion

debe *m* 1. debit 2. debtor side

deber to owe

debe y haber to debits and credits

debidamente *adv* duly

debido *adj* 1. due 2. owing

debido a owing to

débil *adj* 1. slack 2. weak

débito *m* 1. debit 2. charge

de buena fe *adj* bona fide

de capacidad cubic measure

decidir 1. to decide 2. to resolve

decidirse por la opción más fácil to take the soft option

decimal *m* decimal

decisión *f* 1. decision 2. (*fallo*) ruling

decisivo *adj* deciding

declaración *f* 1. declaration 2. statement 3. announcement

declaración *f* **de aduana** customs declaration

declaración *f* **de ingresos nulos** *U.K.* nil return

declaración *f* **de quiebra** declaration of bankruptcy

declaración *f* **de renta** 1. tax return *o* tax declaration 2. declaration of income

declaración *f* **de siniestro** insurance claim

declaración *f* **oficial** official return

declarado *adj* declared

declarar 1. to declare 2. to state

declarar a alguien en quiebra to declare someone bankrupt

declarar mercancías en la aduana to declare goods to customs

declararse en huelga to strike

de comercio commodity exchange

decomisar to forfeit

decomiso *m* 1. forfeiture 2. forfeit

de confianza *adj* reliable

de contenidos packing list *o* packing slip

de control supervisory

decreciente *adj* 1. decreasing 2. falling

decretar to rule

de dimisión notice

deducción *f* deduction

deducción *f* **de impuestos** tax deductions

deducciones *fpl* **personales** personal allowances

deducible *adj* deductible

deducir 1. to deduct 2. (*compensar*) to set against 3. (*inferir*) to deduce 4. (*inferir*) to infer

deducir del sueldo to dock

de envío dispatch note

de exportación *adj* exporting

de fácil manejo *adj* user-friendly

de fácil uso *adj* user-friendly

de favor *adj* complimentary

defectivo *adj* defective

defecto *m* 1. defect 2. fault 3. imperfection

defectuoso *adj* defective

defender to defend

defenderse en juicio to defend a lawsuit

defensa *f* defense

defensor *m* **del pueblo** ombudsman

déficit *m* 1. deficit 2. shortfall

déficit *m* **comercial** trade deficit *o* trade gap

deflación *f* deflation

deflacionista *adj* deflationary

defraudación *f* fraud

de grado inferior *adj* low-level

de hace tiempo *adj* long-standing

dejar (*abandonar*) to leave

dejar de hacer algo to fail

dejar un margen to allow for

dejar un margen del 10% para el porte to allow 10% for shipping

de la casa *adj* in-house

de la esquina corner store

delegación *f* delegation

delegado *mf* 1. delegate 2. deputy

delegado *m* **del personal** *U.K.* worker director

delegar to delegate

del gobierno *adj* government

de libre dedicación adj freelance

delito m **por omisión** nonfeasance

de los corrientes adj instant

del petróleo oil price

del presente mes adj instant

demanda f 1. demand 2. (reclamación) claim

demanda f **de pago** call

demanda f **de pago de acciones** call

demandado defendant

demanda f **efectiva** effective demand

demanda f **estacional** seasonal demand

demanda f **excesiva** run

demandante mf 1. claimant 2. plaintiff

demanda f **por daños y perjuicios** action for damages

demandar to sue

de menor antigüedad junior partner

demora f delay

demorar to delay

demostración f demonstration

demostrar to demonstrate

de muchos años adj long-standing

de obligaciones contract law

de oficina adj clerical

de ordenador computer language

departamental adj departmental

departamento m 1. department 2. division 3. section

departamento m **de atención al cliente** customer service department

departamento m **de compras** 1. purchasing department 2. buying department

departamento m **de contabilidad** 1. accounting department 2. U.K. accounts department

departamento m **de diseño** design department

Departamento m **de Estado** department

departamento m **de exportación** export department

departamento m **de facturación** invoicing department

departamento m **de informática** computer department

departamento m **de 'marketing'** marketing department

departamento m **de personal** personnel department

departamento m **de producción** production department

departamento m **de publicidad** publicity department

departamento m **de reclamaciones** claims department

departamento m **de relaciones públicas** public relations department

departamento m **de reservas** room reservations

depender de to depend on

dependiente mf 1. salesman 2. U.K. shop assistant

de poca calidad adj low-quality

depositante mf depositor

depositar 1. (ingresar) to deposit 2. (ingresar) to bank

depósito m 1. deposit 2. down payment 3. (entrada) deposit 4. (almacén) store 5. (almacén) storeroom 6. (almacén) stockroom 7. (almacenamiento) storage 8. U.K. (almacén de mercancías) goods depot

depósito m **aduanero** bonded warehouse

depósito m **a la vista** demand deposit·

depósito m **a plazo** time deposit

depósito m **a plazo fijo** fixed deposit

depósito m **no reembolsable** non-refundable deposit

depósito m **reembolsable** refundable deposit

depósitos mpl **bancarios** bank deposits

depósitos *mpl* **con interés** interest-bearing deposits

de post-venta after-sales service

depreciación *f* 1. depreciation 2. (*de valor*) depreciation

depreciación *f* **de un activo** writedown

depreciar to depreciate

depreciar el valor de un activo to write down

depreciarse to depreciate

depresión *f* 1. depression 2. slump

de primera calidad *adj* up-market

de primera clase *adj* 1. first-class 2. A1

de promoción *adj* promotional

de prueba probationary

de puerta en puerta *adj* door-to-door

derecho *m* 1. law 2. right ■ *adj* entitlement; right

derecho *m* **civil** civil law

derecho *m* **de aduana** customs duty

derecho *m* **de contratos** contract law

derecho *m* **de ocupación** security of tenure

derecho *m* **de paso** right of way

derecho *m* **de retención** lien

derecho *m* **de veto** right of veto

derechohabiente *m* rightful claimant

derecho *m* **internacional** international law

derecho *m* **marítimo** maritime law

derecho *m* **mercantil** commercial law

derechos *mpl* fee

derechos *mpl* **de autor** royalty

derechos *mpl* **de dársena** port charges *o* port duesfees

derechos *mpl* **de exportación** export duty

derechos *mpl* **de importación** import duty

derechos *mpl* **especiales de giro (DEG)** special drawing rights (SDRs)

derechos *mpl* **portuarios** harbor fees *o* harbor dues

de repuesto spare part

de reserva *adj* backup

derivar de to result from

derrumbamiento *m* collapse

derrumbarse to collapse

desaceleración *f* slowdown

desacelerar to slow down

desaconsejar to advise against

desacreditar to discredit

desacuerdo *m* disagreement

de salario pay slip

desaparecido *adj* 1. unaccounted for 2. missing

desarrollar to develop

desarrollo *m* 1. development 2. growth

desarrollo *m* **de productos** product development

desarrollo *m* **económico** economic development

desbordar to flood

descanso *m* 1. break 2. rest

descargar 1. to unload 2. to offload

descargar mercancías en un puerto to land goods at a port

descarga *f* **y carga de un avión** turnaround

descargo *m* (*deuda*) discharge

descargo *m* **final** final discharge

descender to drop

descenso *m* 1. decline 2. downturn 3. decrease

descentralización *f* decentralization

descentralizar 1. to decentralize 2. to hive off

descontable *adj* discountable

descontar 1. to discount 2. to knock off 3. to deduct

descontar del sueldo to dock

describir to describe

descripción f description

descripción f **comercial** trade description

descripción f **del puesto de trabajo** 1. job description 2. job specification

descubierto m (*sobregiro*) overdraft

descuento m 1. discount 2. rebate

descuento m **al por mayor** wholesale discount

descuento m **básico** basic discount

descuento m **para comerciantes del sector** 1. trade discount 2. trade terms

descuento m **por ausencia de siniestralidad** good driver discount

descuento m **por cantidad** quantity discount

descuento m **por pago al contado** cash discount

descuento m **por volumen** volume discount

descuidado adj negligent

desechable to disposable

desecho m waste

de segunda categoría adv second-class

de segunda clase adv second-class

de segunda mano secondhand

de seguridad backup copy

desembarcar to land

desembolsar 1. to disburse 2. to pay out

desembolso m 1. disbursement 2. expenditure 3. outlay

desembolsos mpl outgoings

desempleado adj unemployed

desempleo m unemployment

desfalcador embezzler

desfalcar to embezzle

desfalco m embezzlement

desfavorable adj unfavorable

desgastar to erode

desgaste m **natural** 1. wear and tear 2. ordinary wear and tear 3. U.K. fair wear and tear

desgaste m **normal** wear and tear

desglosar to break down

desglose m breakdown

desgravable adj tax-deductible

desgravación f concession

desgravación f **fiscal** 1. tax allowance 2. tax relief 3. tax concession

deshacerse de 1. to unload 2. to offload

deshacerse de algo to get rid of something

deshacerse de las existencias sobrantes to dispose of excess stock

deshonorar to dishonor

desistir de una acción to abandon an action

de situación balance sheet

desocupar to vacate

despachar to dispatch

despachar pedidos atrasados to release dues

despachar un pedido to fulfill an order

despacho m 1. (*envío*) dispatch 2. (*oficina*) office

despacho m **aduanero** customs clearance

despacho m **de billetes** 1. ticket office 2. U.K. booking office

despacho m **de pedidos** order fulfillment

desparejado adj odd

despedir 1. to discharge 2. to pay off

despedir a alguien to sack v someone

despedir a un empleado to dismiss an employee

despedir por falta de trabajo to lay off workers

despegar to take off

desperdiciar to waste

desperdicio *m* 1. waste 2. wastage

desperfectos *mpl* breakages

despido *m* 1. dismissal 2. removal 3. *U.K.* (*excedente de plantilla*) redundancy

despido *m* **injusto** 1. unfair dismissal 2. wrongful dismissal

desregulación *f* deregulation

destacado *adj* outstanding

destinatario 1. addressee 2. receiver (who receives)

destino *m* destination

destitución *f* removal

destituir to remove

destreza *f* skill

de supervisión supervisory

desvalorización *f* devaluation

desvalorizar to devalue

detallado *adj* detailed

detallar 1. to detail 2. to itemize 3. to break down

detalle *m* detail

detalles *mpl* particulars

detallista *mf* retailer

detener 1. (*frenar*) to plug 2. (*frenar*) to stop

detener el pago de un cheque to stop payment on a check

deteriorado *adj* 1. damaged 2. shop-soiled

determinar to determine

deuda *f* 1. debt 2. indebtedness 3. obligation

deuda *f* **incobrable** 1. irrecoverable debt 2. write-off

deuda *f* **morosa** bad debt

deudas *fpl* liabilities

deudas *fpl* **a corto plazo** short-term debts

deudas *fpl* **a largo plazo** long-term debts

deudas *fpl* **a pagar** debts due

deudas *fpl* **garantizadas** secured debts

deudas *fpl* **pendientes** outstanding debts

deudor 1. debtor 2. defaulter

deudor *m* **hipotecario** mortgager *o* mortgagor

deudor *m* **judicial** judgment debtor

de usar y tirar to disposable

devaluación *f* devaluation

devaluar to devalue

devengar 1. to earn 2. to bear 3. to yield 4. to accrue

devolución *f* 1. return 2. (*reembolso*) refund

devolución *f* **(de impuestos)** clawback

devolver 1. to return 2. to pay back 3. to refund

devolver por falta de fondos to bounce

devolver una carta al remitente to return a letter to sender

devolver una letra to dishonor a bill

día *m* day

día *m* **de ajuste** quarter day

diagrama *m* diagram

diagrama *m* **de flujo** flow chart

diagrama *m* **de flujos** flow diagram

diario *adj* 1. daily 2. day-to-day

diario *m* **de bolsillo** pocket diary

dictado *m* dictation

dictáfono *m* dictating machine

dictar to dictate

diferencia *f* 1. difference 2. discrepancy

diferencial *adj* differential

diferencias *fpl* **de precio** differences in price

diferente *adj* different

diferido *adj* deferred

diferir 1. to differ 2. (*aplazar*) to defer 3. (*aplazar*) to adjourn

diferir el pago to defer payment

difícil *adj* difficult

dificultad *f* difficulty

difundir a través de la red de emisoras to network

difusión *f* circulation

dígito *m* digit

dilución *f* **del capital** dilution of equity

dimensiones *fpl* 1. dimensions 2. size 3. measurements

dimisión *f* resignation

dimitir to resign

dinero *m* money

dinero *m* **barato** cheap money

dinero *m* **efectivo** cash

dinero *m* **en mano** spot cash

dinero *m* **escaso** tight money

dinero *m* **para gastos menores** petty cash

dinero *m* **para gastos personales** spending money

dinero *m* **suelto** change

diplomado *adj* certificated

dique *m* dock

dirección *f* 1. direction 2. (*gerencia*) management 3. (*señas*) address

dirección *f* **comercial** business address

dirección *f* **conjunta** joint management

dirección *f* **de personal** personnel management

dirección *f* **de reenvío** forwarding address

dirección *f* **postal** accommodation address

dirección *f* **telegráfica** cable address

directamente *adv* direct

directiva *f* directive

directivo *adj* managerial

directo *adj* direct

director 1. director 2. manager

director *m* **adjunto** deputy manager

director *m* **comercial** sales manager

director *m* **de banco** bank manager

director *m* **de exportación** export manager

director *m* **de finanzas** finance director

director *m* **de hotel** hotel manager

director *m* **de "marketing"** marketing manager

director *m* **de planta** floor manager

director *m* **de producción** production manager

director *m* **de proyecto** project manager

director *m* **de publicidad** publicity manager

director *m* **de reclamaciones** claims manager

director *m* **de sucursal** branch manager

director *m* **de una empresa** company director

director *m* **ejecutivo** executive director

director *m* **en funciones** acting manager

director *m* **externo** outside director

director *m* **general** 1. general manager 2. CEO

director *m* **general adjunto** deputy managing director

director *m* **gerente** *mf* 1. managing director; MD 2. general manager

directorio *m* directory

directorio *m* **comercial** classified directory

director *m* **no ejecutivo** non-executive director

director *m* **principal** senior manager *o* senior executive

director *m* **regional** area manager

directriz *f* 1. guideline 2. directive

dirigido a un mercado popular *adj* down-market

dirigir 1. to direct 2. to channel 3. to address 4. (*gestionar*) to manage 5. (*llevar*) to run

dirigir un negocio to control a business

disco *m* disk

disco *m* **duro** hard disk

discrepancia f 1. discrepancy 2. variance

disculpa f apology

disculparse to apologize

discurrir to flow

discusión f 1. discussion 2. argument 3. (*debate*) debate

discutir to discuss

diseñar to design

diseño m design

diseño m **de productos** product design

diseño m **industrial** industrial design

diseño m **registrado** registered design

diskette diskette

disminución f 1. decrease 2. lowering 3. (*impuestos*) abatement

disminución f **de valor** decrease in value

disminuir 1. to decline 2. to decrease 3. to fall off

disolver to dissolve

disolver una sociedad to dissolve a partnership

dispararse to soar

disponer to arrange

disponibilidad f availability

disponible adj 1. available 2. vacant

disposición f provision

dispositivo m device

disquete m diskette

disquetera f disk drive

distinto adj different

distribución f distribution

distribución f **exclusiva** distributorship

distribuidor 1. distributor 2. stockist

distribuir to distribute

distribuir un dividendo to pay a dividend

distrito m 1. district 2. area

distrito m **comercial** commercial district

disuadir to advise against

diversificación f diversification

diversificar to diversify

diverso adj miscellaneous

dividendo m dividend

dividendo m **final** final dividend

dividendo m **mínimo** minimum dividend

dividendo m **por acción** earnings per share *o* earnings yield

dividendo m **por superávit** surplus dividend

dividendo m **provisional** interim dividend

dividir 1. (*separar*) to divide 2. to share 3. (*separar*) to separate

divisas fpl foreign exchange

divisas fpl **de reserva** reserve currency

división f division

divulgación f disclosure

divulgar 1. to disclose 2. to release 3. to publicize

doble adj double

doble imposición f double taxation

doble reserva f double booking

docena f dozen

documentación f documentation

documental adj documentary

documento m document

documento m **adjunto** enclosure

documento m **escrito** instrument

documento m **falso** forgery

documento m **no negociable** nonnegotiable instrument

documentos mpl 1. documents 2. papers

documentos mpl **falsos** faked documents

dólar m dollar

domiciliación f **bancaria** 1. direct debit 2. standing order

domicilio m domicile

domicilio m **particular** home address

domicilio *m* **social** 1. registered office 2. headquarters; HQ

dominante *adj* controlling

dorso *m* back

dotación *f* **de personal** manning

dpto. (= **departamento**) *abbr* (*department*) dept

dueña *f* 1. proprietress 2. landlady

dueño *m* 1. proprietor 2. landlord 3. owner

"dumping" *m* dumping

duplicación *f* duplication

duplicado *m* duplicate

duplicado *m* **de una factura** duplicate of a receipt

duplicar 1. to duplicate 2. to double

duplicarse to double

duro *adj* hard

E

echar al correo 1. *U.K.* to post 2. to mail

echar la culpa to blame

ecológico *adj* environmentally friendly

economía *f* 1. economy 2. economics

economía *f* **de libre mercado** free market economy

economía *f* **de oferta** supply side economics

economía *f* **dirigida** controlled economy

economía *f* **estable** stable economy

economía *f* **madura** mature economy

economía *f* **mixta** mixed economy

economías *fpl* **de escala** economies of scale

economía *f* **sumergida** black economy

económico *adj* 1. economic 2. economical

economista *mf* economist

economista *mf* **de mercado** market economist

economizar 1. to economize 2. to save 3. to save on

edad *f* **de jubilación** retirement age

edificio *m* 1. to building 2. facility 3. premises

edificio *m* **principal** main building

efectivo *adj* 1. effective 2. actual ■ ready cash

efectivo *m* **en caja** cash in hand

efecto *m* 1. effect 2. instrument

efecto *m* **de favor** accommodation bill

efecto *m* **indirecto** spinoff

efecto *m* **negociable** bankable paper

efectos *mpl* **a cobrar** receivables

efecto *m* **secundario** *U.K.* knock-on effect

efectos *mpl* **embargados (vendidos a bajo precio)** distressed merchandise

efectuar to effect

eficacia *f* 1. effectiveness 2. efficiency

eficaz *adj* efficient

eficiencia *f* 1. efficiency 2. effectiveness

eficiente *adj* efficient

ejecución *f* 1. execution 2. implementation 3. enforcement

ejecutar 1. to execute 2. to implement 3. to enforce

ejecutivo *adj* executive ■ executive

ejecutivo *m* **auxiliar** junior executive *o* junior manager

ejecutivo *m* **de cuentas** account executive

ejecutivo *m* **de ventas** sales executive

ejecutivo *m* **en formación** management trainee

ejemplar *m* copy

ejercer 1. to exercise **2.** to perform

ejercer derecho de opción to exercise an option

ejercicio *m* exercise

ejercicio *m* **del derecho de opción** exercise of an option

ejercicio *m* **económico** financial year

ejercicio *m* **fiscal** tax year

elaboración *f* data processing

elaborar 1. to process **2.** (*producto*) to manufacture **3.** (*materias primas*) to process

elaborar cifras to process figures

elasticidad *f* elasticity

elección *f* **1.** election **2.** choice

elegir 1. to elect **2.** to choose

elemento *m* factor

elevador *m* **de granos** elevator

eludir to evade

elusión *f* evasion

elusión *f* **de impuestos** tax avoidance

e-mail email

embalador packer

embalaje *m* **1.** packaging **2.** packing **3.** package

embalaje *m* **de exposición** display pack

embalaje *m* **de plástico tipo burbuja 1.** blister pack **2.** bubble pack

embalaje *m* **hermético** airtight packaging

embalaje *m* **vacío** dummy pack

embalar 1. to pack **2.** (*caja*) to case **3.** (*caja*) to crate

embalar mercancías en cajas de cartón to pack goods into cartons

embarcadero *m* wharf

embarcar to embark

embarcarse to board

embarcarse en to embark on

embargador sequestrator

embargar 1. to embargo **2.** to seize **3.** to sequester *o* to sequestrate

embargo *m* **1.** embargo **2.** seizure **3.** sequestration

embarque *m* embarkation

embaucar to fiddle

embolsar to pocket

embotellamiento *m* bottleneck

emergencia *f* emergency

emisión *f* issue

emisión *f* **de acciones 1.** stock issue **2.** *U.K.* share issue

emisión *f* **de acciones gratuitas** scrip issue

emisión *f* **de derechos** rights issue

emisión *f* **gratuita** bonus issue

emisión *f* **publicitaria** commercial

emisor underwriting syndicate

emitir to issue

emolumentos *mpl* fee

empaletar to palletize

empaquetador packer

empaquetar 1. to parcel **2.** to pack

empezar 1. to start **2.** to begin

empezar un negocio a cero to cold start

emplazamiento *m* summons

empleado 1. employee **2.** employed

empleado *m* **del servicio de información** information officer

empleado *m* **de oficina** clerk

empleado *m* **para mantener llenos los estantes** shelf filler

emplear 1. to employ **2.** to use

emplear de nuevo to re-employ

emplear más personal to take on more staff

empleo *m* 1. employment 2. appointment 3. job

empleo *m* **a tiempo parcial** part-time work *o* part-time employment

empleo *m* **de la capacidad** capacity utilization

empleo *m* **eventual** temporary employment

empleo *m* **fijo** staff appointment

empleo *m* **seguro** secure job

emprendedor *adj* go-ahead

emprender to undertake

emprender un negocio to go into business

empresa *f* 1. enterprise 2. business 3. concern 4. firm 5. undertaking 6. setup 7. venture

empresa *f* **a pequeña escala** small-scale enterprise

empresa *f* **comercial** commercial undertaking

empresa *f* **competidora** rival company

empresa *f* **con fines de lucro** profit-oriented company

empresa *f* **conjunta** joint venture

empresa *f* **de alquiler de maquinaria** plant-hire firm

empresa *f* **de transporte público** common carrier

empresa *f* **de transportes** carrier

empresa *f* **de ventas por correo** mail-order business *o* mail-order firm

empresa *f* **en ruinas** wreck

empresa *f* **familiar** family company

empresa *f* **mediana** middle-sized company

empresa *f* **privada** private enterprise

empresa *f* **que comercia con otra** trading partner

empresarial *adj* entrepreneurial

empresario 1. employer 2. entrepreneur

empresas *fpl* **rivales** competing firms

empréstito *m* loan capital

empuje *m* drive

en aguas territoriales *adv* offshore

en aumento *adj* increasing ■ on the increase

en bancarrota *adj* bankrupt

en blanco *adj* blank

encargado manager

encargado *m* **de compras** buyer

encargado *m* **del libro de compras** *U.K.* bought ledger clerk

encargado *m* **del libro de ventas** sales ledger clerk

encargar 1. (*confiar*) to entrust 2. (*hacer un pedido*) to order

encargarse de to undertake

encarte *m* **publicitario (de una revista)** magazine insert

encauzar to channel

enchufe *m* 1. plug 2. connection 3. (*influencia*) contact

encogimiento *m* shrinkage

en común *adv* jointly

en condiciones favorables on favorable terms

en conjunto *adv* overall

en construcción under construction

encontrar 1. to find 2. to meet

encontrarse (con) to meet

en cuanto a regarding

encubrimiento *m* **de activos** concealment of assets

encuesta *f* 1. opinion poll 2. questionnaire

endémico *adj* chronic

endeudado *adj* indebted

endeudarse 1. to get into debt 2. to run into debt

endosante *mf* endorser

endosar un cheque to endorse a check

endosatario endorsee

endoso *m* endorsement

en efectivo *adv* cash

en el centro de la ciudad *adv* downtown

en el extranjero *adv* overseas

energía *f* 1. (*electricidad*) energy 2. energy 3. drive

en fecha futura *adv* forward

en funciones *adj* acting

enjuiciar to prosecute

enlace *m* tie-up

en las condiciones acordadas on agreed terms

en línea on line *o* online

en manos de los tribunales *adj* sub judice

en marcha *adj* going

enmendar to amend

enmienda *f* amendment

en nombre de on behalf of

en plena dedicación *adj* full-time

en pleno auge boom industry

en promoción *adj* promotional

en quiebra *adj* bankrupt

ensayo *m* 1. test 2. trial

enseñar 1. to show 2. to teach

en su defecto failing that

en su totalidad *adv* outright

entablar to enter into

entablar negociaciones to open negotiations

entablar un pleito to take legal action

entender to understand

entrada *f* 1. entrance 2. admission 3. entering 4. entry 5. (*billete*) ticket 6. (*depósito*) down payment 7. (*depósito*) deposit

entrada *f* **de favor** complimentary ticket

entradas *fpl* receipts

entrar en to enter

entrar en dársena to dock

entrar en vigor to operate

entrega *f* delivery

entrega *f* **con acuse de recibo** 1. certified mail 2. *U.K.* recorded delivery

entrega *f* **futura** future delivery

entrega *f* **gratuita** free delivery

entregar 1. to deliver 2. to hand in 3. to hand over

entrega *f* **urgente** express delivery

entrevista *f* interview

entrevistado interviewee

entrevistador interviewer

entrevistar to interview

en trozos pequeños *adv* fine

enumerar to list

en una disputa to arbitrate in a dispute

en uso employed

envasado *adj* shrink-wrapped

envasar to pack

envase *m* 1. (*embalaje*) packing 2. (*embalaje*) packaging 3. (*embalaje*) package 4. (*embalaje*) pack 5. (*recipiente*) container

envase *m* **al vacío** shrink-wrapping

envase *m* **no retornable** non-returnable packing

envases *mpl* **devueltos** returned empties

en venta for sale

enviar 1. to send 2. to dispatch 3. *U.K.* to post

enviar por carga aérea to airfreight

enviar por correo to express

enviar por correo aéreo to airmail

enviar por fax to fax

enviar por télex to telex

enviar una carga por vía marítima to send a shipment by sea

enviar una factura por correo to send an invoice by mail

enviar un paquete por correo aéreo to send a package by airmail

enviar un paquete por vía terrestre o marítima to send a package by surface mail

envío *m* 1. (*carga*) dispatch 2. (*carga*) shipment 3. (*expedición*) dispatch 4. (*expedición*) shipping 5.

(*expedición*) forwarding 6. (*expedición*) consignment 7. (*giro*) remittance 8. (*remesa*) consignment

envío *m* **agrupado de mercancías** consolidated shipment

envío *m* **de publicidad por correo** 1. direct mailing 2. mailing shot

envío *m* **de revistas por correo** magazine mailing

envío *m* **por correo** mailing

envíos *mpl* **a granel** bulk shipments

envoltorio *m* wrapper *o* wrapping

envolver 1. to wrap up 2. to parcel

epígrafes *mpl* **de un acuerdo** heads of agreement

equilibrar to balance

equilibrio *m* balance

equipaje *m* 1. *U.K.* luggage 2. baggage

equipaje *m* **de mano** hand luggage

equipaje *m* **no reclamado** unclaimed baggage

equipar to equip

equiparación *f* equalization

equipo *m* equipment

equipo *m* **de consumidores** consumer panel

equipo *m* **defectuoso** faulty equipment

equipo *m* **de oficina** office equipment

equipo *m* **de ventas** sales team

equipo *m* **directivo** management team

equipo *m* **pesado** heavy equipment

equipos *mpl* **de oficina** business equipment

equitativo *adj* fair

equivocación *f* 1. mistake 2. error

equivocado *adj* wrong

erosionar to erode

errar to miss

erróneo *adj* 1. erroneous 2. wrong

error *m* 1. error 2. slip 3. mistake

error *m* **aleatorio** random error

error *m* **de cálculo** miscalculation

error *m* **de copia** clerical error

error *m* **de oficina** clerical error

error *m* **de ordenador** computer error

escala *f* 1. scale 2. range

escala *f* **de rendimiento** earning capacity

escala *f* **de salarios** wage scale

escala *f* **móvil de salarios** incremental scale

escalar to escalate

escala *f* **salarial** wage scale

escalonar to stagger

escaparate *m* 1. shop window 2. window display

escasez *f* shortage

escasez *f* **de mano de obra** manpower shortage

escaso short of

escogido *adj* choice

escribir to write

escribir a alguien to correspond with someone

escribir sin abreviar to write out

escrito *adj* handwritten ■ writing

escritorio *m* desk

escritura *f* 1. writing 2. handwriting 3. (*título*) deed

escritura *f* **de cesión** deed of assignment

escritura *f* **de constitución** articles of association

escritura *f* **de convenio** deed of covenant

escritura *f* **de sociedad** deed of partnership

escritura *f* **de transferencia** deed of transfer

escudo *m* (*moneda*) escudo

escuela *f* **de secretariado** secretarial college

escuela *f* **empresarial** business school

escuela *f* **superior de comercio** commercial college

esencial *adj* essential

esfuerzo *m* effort

espacio *m* 1. space 2. room

espacio *m* **en blanco** blank

espacio *m* **para oficinas** office space

espacio *m* **publicitario** advertising space

especial *adj* special

especialista *mf* specialist

especialización *f* specialization

especializado *adj* skilled

especializar to specialize

especificación *f* specification

especificar 1. to specify 2. to itemize

esperar instrucciones to await instructions

espionaje *m* **industrial** industrial espionage

esquina *f* corner

estabilidad *f* 1. stability 2. steadiness

estabilidad *f* **de los precios** price stability

estabilización *f* stabilization

estabilizar(se) to stabilize

estabilizar los precios to peg prices

estabilizarse to level off *o* to level out

estable *adj* stable

establecer 1. to establish 2. to set 3. to base

establecerse 1. to set up in business 2. to settle

establecimiento *m* establishment

establecimiento de contactos en el mundo de negocios networking

estación *f* 1. season 2. (*tren*) station 3. (*de ordenador*) workstation

estacional *adj* seasonal

estación *f* **de ferrocarril** railway station

estación *f* **de mercancías** freight depot

estadísticas *fpl* statistics

estadístico *adj* statistical ■ statistician

estado *m* (*condición*) state

estado *m* **de cuenta** bank balance

estado *m* **de cuenta mensual** monthly statement

estado *m* **de cuentas** statement of account

estado *m* **de cuentas semestral** half-yearly statement

estado *m* **de flujo de caja** cash flow statement

estadounidense American ■ *adj* American

estafa *f* fraud

estafador racketeer

estampilla *f* stamp

estancado *adj* stagnant

estancamiento *m* stagnation

estancia *f* stay

estándar *adj* standard

estandarización *f* standardization

estandarizar to standardize

estantería *f* 1. shelf 2. shelving 3. (*vitrina*) display stand *o* display unit

estar de acuerdo to agree with

estar en punto muerto to deadlock

estatal *adj* government

estatutos *mpl* articles of association

estibador *m* stevedore

estimación *f* 1. estimate 2. estimation

estimado *adj* estimated

estimar to estimate

estimular to boost

estimular la economía to stimulate the economy

estímulo *m* 1. stimulus 2. boost 3. incentive

estipulación *f* 1. stipulation 2. provision

estipular to stipulate

estratagema *f* device

estrategia *f* strategy

estrategia f **comercial** business strategy

estrategia f **de 'marketing'** marketing strategy

estratégico adj strategic

estropear to spoil

estropearse to break down

estructura f structure

estructura f **cuadricular** grid structure

estructural adj structural

estructurar to structure

estudiar to study

estudio m 1. study 2. survey

estudio m **de desplazamientos y tiempos** time and motion study

estudio m **de mercado** market research

estudios mpl **sobre el terreno** field work

etapa f stage

etiqueta f label

etiqueta f **(de señas)** address label

etiqueta f **de correo aéreo** airmail sticker

etiqueta f **de precio** 1. price label 2. price tag o price ticket

etiquetado m labeling

etiquetar to label

euro m euro

eurocheque m Eurocheque

eurodivisa f Eurocurrency

eurodólar m Eurodollar

euromercado m Euromarket

europeo adj European

evadir to evade

evadir impuestos to evade tax

evaluación f 1. valuation 2. evaluation

evaluación f **de la rentabilidad** measurement of profitability

evaluar 1. to evaluate 2. to assess 3. to value

evaluar los costes to evaluate costs

evasión f evasion

evasión f **de capital(es)** flight of capital

evasión f **de impuestos** 1. tax evasion 2. tax avoidance

eventual adj prospective

eventualidad f contingency

evitar 1. to avoid 2. to prevent

exactamente adv exactly

exacto adj 1. exact 2. accurate

examen m 1. examination 2. test 3. (inspección) examination

examinar to examine

excedencia f leave of absence

excedente m 1. surplus 2. excess

excedente m **de plantilla** U.K. redundancy

excedente m **laboral** overmanning

exceder to exceed

excelente adj 1. excellent 2. first-class

excepcional adj exceptional

excepto 1. except 2. excluding

excesivo adj excessive

exceso m 1. excess 2. surplus

exceso m **de capacidad** excess capacity

exceso m **de equipaje** excess baggage

exceso m **de existencias** overstocks

exceso m **de personal** overmanning

excluir to exclude

exclusión f exclusion

exclusiva f sole right

exclusividad f exclusivity

exclusivo adj sole

excusa f apology

exención f exemption

exención f **fiscal** tax exemption

exención fiscal exemption from tax

exento adj exempt

exento de alquiler adj rent-free

exento de impuestos adj 1. exempt from tax 2. tax-exempt

exhibición f 1. exhibition 2. display

exhibidor demonstrator

exhibir to display

exigir 1. to require **2.** to demand **3.** to claim

exigir el reembolso to ask for a refund

eximir to exempt

existencias *fpl* **1.** stock **2.** inventory

existencias *fpl* **finales** closing stock

existencias *fpl* **iniciales 1.** beginning inventory **2.** *U.K.* opening stock

éxito *m* success

expandir to expand

expansión *f* expansion

expansión *f* **industrial** industrial expansion

expedición *f* **1.** forwarding **2.** shipping **3.** consignment

expedidor shipper

expediente *m* **1.** dossier **2.** file **3.** record

expedir 1. to ship **2.** to dispatch

experimentado *adj* experienced

experimentar una recuperación to stage a recovery

experto *adj* experienced

expiración *f* **1.** expiration **2.** expiry

expirar to expire

explicación *f* explanation

explicar to explain

explorar to explore

explotar to exploit

exponer 1. to exhibit **2.** to display **3.** (*describir*) to describe

exportación *f* export

exportaciones *fpl* exports

exportador exporter ■ *adj* exporting

exportar to export

exposición *f* **1.** display **2.** exhibition **3.** show **4.** (*riesgo*) exposure

expositor exhibitor

expresar to express

expreso *adj* express

expropiación *f* **forzosa** compulsory purchase

extender 1. to extend **2.** to make out

extender un cheque to write (out) a check

extensión *f* extension

exterior *adj* **1.** external **2.** (*externo*) outside

externo *adj* **1.** external **2.** outside

extirpar to excise

extra *adj* extra

extracto *m* **de cuentas** bank statement

(en el) extranjero *m* abroad

extranjero *adj* **1.** overseas **2.** foreign ■ overseas

extraoficial *adj* unofficial

extraoficialmente off the record

extraordinario *adj* extraordinary

extras *mpl* extras

extras *mpl* **opcionales** optional extras

F

fábrica *f* **1.** (*planta*) plant **2.** (*planta*) factory

fabricación *f* **1.** manufacturing **2.** manufacture

fabricante *m* **1.** manufacturer **2.** producer

fabricar 1. to manufacture **2.** to produce

fabricar coches en serie to mass-produce cars

fabricar en serie to mass-produce

fácil *adj* easy

facilidad f facility
facilidad f **de venta** salability
facilidades fpl **de crédito** credit facilities
facilidades fpl **de pago** easy terms
factibilidad f feasibility
factor m factor
factor m **decisivo** deciding factor
factor m **del coste** cost factor
factor m **de riesgo (en una inversión)** downside factor
factores mpl **cíclicos** cyclical factors
factores mpl **de producción** factors of production
factor m **negativo** minus factor
factor m **positivo** plus factor
factura f 1. bill 2. invoice
facturación f 1. billing 2. invoicing 3. (*ingresos*) sales revenue
factura f **de hotel** hotel bill
factura f **detallada** 1. itemized invoice 2. detailed account
factura f **por duplicado** duplicate receipt
factura f **pro forma** pro forma (invoice)
facturar 1. to bill 2. to invoice
facturar el equipaje to check in
facturas fpl **impagadas** unpaid invoices
fallar 1. to fail 2. to miss
fallecido adj dead
fallo m 1. fault 2. (*decisión*) ruling
falseado adj false
falsear to fiddle
falsificación f 1. falsification 2. forgery 3. fake
falsificado adj counterfeit
falsificar 1. to falsify 2. to forge 3. to fake 4. (*embaucar*) to fiddle
falsificar dinero to counterfeit
falso adj 1. false 2. (*falsificado*) counterfeit
falta f 1. fault 2. (*escasez*) shortage
falta f **de entrega** non-delivery
falta f **de fondos** lack of funds

fama f fame
fase f 1. phase 2. stage
favorable adj favorable
fax m fax
fecha f date
fecha f **de amortización** redemption date
fecha f **de caducidad** 1. expiration date 2. sell-by date 3. *U.K.* expiry date
fecha f **de cumplimiento** completion date
fecha f **de entrada en vigor** effective date
fecha f **de entrega** delivery date
fecha f **de lanzamiento** launching date
fecha f **de recepción** date of receipt
fecha f **de rescate** redemption date
fecha f **de vencimiento** maturity date
fechador m date stamp
fecha f **inicial** starting date
fecha f **límite** closing date
fechar to date
fecha f **tope** 1. closing date 2. deadline
feria f 1. show 2. fair
feria f **comercial** trade fair
ferrocarril m 1. rail 2. railroad 3. *U.K.* railway
"ferry" m ferry
ferry roll-on roll-off roll on/roll off ferry
fiabilidad f reliability
fiable adj reliable
fiador 1. guarantor 2. surety
fianza f 1. guarantee 2. security 3. surety
ficha f index card
ficha f **de ordenador** file
ficha f **de registro** filing card
fichero m 1. file 2. card catalog 3. (*de ordenador*) computer file
fichero m **de tarjetas** card-index file
ficticio dummy pack

fidelidad *f* **a la marca** brand loyalty

fidelidad *f* **a un establec-imiento** customer loyalty

fiesta *f* **nacional** public holiday

fiesta *f* **oficial** 1. *U.K.* statutory holiday 2. bank holiday

fijación *f* fixing

fijación *f* **colectiva de precios** common pricing

fijación *f* **de los precios** pricing

fijación *f* **de precios competi-tivos** competitive pricing

fijación *f* **de precios marginal** marginal pricing

fijar 1. to fix 2. to arrange 3. to set

fijar los daños to assess damages

fijar objetivos to set targets

fijar una reunión para las 3 de la tarde to fix a meeting for 3 p.m.

fijo *adj* 1. fixed 2. set 3. (*uniforme*) flat

filial *adj* affiliated ■ subsidiary

fin *m* end

final *adj* 1. final 2. closing ■ end

finalización *f* completion

finalizar 1. to finalize 2. (*terminar*) to end

financiación *f* 1. funding 2. financing

financiación *f* **del déficit pre-supuestario** deficit financing

financiamiento *m* financing

financiar 1. to finance 2. to fund

financiar una operación to finance an operation

financieramente *adj* financially

financiero *adj* financial

finanzas *fpl* 1. finance 2. finances

finanzas *fpl* **públicas** public finance

fin *m* **de mes** month end

fingir to fake

finiquito *m* settlement

firma *f* 1. signature 2. (*empresa*) firm

firma *f* **de un contrato** comple-tion of a contract

firmante *mf* signatory

firmar to sign

firmar como testigo to witness

firmar un cheque to sign a check

firmar un contrato to sign a contract

firme *adj* 1. firm 2. strong

fiscal *adj* fiscal ■ prosecution counsel

fletador charterer

fletamento *m* (*flete*) freightage

fletar 1. to charter 2. (*cargar*) to take on freight

fletar un avión to charter an air-craft

flete *m* 1. freight 2. charter 3. freightage

flete *m* **aéreo** air freight

flete *m* **de vuelta** homeward freight

flexibilidad *f* flexibility

flexible *adj* flexible

flojo *adj* 1. slack 2. loose 3. (*débil*) weak

florecer to flourish

floreciente *adj* 1. booming 2. flourishing

flotación *f* float

flotante *adj* floating

(hacer) flotar una divisa to float

fluctuación *f* fluctuation

fluctuante to fluctuating

fluctuar to fluctuate

fluir to flow

flujo *m* flow

flujo *m* **de caja** cash flow

flujo de caja descontado *abbr* (*discounted cash flow*) DCF

flujo *m* **de caja descontado** discounted cash flow

flujo *m* **de caja negativo** nega-tive cash flow

flujo *m* **de caja positivo** posi-tive cash flow

FMI (Fondo Monetario Internacional) *abbr* (*International Monetary Fund*) IMF

folleto *m* 1. leaflet 2. prospectus

folleto *m* **publicitario** brochure

folleto *m* **publicitario enviado por correo** mailing piece

fondo *m* 1. bottom 2. (*finanzas*) fund

fondo *m* **de caja** 1. cash float 2. float

fondo *m* **de comercio** goodwill

fondo *m* **de pensiones** pension fund

Fondo Monetario Internacional (FMI) International Monetary Fund (IMF)

fondo *m* **para imprevistos** contingency fund

fondos *mpl* petty cash

fondos *npl* **de inversión** 1. *U.K.* unit trust 2. mutual fund

fondos *mpl* **mutuos** 1. *U.K.* unit trust 2. mutual fund

fondos *mpl* **públicos** public funds

formación *f* training

formación *f* **de mandos** management training

formación *f* **en el puesto de trabajo** in-house training

formación *f* **profesional en el trabajo** on-the-job training

formación *f* **profesional fuera del trabajo** off-the-job training

formal *adj* formal

formalidad *f* formality

formalidades *fpl* **aduaneras** customs formalities

formar 1. to form 2. to train

formarse to train

formulario *m* form

formulario *m* **de declaración de la renta** tax form

formulario *m* **de solicitud** application form

fórmulas *fpl* **judiciales** form of words

fotocopia *f* 1. photocopy 2. photocopying

fotocopiadora *f* 1. copier 2. photocopier

fotocopiaje *m* photocopying

fotocopiar to photocopy

fracasado *adj* unsuccessful

fracasar 1. to fail 2. to flop 3. to wreck

fracaso *m* 1. failure 2. flop

frágil *adj* fragile

franco *m adj* 1. free 2. (*libre*) franco ■ (*moneda*) franc

franco a bordo *adj* free on board ■ FOB *o* f.o.b.

franco *m* **a domicilio** 1. freight paid 2. *U.K.* carriage paid

franco de porte *adj* 1. freight free 2. *U.K.* carriage free

franco *m* **en almacén** price ex warehouse

franco *m* **en fábrica** price ex works

franco *m* **n muelle** price ex quay

franco sobre vagón *adj, adv* free on rail

franco vagón FF.CC. *adj, adv* free on rail

franquear 1. to frank 2. to stamp

franqueo *m* postage

franqueo *m* **concertado** postage paid ■ *adj* postpaid

(gastos de) franqueo y embalaje postage and packing

franqueo y embalaje *abbr* (*postage and packing*) p & p

franquicia *f* 1. franchise 2. franchising

franquiciador franchiser

franquiciar to franchise

fraude *m* fraud

fraude *m* **fiscal** tax evasion

fraudulentamente *adv* fraudulently

fraudulento *adj* fraudulent

frecuencia *f* **de visitas de un representante** call rate

frecuente *adj* 1. frequent 2. common

frenar 1. to plug 2. to stop

freno *m* 1. brake 2. check

frontera *f* border

fuego *m* 1. fire 2. game

fuente *f* **de ingresos** source of income

fuera de actas off the record

fuera de control out of control

fuera de horas de oficina outside office hours

fuera de horas punta *adj* off-peak

fuerte *adj* strong

fuerte competencia *f U.K.* keen competition

fuerza *f* strength

fuerza *f* **mayor** 1. act of God 2. force majeure

fuerzas *fpl* **del mercado** market forces

fuga *f* flight

fuga *f* **de capital(es)** flight of capital

funcionamiento *m* 1. (*maquinaria*) operating 2. (*maquinaria*) running 3. (*rendimiento*) performance

funcionario 1. official 2. civil servant

funcionario *f* **de aduanas** customs officer *o* customs official

funda *f* cover

fundamental *adj* 1. basic 2. fundamental

fundar una compañía 1. to set up a company 2. *U.K.* to float a company

furgoneta *f* **de reparto** delivery van *o* delivery truck

fusión *f* merger

fusionar to merge

futuros *mpl* futures

G

galería *f* **comercial** 1. shopping mall 2. shopping arcade

gama *f* range

gama *f* **de precios** price range

gama *f* **de productos** product line

gama *f* **de productos de una compañía** product mix

ganancia *f* 1. gain 2. profit 3. return

ganancia *f* **neta** clear profit

ganancias *fpl* earnings

ganancias *fpl* **netas** net earnings *o* net income

ganar 1. to gain 2. (*sueldo*) to earn

ganar dinero to make money

ganga *f* bargain

garante *mf* 1. backer 2. guarantor 3. surety

garantía *f* 1. guarantee 2. warranty 3. collateral 4. (*fianza*) surety 5. (*fianza*) security

garantizar 1. to guarantee 2. to warrant

garantizar el pago to underwrite

gasolina a precio reducido cut-price gasoline

gastar to spend

gastar excesivamente to overspend

gastar más de lo presupuestado to overspend one's budget

gastar menos to underspend

gasto *m* 1. expense 2. expenditure 3. outlay

gasto *m* **de tramitación** handling charge

gastos *mpl* expenses

gastos *mpl* **a cobrar a la entrega** charges forward

gastos *mpl* **adicionales y complementarios** extra charges

gastos *mpl* **administrativos** administrative expenses

gastos *mpl* **aparte** extras

gastos *mpl* **bancarios** bank charges

gastos *mpl* **corrientes** running costs *o* running expenses

gastos *mpl* **de acarreo** haulage costs *o* haulage rates

gastos *mpl* **de capital** capital expenditure

gastos *mpl* **de consumo** consumer spending

gastos *mpl* **de demora** demurrage

gastos *mpl* **de descarga** landing fees

gastos *mpl* **de embalaje** packing charges

gastos *mpl* **de explotación** 1. operating costs *o* operating expenses 2. operational costs

gastos *mpl* **de franqueo** postal charges *o* postal rates

gastos *mpl* **del consumidor** consumer spending

gastos de mantenimiento running costs *o* running expenses

gastos *mpl* **de producción** 1. overhead 2. overhead costs *o* overhead expenses

gastos *mpl* **de publicidad** publicity expenditure

gastos *mpl* **de transporte** freight costs

gastos *mpl* **generales** 1. overhead 2. overhead costs *o* overhead expenses

gastos *mpl* **generales de fabricación** manufacturing overhead

gastos *mpl* **iniciales** start-up costs

gastos *mpl* **menores** 1. petty expenses 2. incidental expenses

gastos *mpl* **no autorizados** unauthorized expenditure

gastos *mpl* **reembolsables** out-of-pocket expenses

gastos *mpl* **totales** total expenditure

general *adj* 1. general 2. across-the-board 3. (*completo*) full-scale ■ *adv* overall

género *m* merchandise

genuino *adj* genuine

gerente *mf* manager

gestión *f* management

gestionar 1. to negotiate 2. to manage

gestionar deudas con descuento to factor

gestión *f* **de cartera** portfolio management

gestión *f* **de deudas con descuento** factoring

gestión *f* **lineal** line management

girar to draw

girar (volumen de ventas) to turn over

girar en descubierto to overdraw

giro *m* 1. (*envío*) remittance 2. (*letra*) draft

giro *m* **a la vista** sight draft

giro *m* **bancario** 1. *U.K.* bank bill 2. (*letra bancaria*) bank draft 3. (*letra bancaria*) banker's draft 4. *U.K.* (*letra bancaria*) giro system

giro *m* **postal** 1. money order 2. postal order

giro *m* **postal internacional** foreign money order

global *adj* 1. comprehensive 2. (*mundial*) worldwide ■ *adv* overall

gobierno *m* government

graduado *adj* graduated

gradual *adj* gradual

gráfica *f* 1. graph 2. chart

gráfico *m* 1. graph 2. chart

gráfico *m* **circular** pie chart

gráfico *m* **de barras** bar chart

gráfico *m* **de ventas** sales chart

gráfico *m* **sectorial** pie chart

gramo *m* gram *o* gramme

grande *adj* 1. large 2. big 3. (*importante*) heavy

gran demanda *f U.K.* keen demand

grandes almacenes *mpl* 1. store 2. department store

grandes costes *mpl* heavy costs *o* heavy expenditure

gran gasto *m* heavy costs *o* heavy expenditure

grapa *f* staple

grapadora *f* stapler

grapar to staple

grapar papeles to staple papers together

gratificación *f* **por méritos** merit award *o* merit bonus

gratis *adj, adv* gratis ■ *adj* 1. free 2. free of charge ■ *adv* free

gratuitamente *adv* free

gratuito *adj* free

gravamen *m* lien

gravamen *m* **sobre las importaciones** import levy

gravar 1. to impose 2. to levy

gravar con un impuesto to tax

gremio *m* guild

grúa *f* crane

gruesa *f abbr* (*144*) gross *n*

grupo *m* group

grupo *m* **de trabajo** working party

grupos *mpl* **socioeconómicos** socio-economic groups

guardar 1. (*dinero*) to save 2. to store 3. (*ordenador*) to back up 4. (*ordenador*) to save 5. (*tener*) to hold

guardia *m* **de seguridad** security guard

guerra *f* **de precios** price(-cutting) war

guía *f* **comercial** 1. commercial directory 2. trade directory

guía *mf* **de turismo** courier

guía *f* **telefónica** 1. telephone book 2. telephone directory

guía *f* **urbana** street directory

H

haber *m* 1. credit balance 2. to credit side

habilidad *f* skill

habitación *f* room

habitaciones *fpl* **de hotel** hotel accommodations

habitante *mf* 1. inhabitant 2. occupant 3. (*residente*) resident

habitual *adj* 1. usual 2. routine

hacer 1. to do 2. to make

hacer bajar los precios to force prices down

hacer cumplir to enforce

hacer efectivo *U.K.* to encash

hacer falta to take

hacer frente (a) to cope

hacer funcionar to run

hacer negocios to transact business

hacer publicidad con mucho bombo to hype

hacerse cargo to take over

hacerse un seguro to take out a policy

hacer subir los precios to force prices up

hacer trabajo eventual to temp

hacer una lista to list

hacer un asiento to post an entry

hacer un borrador to draft

hacer un depósito to pay money down

hacer un inventario 1. to inventory 2. to take stock

hacer un muestreo to sample

hacer un pedido to order

hacia abajo *adv* downward

hacia el centro *adv* downtown

Hacienda f **Pública** treasury
hasta up to
hecho a medida adj custom-built o custom-made
hectárea f hectare
herramienta f 1. implement 2. tool
hipermercado m 1. hypermarket 2. superstore
hipoteca f mortgage
hipotecar to mortgage
historial m record
hoja f **de cálculo** spreadsheet
hoja f **de papel** sheet of paper
hoja f **de sueldo** pay slip
"holding" holding company
hombre m man
hombre m **de confianza** right-hand man
hombre m **de negocios** businessman
honorarios mpl 1. fee 2. honorarium
hora f hour
hora f **de apertura** opening time
hora f **de cierre** closing time
hora-hombre f man-hour
horario m timetable
horario m **bancario** banking hours
horario m **comercial** opening hours
horario m **de oficina** office hours
horario m **de presentación en el aeropuerto** check-in time
horas fpl **de oficina** business hours
horas fpl **extraordinarias** overtime
horas fpl **punta** 1. peak period 2. rush hour
hotel m hotel
hotel m **homologado** U.K. graded hotel
hueco m gap
hueco m **de un mercado** niche
hueco m **en el mercado** gap in the market

huelga f strike
huelga f **de brazos caídos** sit-down strike
huelga f **de celo** 1. go-slow 2. work-to-rule
huelga f **de protesta** protest strike
huelga f **de solidaridad** sympathy strike
huelga f **general** general strike
huelga f **salvaje** wildcat strike
huelguista mf striker
hundimiento m collapse
hundirse 1. to collapse 2. to sink 3. (caer en picado) to slump
(pequeño) hurto m pilferage o pilfering
hurto m **en las tiendas** shoplifting

I

igual adj equal
igualar to equal
igualdad f 1. equality 2. parity
ilegal adj illegal
ilegalidad f illegality
ilegalmente adv illegally
ilícito adj illicit
imagen f **de marca** brand image
imagen f **pública** public image
imagen f **pública de una empresa** corporate image
imitación f 1. imitation 2. fake
impagado adj unpaid
impago m **de una deuda** non-payment
impar to odd
impedir to prevent
imperfección f imperfection

imperfecto *adj* imperfect

imponer to impose

imponible *adj* taxable

importación *f* 1. import 2. importing 3. importation

importaciones *fpl* imports

importaciones *fpl* **visibles** visible imports

importación-exportación *adj* import-export

importador importer ■ *adj* importing

importancia *f* importance

importante *adj* 1. important 2. major 3. (*grande*) heavy

importar 1. to import 2. (*valer*) to matter

importe *m* amount

importe *m* **debido** amount owing

importe *m* **pagado** amount paid

imposible de conseguir *adj* unobtainable

imposición *f* 1. (*depósito*) deposit 2. (*impuesto*) taxation

imposición *f* **alta** high taxation

imposición *f* **a plazo** time deposit

imposición *f* **directa** direct taxation

imposición *f* **en efectivo** cash deposit

imposición *f* **indirecta** indirect taxation

impositor depositor

imprenta *f* printer

imprescindible *adj* essential

impresión *f* printout

impreso *m* form

impreso *m* **de declaración de aduana** customs declaration form

impreso *m* **de solicitud** application form

impresora *f* 1. printer 2. computer printer

impresora *f* **de líneas** line printer

impresora *f* **de rueda de margarita** daisy-wheel printer

impresora *f* **láser** laser printer

impresora *f* **matricial** dot-matrix printer

imprimir to print out

impuesto *m* 1. tax 2. taxation

impuesto *m* **ad valorem** ad valorem tax

impuesto *m* **atrasado** back tax

impuesto *m* **básico** basic tax

impuesto *m* **de circulación** road tax

impuesto *m* **del timbre** stamp duty

impuesto *m* **de sociedades** corporation tax

impuesto *m* **de venta** purchase tax

impuesto *m* **directo** direct tax

impuesto *m* **indirecto** indirect tax

impuesto *m* **no incluido** exclusive of tax

impuesto *m* **pagado** tax paid

impuesto *m* **para financiar la formación profesional** *U.K.* training levy

impuesto *m* **progresivo** *U.K.* graded tax

impuesto *m* **progresivo sobre la renta** graduated income tax

impuestos *mpl* duty

impuestos *mpl* **incluidos** inclusive of tax

impuesto *m* **sobre el consumo** excise duty

impuesto *m* **sobre el valor añadido (IVA)** value added tax (VAT)

impuesto *m* **sobre el volumen de ventas** turnover tax

impuesto *m* **sobre la renta** income tax

impuesto *m* **sobre las plusvalías** capital gains tax

impuesto *m* **sobre las ventas de bienes o servicios** output tax

impuesto *m* **sobre la venta** sales tax

impuestos *mpl* **retenidos en el origen** tax deducted at source

impulsar to boost

impulso *m* 1. impulse 2. boost

inalcanzable *adj* unobtainable

inalterado *adj* unchanged

inasequible *adj* unavailable

inauguración *f* opening

inaugural *adj* opening

incapaz *adj* incapable

incautación *f* seizure

incautar to seize

incendio *m* fire

incentivo *m* incentive

incluido *adj* inclusive

incluir 1. to include 2. to incorporate

inclusive *adj* inclusive

inclusivo *adj* inclusive

incobrable bad debt

incompetencia *f* 1. (*incapacia*) incompetence 2. (*ineficacia*) inefficiency

incompetente *adj* 1. (*incapaz*) incompetent 2. (*ineficaz*) inefficient

incondicional *adj* unconditional

incorporado *adj* built-in

incorporar to incorporate

incorrectamente *adv* incorrectly

incorrecto *adj* incorrect

incremental *adj* incremental

incrementar to increase

incremento *m* 1. increment 2. increase

incumplimiento *m* default

incumplir 1. to default 2. to break

incumplir los pagos to default on payments

incurrir en to incur

indemnidad *f* indemnity

indemnización *f* 1. indemnity 2. indemnification

indemnización *f* **por daños y perjuicios** compensation for damage

indemnizar 1. to indemnify 2. (*resarcir*) to make good 3. (*compensar*) to compensate

indemnizar a alguien por una pérdida to indemnify someone for a loss

independiente *adj* independent

indexación *f* indexation

indicador *m* 1. indicator 2. index number

indicadores *mpl* **económicos** economic indicators

indicar 1. to show 2. to specify 3. (*citar referencia*) to quote

índice *m* 1. index 2. index number 3. (*alfabético*) index

índice *m* **de crecimiento** growth index

índice *m* **del coste de vida** cost-of-living index

índice *m* **de ocupación** occupancy rate

índice *m* **de precios al consumo** retail price index

índice *m* **de precios al consumo (IPC)** consumer price index

índice *m* **de precios al por mayor** wholesale price index

índice *m* **ponderado** weighted index

indiciación *f* indexation

indirecto *adj* indirect

indisponibilidad *f adj* unavailability

industria *f* industry

industria *f* **clave** key industry

industria *f* **con alto coeficiente de capital** capital-intensive industry

industria *f* **de los servicios** tertiary industry

industria *f* **de servicios** service industry

industrial *adj* industrial ■ industrialist

industrialización *f* industrialization

industrializar to industrialize

industria f **nacionalizada** nationalized industry

industria f **pesada** heavy industry

industria f **principal** staple industry

industria f **próspera** boom industry

industria f **secundaria** secondary industry

industria f **terciaria** tertiary industry

ineficacia f inefficiency

ineficaz adj inefficient

inexplicado adj 1. unexplained 2. unaccounted for

inferior adj lower

inflación f inflation

inflacionario adj inflationary

inflación f **de costes** cost-push inflation

inflacionista adj inflationary

influencia f influence

influenciar to influence

influir to influence

información f information

información f **de vuelos** flight information

información f **privilegiada** insider dealing

información f **publicitaria** sales literature

informar 1. to inform 2. to report 3. (advertir) to advise 4. (dar instrucciones) to brief

informar sobre la marcha to report on progress

informático adj computerized

informatizado adj computerized

informatizar to computerize

informe m 1. report 2. survey 3. statement 4. (registro) record

informe m **anual** annual report

informe m **confidencial** confidential report

informe m **de viabilidad (de un proyecto)** feasibility report

informe m **provisional** interim report

informe m **sobre la marcha de un trabajo** progress report

infracción f **aduanera** infringement of customs regulations

infracción f **fiscal** tax offense

infraestructura f infrastructure

infringir 1. to break 2. to infringe

infringir la ley to break the law

ingeniero m **de obra** site engineer

ingeniero m **de producto** product engineer

inglés adj 1. English 2. British

ingresar 1. to bank 2. to deposit

ingresar en to join

ingresar en caja to take

ingreso m 1. revenue 2. (depósito) deposit 3. (entrada) entry 4. (entrada) admission 5. (afiliación) membership

ingreso m **fijo** regular income

ingresos mpl 1. income 2. (recaudación) take 3. earnings 4. (entradas) receipts

ingresos mpl **brutos** gross earnings

ingresos mpl **de un negocio** takings

ingresos mpl **de ventas** sales revenue

ingresos mpl **invisibles** invisible earnings

ingresos mpl **libres de impuestos** non-taxable income

ingresos mpl **netos** 1. net earnings o net income 2. net receipts

ingresos mpl **por alquiler** rental income

ingresos mpl **por publicidad** revenue from advertising

ingreso m **total** total revenue

iniciación f induction

iniciado m insider

inicial adj 1. initial 2. starting 3. opening

iniciar 1. to initiate 2. to pioneer

iniciar conversaciones to initiate discussions

iniciativa f initiative

inicio *m* start

injusto *adj* unfair

inmediatamente *adv* immediately

inmediato *adj* 1. immediate 2. instant 3. prompt

inmovilizar capital lock up capital

innovación *f* innovation

innovador *adj* innovative ■ innovator

innovar to innovate

inquietud *f* 1. concern 2. worry

inquilino 1. tenant 2. lessee 3. occupant

inquilino *m* **en posesión** sitting tenant

inscribir (*registrar*) to enter

inscribir (en un registro) to register

inscribirse (*registrarse*) to register

inscribir una compañía en un registro to register a company

inscripción *f* 1. registration 2. (*entrada*) entering

insignificante *adj* 1. petty 2. negligible

insistir en to hold out for

insolvencia *f* 1. insolvency 2. bankruptcy

insolvente *adj* 1. insolvent 2. bankrupt

inspección *f* 1. inspection 2. survey 3. examination

inspección *f* **aduanera** customs examination

inspeccionar 1. to inspect 2. to survey

inspección *f* **de daños** damage survey

inspector 1. inspector 2. controller

inspector *m* **de calidad** quality controller

inspector *m* **de fábrica** factory inspector

inspector *m* **de Hacienda** tax inspector

inspector *m* **de obra** surveyor

instalaciones *fpl* facilities

instalaciones *fpl* **de almacenaje** storage facilities

instalaciones *fpl* **portuarias** harbor facilities

instalar la maquinaria en una fábrica to tool up

instantáneo *adj* instant

institución *f* institution

institucional *adj* institutional

institución *f* **financiera** financial institution

instituir to institute

instituto *m* institute

instrucción *f* 1. instruction 2. directive

instrucciones *fpl* directions for use

instrucciones *fpl* **de envío** 1. forwarding instructions 2. shipping instructions

instrumento *m* 1. instrument 2. implement 3. (*medio*) medium

instrumento *m* **negociable** negotiable instrument

insuficiencia *f* 1. insufficiency 2. shortfall

intangible *adj* intangible

integración *f* **horizontal** horizontal integration

integración *f* **vertical** vertical integration

intensificar (el control) to tighten up on

intercambiable *adj* exchangeable

intercambiar 1. to exchange 2. to swap 3. to swop

intercambio *m* 1. exchange 2. swap 3. swop

interés *m* 1. interest 2. (*atracción*) appeal

interés *m* **acumulado** accrued interest

interés *m* **acumulativo** cumulative interest

interesar 1. to interest 2. (*atraer*) to appeal to 3. to attract

interés *m* **compuesto** compound interest

interés *m* **elevado** high interest

intereses *mpl* **creados** vested interest

interés *m* **fijo** fixed interest

interés *m* **personal** vested interest

interés *m* **simple** simple interest

interfaz *m* interface

interino *adj* acting ■ temp

interior *adj* **1.** internal **2.** inland **3.** (*nacional*) domestic

intermediario **1.** intermediary **2.** middleman **3.** (*agente*) broker **4.** (*agente*) mediator

internacional *adj* international

Internet *n* Internet

interno *adj* **1.** in-house **2.** (*de la casa*) internal

interpretar to interpret

intérprete *mf* interpreter

interrumpir to discontinue

interrupción *f* **1.** interruption **2.** breakdown

intervención *f* audit

intervenir to audit

interventor auditor

introducción *f* introduction

introducir to introduce

introducir datos to input information

introducir gradualmente to phase in

inundación *f* flood

inundar to flood

inundar el mercado to glut

invalidación *f* invalidation

invalidar 1. to void **2.** to invalidate

invalidez *f* invalidity

inválido *adj* **1.** invalid **2.** void

invariable *adj* unchanged ■ constant

inventariar to inventory

inventario *m* **1.** inventory **2.** *U.K.* stocktaking **3.** stock list

inventario *m* **de posición (en almacén)** pick list

inversión *f* **1.** investment **2.** (*revocación*) reversal

inversiones *fpl* **de interés fijo** fixed-interest investments

inversiones *fpl* **en valores seguros** blue-chip investments

inversiones *fpl* **exteriores** foreign investments

inversionista *mf* investor

inversión *f* **segura 1.** safe investment **2.** secure investment

inversión *f* **sin riesgo** risk-free investment

inversor investor

inversores *mpl* **institucionales** institutional investors

invertir to invest

investigación *f* **1.** investigation **2.** research **3.** (*petición de informes*) inquiry

investigación *f* **de conflictos 1.** problem solving **2.** troubleshooting

investigación *f* **de mercado** market research

investigación *f* **sobre el consumo** consumer research

investigación y desarrollo (I+D) research and development; R&D

investigador research worker *o* researcher

investigar 1. to investigate **2.** to research **3.** (*perseguir*) to follow up

invitación *f* invitation

invitar to invite

ir to go

ir a la huelga 1. to strike **2.** to go on strike

ir de compras shopping

ir de tiendas shopping

ir haciendo to get along

irregular to irregular

irregularidades *fpl* irregularities

irrevocable *adj* irrevocable

irse to leave

itinerario *m* itinerary

IVA (impuesto sobre el valor añadido) *abbr U.K.* (*value added tax*) VAT

IVA (sobre los bienes y servicios adquiridos por una empresa) input tax
izquierdo *adj* left

JK

jefe manager ■ *adj* 1. ■ 1. chief; head 2. *informal* boss
jefe *m* **de almacén** stock controller
jefe *m* **de compras** purchasing manager
jefe *m* **de departamento** 1. departmental manager 2. head of department
jefe *m* **de distribución** distribution manager
jefe *m* **de equipo de ventas** field sales manager
jefe *m* **de oficina** chief clerk
jefe *m* **de personal** personnel manager
jefe *m* **de publicidad** advertising manager
jefe *m* **de sección** departmental manager
jefe *m* **ejecutivo** chief executive; CEO
jornada *f* day
joven *adj* young
jubilación *f* retirement
jubilarse to retire
judicial *adj* legal
juego *m* set
juego *m* **completo en caja de presentación** boxed set
juez *mf* 1. judge 2. adjudicator

juicio *m* 1. lawsuit 2. court case 3. trial 4. (*sentencia*) judgment *o* judgement
junta *f* **de directores** management
junta *f* **directiva** board of directors
junta *f* **general** general meeting
junta *f* **general anual** 1. annual meeting 2. *U.K.* annual general meeting; AGM
juntar to join
jurídico *adj* legal
jurisdicción *f* jurisdiction
justificar 1. to justify 2. to warrant 3. (*responder*) to account for
justo *adj* fair
juzgado *m* court
juzgar to judge
kilo *m* kilo *o* kilogram
kilogramo *m* kilo *o* kilogram
kilometraje *m* mileage allowance

L

laboral *adj* occupational
lado *m* side
laguna *f* **fiscal** tax loophole
lanzamiento *m* 1. launch 2. launching 3. float 4. rollout
lanzamiento *m* **de una nueva compañía** *U.K.* flotation
lanzamiento *m* **de una sociedad** *U.K.* floating of a company
lanzar to launch
lanzar al mercado 1. to bring out 2. to release
la Red web *n*: the web
largo *adj* long

largo plazo *adj* long-term

la Web web *n*: the web

"leasing" *m* leasing

legal *adj* 1. legal 2. lawful 3. statutory

legalizar to authenticate

legible por ordenador *adj* computer-readable

legislación *f* legislation

legítimo *adj* rightful

lenguaje *m* **burocrático** officialese

lenguaje *m* **de programación** programming language

lenguaje *m* **informático** computer language

lento *adj* slow

letra *f* 1. handwriting 2. writing 3. (*bancaria*) bill 4. (*bancaria*) draft

letra *f* **a largo plazo** long-dated bill

letra *f* **al propio cargo** 1. note of hand 2. promissory note

letra *f* **bancaria** *U.K.* bank bill

letra *f* **de cambio** bill of exchange

letras *fpl* **a cobrar** bills receivable

letras *fpl* **a corto vencimiento** short-dated bills

letras *fpl* **a pagar** bills payable

letras *fpl* **por cobrar** bills for collection

letrero *m* 1. notice 2. sign

levantar to lift

levantar acta to minute

levantar una sesión to close a meeting

levantar un embargo to lift an embargo

ley *f* law

ley *f* **de la oferta y la demanda** law of supply and demand

ley *f* **de prescripción** statute of limitations

ley *f* **de rendimientos decrecientes** law of diminishing returns

ley *f* **de sociedades anónimas** company law

liberación *f* release

liberalización *f* deregulation

liberalizar to decontrol

liberar 1. to free 2. to release

libra *f* pound

librado drawee

librador drawer

libra *f* **esterlina** 1. pound sterling 2. sterling

libramiento *m* order

libre *adj* 1. free 2. vacant 3. (*franco*) franco

libre cambio free trade

libre comercio free trade

libre de derechos de aduana *adj* free of duty

libre de impuestos *adj* 1. duty-free 2. free of tax 3. tax-free

libreta *f* **de ahorros** bank book

libro *m* book

libro *m* **de caja** cash book

libro *m* **de pedidos** order book

libro *m* **de registro** register

libro *m* **de ventas** sales book

libro *m* **diario** journal

libro *m* **mayor** ledger

libro *m* **mayor de compras** 1. purchase ledger 2. *U.K.* bought ledger

libro *m* **mayor de resultados** nominal ledger

libro *m* **mayor de ventas** sales ledger

libro *m* **registro de accionistas** register of stockholders

licencia *f* 1. license 2. permit 3. permission 4. (*autorización*) licensing

licencia *f* **de exportación** export license *o* export permit

licencia *f* **de importación** import license *o* import permit

licenciado *m* **en prácticas** graduate trainee

licencia *f* **por maternidad** maternity leave

licitación *f* bidding

licitador *m* 1. tenderer 2. bidder

licitar para un contrato to tender for a contract

lícito *adj* 1. lawful 2. legal

líder *m* **del mercado** market leader

limitación *f* 1. limitation 2. restriction

limitado *adj* limited

limitar 1. to limit 2. to restrict

limitar el crédito to restrict credit

límite *m* 1. limit 2. ceiling

límite *m* **de crédito** 1. credit limit 2. lending limit

límite *m* **de descubierto bancario** *U.K.* overdraft facility

límite *m* **de precios** price ceiling

línea *f* line

línea *f* **aérea** airline

línea *f* **de carga** load line

línea *f* **de crédito** line of credit

línea *f* **de flotación** load line

línea *f* **de productos** product line

línea *f* **exterior** outside line

lineal straight line depreciation

línea *f* **telefónica** telephone line

liquidación *f* 1. liquidation 2. winding up 3. (*rebajas*) sale

liquidación *f* **de activo** realization of assets

liquidación *f* **de inventario** 1. inventory sale 2. *U.K.* stocktaking sale

liquidación *f* **de una deuda** clearing

liquidación *f* **forzosa** compulsory liquidation

liquidación *f* **total por cierre** 1. going-out-of-business sale 2. *U.K.* closing-down sale

liquidación *f* **voluntaria** voluntary liquidation

liquidar to sell off

liquidar existencias 1. to clear 2. to liquidate stock

liquidar propiedades to realize property *o* to assets

liquidar una compañía to liquidate a company

liquidar una cuenta to settle an account

liquidar una deuda to clear a debt

liquidar una sociedad to wind up

liquidez *f* liquidity

lira *f* lira

lista *f* list

lista *f* **de bultos** packing list *o* packing slip

lista *f* **de correos** 1. *U.K.* general delivery 2. poste restante

lista *f* **de destinatarios** mailing list

lista *f* **de direcciones** address list

lista *f* **de existencias** stock list

lista *f* **del contenido de un paquete** docket

lista *f* **de precios** 1. price list 2. scale of charges

lista *f* **de precios fija** fixed scale of charges

listado *m* **de ordenador** computer listing

lista *f* **negra** black list

listo *adj* ready

litro *m* liter

llamada *f* call

llamada *f* **a cobro revertido** 1. collect call 2. *U.K.* transferred charge call 3. *U.K.* reverse charge call

llamada *f* **de fuera** incoming call

llamada *f* **internacional** international call

llamada *f* **local** local call

llamada *f* **rutinaria** routine call

llamadas *fpl* **internacionales directas** international direct dialing

llamada *f* **telefónica** 1. phone call 2. telephone call

llamar 1. to telephone **2.** to phone back

llamar (por teléfono) 1. to call **2.** to phone

llamar a cobro revertido 1. *U.K.* to reverse the charges **2.** to call collect

llave *f* key

llegada *f* arrival

llegadas *fpl* arrivals

llegar 1. to arrive **2.** to reach

llegar al máximo to peak

llegar a un acuerdo to reach an agreement

llenar to fill a gap

lleno *adj* full

llevar 1. to take **2.** to carry **3.** to transport **4.** (*dirigir*) to run **5.** (*producir*) to bear

llevar a alguien ante los tribunales to take someone to court

llevar negociaciones to conduct negotiations

llevar un negocio to carry on a business

lo antes posible *abbr* (*as soon as possible*) asap

local *adj* local ■ (*edificio*) premises

local *m* **comercial** business premises

local *m* **de exposición** stand

local *m* **sin vivienda incorporada** lock-up premises

logotipo *m* logo

lo mejor *adj* best

lonja *f* **1.** commodity market **2.** commodity exchange

los miembros membership

los socios membership

lote *m* **1.** batch **2.** lot

lucrativo *adj* **1.** money-making **2.** profit-making **3.** profitable

lugar *m* **1.** place **2.** site **3.** venue **4.** spot

lugar *m* **de reunión** meeting place

lugar *m* **de trabajo** place of work

M

macroeconomía *f* macro-economics

magistratura *f* **del trabajo** industrial tribunal

mala administración *f* **1.** maladministration **2.** mismanagement

mala calidad *f* poor quality

mala compra *f* bad buy

malentendido *m* misunderstanding

mal equipado *adj* underequipped

maleta *f* case

maletas *fpl* **1.** *U.K.* luggage **2.** baggage

maletín *m* briefcase

malgastar to waste

mal pagado *adj* underpaid

malversación *f* **1.** misappropriation **2.** embezzlement

malversador embezzler

malversar 1. to misappropriate **2.** to embezzle

mandante *m* principal

mandar por correo 1. to mail **2.** *U.K.* to post

mandar por correo electrónico to email

mandar por e-mail to email

mandar trabajo fuera to farm out work

mandato *m* **1.** mandate **2.** writ **3.** (*periodo*) tenure **4.** (*campo de aplicación*) terms of reference

mando *m* control

mando *m* **a distancia** remote control

mandos *mpl* **intermedios** middle management

manejable *adj* manageable

manejar 1. to handle **2.** to operate

manejo *m* handling

manejo *m* **de materiales** materials handling

manera *f* means

manifiesto *m adj* manifest

manipulación *f* handling

mano *f* **de obra 1.** manpower **2.** work force **3.** labor force

mano *f* **de obra barata** cheap labor

mano *f* **de obra cualificada** skilled labor

mano *f* **de obra local** local labor

mantener 1. (*conservar*) to maintain **2.** to keep up **3.** (*sostener*) to maintain

mantenimiento *m* maintenance

mantenimiento *m* **de relaciones** maintenance of contacts

mantenimiento *m* **de suministros** maintenance of supplies

manual *adj* manual ■ manual

manual *m* **de funcionamiento** operating manual

manual *m* **de mantenimiento** service manual

manufacturar to manufacture .

manzana *f* (*edificios*) block

maqueta *f* **1.** mock-up **2.** model

máquina *f* machine

máquina *f* **de cambio** change machine

máquina *f* **franqueadora** franking machine

maquinaria *f* **1.** plant **2.** machinery

maquinaria *f* **pesada** heavy machinery

maquinista *mf* operator

marca *f* **1.** brand **2.** (*señal*) mark

marca *f* **comercial 1.** trademark *o* trade name **2.** brand name

marcador *m* marker pen

marcar 1. to mark **2.** (*teléfono*) to dial

marcar directamente to dial direct

marca *f* **registrada** registered trademark

marcar un número to dial a number

marcha *f* progress

marcharse to leave

marco *m* frame

marco *m* **alemán** deutsche mark

margen *m* margin

margen *m* **de beneficio 1.** profit margin **2.** mark-up

margen *m* **de beneficio bruto** gross margin

margen *m* **de cobertura** backwardation

margen *m* **de error** margin of error

margen *m* **neto** net margin

marginal *adj* marginal

marina *f* **mercante** merchant marine

marino *adj* marine

marítimo *adj* maritime

"marketing" *m* marketing

más *adv* more ■ plus

masa *f* mass

más antiguo *adj* senior

más bajo *adj* lower

más joven *adj* **1.** junior **2.** younger

master en administración de empresas *abbr* (*Master's in Business Administration*) M.B.A. ■ Master's degree in Business Administration

más vendido *adj* top-selling

material *m* **de embalaje** packaging material

material *m* **de exposición** display material

materias *fpl* **primas** raw materials

materias *fpl* **primas cotizadas en el mercado de futuros** commodity futures

matrícula *f* **1.** registration **2.** registration fee

matriz *f* (**de un talonario**) counterfoil

matriz *f* **de un talonario** check stub

maximización *f* maximization

maximizar to maximize

máximo *adj* maximum ■ maximum

mayor *adj* **1.** (*importante*) major **2.** (*principal*) main **3.** (*superior*) senior

mayoría *f* majority

mayorista *mf* **1.** wholesale dealer **2.** wholesaler

mechera *f* shoplifter

media *f* mean

mediación *f* mediation

media docena *f* half a dozen *o* a half-dozen

mediador mediator

mediador *m* **de conflictos 1.** problem solver **2.** troubleshooter

mediana *f* median

mediano *adj* **1.** medium **2.** medium-sized **3.** average

media *f* **ponderada** weighted average

mediar to mediate

medición *f* **de la rentabilidad** measurement of profitability

medida *f* **de tiempo** timing

medida *f* **de volumen** cubic measure

medidas *fpl* measurements

medidas *fpl* **de precaución** safety precautions

medidas *fpl* **de seguridad** safety measures

medidas *fpl* **de seguridad (en una oficina)** office security

medidas *fpl* **fiscales** fiscal measures

medio *adj* ■ mean; medium ■ *adj* ■ average; (*manera*) means ■ *adj* **1.** medium **2.** (*mitad*) half

mediocre *adj* **1.** mediocre **2.** low-quality

medios *mpl* **1.** (*instalaciones*) facilities **2.** (*recursos*) means

medios *mpl* **de comunicación** mass media

medios *mpl* **de transporte** transportation facilities

medios *mpl* **fraudulentos** false pretenses

(el/la) mejor best

mejora *f* **1.** upturn **2.** improvement

mejorar to recover

mejor postor highest bidder

memorandum *m* memo

memoria *f* **1.** memory **2.** (*informe*) report

mencionar 1. to mention **2.** to refer

menor *adj* **1.** junior **2.** younger

menos *adj* minus ■ *adv* less

menos de under

menos de lo necesario (*escaso*) short of

mensaje *m* message

mensajero 1. messenger **2.** courier

mensual *adj* monthly

mensualmente *adv* monthly

mercadeo *m* merchandizing

mercader *m* to merchant

mercado *m* **1.** market **2.** marketplace **3.** (*salida*) outlet

mercado *m* **a futuros** forward market

mercado *m* **alcista** bull market

mercado *m* **bajista** bear market

mercado *m* **cautivo** captive market

mercado *m* **cerrado** closed market

Mercado Común Europeo Common Market

mercado *m* **débil** weak market

mercado *m* **de compradores** buyer's market

mercado *m* **de divisas** foreign exchange market

mercado *m* **de valores** stock market

mercado *m* **de vendedores** seller's market

mercado *m* **interior 1.** home market **2.** domestic market

mercado *m* **libre** open market

mercado *m* **limitado** limited market

mercado *m* **mundial** world market

mercado *m* **nacional** 1. home market 2. domestic market

mercado *m* **negro** black market

mercado *m* **potencial** potential market

mercado *m* **previsto** target market

mercados *mpl* **extranjeros** overseas markets

mercados *mpl* **monetarios** money markets

mercadotecnia *f* marketing

Mercado Unico Europeo Single European Market

mercancía *f* commodity

mercancía *f* **exportada** export

mercancías *fpl* 1. goods 2. merchandise

mercancías *fpl* **a precio reducido** cut-price goods

mercancías *fpl* **con impuestos aduaneros pagados** duty-paid goods

mercancías *fpl* **dañadas por un incendio** fire-damaged goods

mercancías *fpl* **en tránsito** goods in transit

mérito *m* merit

mermas *fpl* leakage

mes *m* month

mesa *f* **de despacho** desk

mes *m* **civil** calendar month

meta *f* target

mezclado *adj* mixed

microeconomía *f* micro-economics

microordenador *m* microcomputer

miembro *m* member

millón *m* million

millonario millionaire

mil millones *mpl* billion

mínimo *m* low ■ *adj* ■ minimum; minimum

ministerio *m* department

ministerio *m* **de Hacienda** Exchequer

ministro *m* **del gobierno** secretary

minoría *f* minority

minorista *mf* 1. retail dealer 2. retailer

minusvalías *fpl* capital loss

minuto *m* minute

misceláneo *adj* miscellaneous

misión *f* **comercial** trade mission

mitad *f* half

mixto *adj* mixed

modelo *mf* 1. model 2. standard

modelo *m* **a escala** 1. model 2. mock-up

modelo *m* **de prueba** demonstration model

modelo *m* **económico** economic model

modem *m* modem

moderado *adj* moderate

moderar to moderate

moderno *adj* 1. modern 2. up to date

modificación *f* alteration

modificar to alter

modo *m* mode

modo *m* **de empleo** directions for use

modo *m* **de pago** mode of payment

moneda *f* 1. coin 2. currency

moneda *f* **bloqueada** blocked currency

moneda *f* **convertible** 1. convertible currency 2. hard currency

moneda *f* **débil** soft currency

moneda *f* **de curso legal** 1. legal currency 2. legal tender

moneda *f* **estable** stable currency

moneda **extranjera** to exchange

moneda *f* **extranjera** foreign currency

moneda *f* **fuerte** strong currency

moneda *f* **inflacionista** inflated currency

moneda *f* **suelta** 1. change 2. small change

monetario *adj* monetary

monopolio 1. monopoly 2. corner

monopolio *m* **absoluto** absolute monopoly

monopolización *f* monopolization

monopolizar to monopolize

montacargas *m* elevator

montaje *m* assembly

moratoria *f* moratorium

moroso slow payer

mostrador *m* counter

mostrador *m* **de facturación** check-in (counter)

mostrar to show

mostrar (el funcionamiento de algo) to demonstrate

mostrar un beneficio to show a profit

motivación *f* motivation

motivado *adj* motivated

motor *m* drive

móvil cellular telephone

movilidad *f* mobility

movilizar to mobilize

movilizar capital to mobilize capital

movimiento *m* movement

movimientos *mpl* **de capital** movements of capital

movimientos *mpl* **de existencias** stock movements

mudanza *f* removal

mudar to remove

mudar(se) to move

muebles *mpl* **de oficina** office furniture

muelle *m* 1. quay 2. dock 3. wharf

muerto *adj* dead

muestra *f* 1. trial sample 2. sample

muestra *f* **aleatoria** random sample

muestra *f* **de inspección** check sample

muestra *f* **gratuita** free sample

muestra *f* **pequeña** swatch

muestreo *m* sample

muestreo *m* **aleatorio** random sampling

muestreo *m* **de aceptación** acceptance sampling

muestreo *m* **por áreas** sampling

mujer *f* **de negocios** businesswoman

multa *f* 1. fine 2. penalty

multar to fine

multilateral *adj* multilateral

multinacional *f* multinational

múltiple *adj* multiple

multiplicación *f* multiplication

multiplicar to multiply

multitud *f* 1. crowd 2. multitude

mundial *adj* worldwide

mundialmente *adv* worldwide

mundo *m* world

mutua *f* **de seguros** mutual (insurance) company

mutuo *adj* mutual

muy bien *adv* fine

muy bien pagado *adj* highly-paid

muy capacitado *adj* highly qualified

muy caro *adj* highly-priced

muy cualificado *adj* highly qualified

muy moderno *adj* state-of-the-art

N

nacional *adj* 1. national 2. domestic

nacionalización *f* nationalization

nación *f* **más favorecida** most-favored nation

nada *f* nil ■ *pron* nothing

naufragar to wreck

naufragio *m* wreck

nave *f* **de carga** loading bay

necesario *adj* necessary

necesidad *f* need

necesitar to need

negar(se) to refuse

negarse a cumplir un acuerdo to repudiate an agreement

negativa *f* refusal

negligencia *f* negligence

negociable *adj* negotiable

negociación *f* 1. bargaining 2. negotiation

negociaciones *fpl* **conjuntas** joint discussions

negociaciones *fpl* **salariales** wage negotiations

negociador negotiator

negociar 1. to negotiate 2. to bargain

negociar (en) to deal in

negocio *m* 1. bargain 2. deal 3. (*empresa*) business 4. (*empresa*) concern

negocio *m* **descuidado** neglected business

negocio *m* **deshonesto (pero no ilegal)** sharp practice

negocio *m* **duro** 1. hard bargain 2. hard bargaining

negocio *m* **ilícito** racketeering

negocios *mpl* business

negocios: por asuntos de negocios business: on business

negocio *m* **suplementario** sideline

neto *adj* net

nivel *m* level

nivelarse to level off *o* to level out

nivel *m* **de existencias** stock level

niveles *mpl* **de dotación de personal** manning levels

niveles *mpl* **de salarios** wage levels

noche *f* night

no cualificado *adj* unskilled

no cuelgue hold the line please *o* please hold

no cumplir un objetivo to miss a target

no encontrar to miss

no entregado *adj* undelivered

no incluido exclusive of ■ *adj* extra

nombramiento *m* appointment

nombramiento *m* **de administrador judicial** letters of administration

nombrar to appoint

nombrar por coopción to co-opt someone

nombre *m* **comercial** 1. brand name 2. trademark *o* trade name

nombre: en nombre de behalf: on behalf of

no oficial *adj* unofficial

norma *f* 1. norm 2. standard 3. (*regla*) law 4. (*regla*) rule

normal *adj* 1. (*estándar*) normal 2. (*estándar*) standard 3. (*corriente*) regular 4. (*corriente*) usual

normalización *f* standardization

normalizar to standardize

normas *fpl* regulations

normas *fpl* **de conducta** code of practice

normas *fpl* **de producción** production standards

normas *fpl* **de seguridad** safety regulations

no subvencionado *adj* unsubsidized

nota *f* note

notable *adj* outstanding

nota *f* **de abono** credit note

nota *f* **de adeudo** debit note

nota *f* **de aviso** advice note

nota *f* **de cobertura** cover note

nota *f* **de crédito** credit note

nota *f* **de envío** 1. consignment note 2. shipping note

nota *f* **de expedición** 1. dispatch note 2. consignment note 3. shipping note

notario *m* notary public

notario *m* **especialista en escrituras de trapaso** conveyancer

noticia *f* 1. news 2. item

notificación *f* 1. notice 2. notification

notificación *f* **de despido** notice

notificación *f* **de renovación** renewal notice

notificar to notify

novedad *f* departure

no vendido *adj* unsold

no verificado *adj* unaudited

nuevo nombramiento *m* reappointment

nuevo pedido *m* reorder

nulo *adj* 1. null 2. void

numerar to number

numérico numeric *o* numerical

número *m* 1. number 2. (*ejemplar*) copy 3. (*ejemplar*) issue

número *m* **de apartado de correos** box number

número *m* **de cheque** check number

número *m* **de cuenta del Girobank** *U.K.* giro account number

número *m* **de factura** invoice number

número *m* **de llamada gratuita** toll free number

número *m* **de lote** batch number

número *m* **de matrícula** registration number

número *m* **de pedido** order number

número *m* **de referencia** reference number

número *m* **de registro** registration number

número *m* **de serie** serial number

número *m* **de teléfono** 1. phone number 2. telephone number

números *mpl* **impares** odd numbers

O

obedecer 1. to obey 2. to comply with

objetivo *m* objective ■ *adj* 1. ■ 1. objective; target 2. aim

objetivo *m* **de producción** production target

objetivo *m* **de ventas** sales target

objetivos *mpl* **a largo plazo** long-term objectives

objeto *m* **de una OPA** takeover target

objetos *mpl* **salvados** salvage

obligación *f* 1. obligation 2. duty

obligaciones *fpl* 1. loan stock 2. (*responsabilidades*) responsibilities

obligaciones *fpl* **a corto plazo** current liabilities

obligacionista *mf* debenture holder

obligación *f* **perpetua** irredeemable bond

obligación *f* **redimible** callable bond

obligatorio *adj* 1. compulsory 2. binding

obrero 1. workman 2. worker 3. manual worker

obreros *mpl* **cualificados** skilled workers

obreros *mpl* **semicualificados** semi-skilled workers

obsequiar to present

obsequio *m* 1. free gift 2. gift 3. present

obsequio *m* **publicitario** premium offer

obsolescencia *f* obsolescence

obsolescente *adj* obsolescent

obsoleto *adj* obsolete

obtener 1. to obtain 2. to get

obtener beneficios brutos to gross

obtener beneficios netos to net

obtener el título de to qualify as

obtener la libertad de alguien bajo fianza to bail someone out

ocupación *f* 1. (*empleo*) occupation 2. (*empleo*) employment 3. (*posesión*) tenure 4. (*posesión*) occupancy

ocupación *f* **temporal** temporary employment

(línea) ocupada *adj* engaged

ocupado *adj* 1. busy 2. engaged

ocupante *mf* occupant

ocuparse de to attend to

ocupar un vacío to fill a gap

oferta *f* 1. offer 2. (*puja*) bid 3. (*suministro*) supply 4. (*trabajo*) tendering 5. (*trabajo*) tender

oferta *f* **de adquisición disputada** contested takeover

oferta *f* **de lanzamiento** introductory offer

oferta *f* **de ocasión** bargain offer

oferta *f* **de venta** offer for sale

oferta *f* **en metálico** cash offer

oferta *f* **especial** special offer

oferta *f* **final** closing bid

oferta *f* **inicial** opening bid

oferta *f* **monetaria** money supply

oferta *f* **pública de adquisición (OPA)** takeover bid

ofertas *fpl* bidding

ofertas *fpl* **de trabajo** 1. appointments vacant 2. situations vacant

ofertas *fpl* **lacradas** sealed tenders

oferta *f* **y demanda** supply and demand

oficial *adj* official

oficina *f* office

oficina *f* **central** head office

oficina *f* **central de correos** general post offfice

oficina *f* **de colocación** employment agency *o* employment bureau

oficina *f* **de distribución modificable** open-plan office

oficina *f* **de expedición** dispatch department

oficina *f* **de información** information bureau

oficina *f* **de informática** computer bureau

oficina *f* **del registro civil** registry office

oficina *f* **de reclamaciones** complaints department

oficina *f* **general** general office

oficina *f* **principal** main office

oficinas *fpl* **de alquiler** offices to rent

oficinista *mf* clerk

oficioso *adj* unofficial

ofrecer to offer

ofrecer un precio to quote

OIT (Organización Internacional del Trabajo) *abbr* (*International Labour Organization*) ILO

omisión *f* omission

omitir to omit

opcional *adj* optional

opción *f* **de compra** option to purchase

OPEP (Organización de los Países Exportadores de Petróleo) *abbr* (*Organization of Petroleum Exporting Countries*) OPEC

operación *f* 1. operation 2. transaction 3. operating

operacional *adj* operational

operación *f* **al contado** cash transaction

operación *f* **en multiples divisas** multicurrency operation

operaciones *fpl* **en bolsa** dealing

operación *f* **fraudulenta** fraudulent transaction

operación *f* **llaves en mano** turnkey operation

operador *m* **de cambios** foreign exchange broker *o* dealer

operador *m* **de teclado** keyboarder

operar to operate

operario 1. operator 2. worker

operativo *adj* operative

opinión *f* **pública** public opinion

oportunamente *adv* duly

oportunidad *f* opportunity

oportunidades *fpl* **de mercado** market opportunities

optar (*decidir*) to decide

optar por una línea de conducta to decide on a course of action

optativo *adj* optional

orden *m* 1. order 2. (*mandato*) writ 3. (*mandato*) warrant

ordenador *m* computer

ordenador *m* **personal** personal computer; PC

orden *m* **alfabético** alphabetical order

ordenar 1. to order 2. to arrange 3. to put in order

orden *m* **cronológico** chronological order

orden *f* **de compra** purchase order

orden *f* **de domiciliación (bancaria)** banker's order

orden *f* **de expedición** delivery order

orden *m* **del día** agenda

orden *f* **de pago** 1. order 2. payment order

ordinario *adj* 1. ordinary 2. regular

organigrama *m* 1. organization chart 2. flow chart 3. flow diagram

organismo *m* organization

organismo *m* **paraestatal** quango

organización *f* organization

Organización de los Países Exportadores de Petróleo (OPEP) Organization of Petroleum Exporting Countries (OPEC)

Organización Internacional del Trabajo (OIT) International Labour Organization (ILO)

organización *f* **lineal** line organization

organización y métodos organization and methods

organizar 1. to organize 2. to arrange

organizativo *adj* organizational

órgano *m* **administrativo** administrative body *o* authority

órgano *m* **decisorio** decision-making body

órganos *mpl* **de gestión** managerial posts

origen *m* origin

original *adj* original ■ original

oro *m* bullion

oscilación *f* fluctuation

oscilar 1. (*fluctuar*) to fluctuate 2. (*variar*) to range

otorgar 1. to grant 2. to award

P

pactar (*convenir*) to covenant
pacto *m* 1. covenant 2. agreement
padrino *m* sponsor
paga *f* pay
pagadero *adj* payable
pagadero a la entrega payable on delivery
pagadero a la vista payable on demand
pagadero a sesenta días payable at sixty days
pagadero por adelantado payable in advance
paga *f* **de vacaciones** 1. vacation pay 2. *U.K.* holiday pay
pagado *adj* 1. paid 2. prepaid
pagador payer
paga *f* **extraordinaria de Navidad** Christmas bonus
pagar 1. to pay 2. to pay out 3. to defray 4. (*devolver*) to repay
pagar (costes) to bear
pagar al contado to pay cash
pagar a plazos to pay in installments
pagar con cheque to pay by check
pagar con tarjeta de crédito to pay by credit card
pagaré *m* 1. accommodation bill 2. promissory note 3. note of hand ■ *abbr* (*I owe you*) (*vale*) IOU
pagaré *m* **de interés fijo** debenture
pagar en efectivo to pay cash
pagar intereses to pay interest
pagar la cuenta y marcharse to check out

pagar los intereses de una deuda to service a debt
pagar por adelantado 1. to prepay 2. to pay in advance
pagar una cuenta to pay a bill
pagar una deuda 1. to discharge a debt 2. to redeem a debt 3. to pay up
pagar una factura 1. to pay an invoice 2. to settle 3. to honor a bill
pagar una reclamación to settle a claim
páginas *fpl* **amarillas** yellow pages
pago *m* 1. payment 2. repayment 3. (*de una deuda*) discharge 4. (*finiquito*) settlement
pago *m* **a cuenta** 1. interim payment 2. payment on account
pago *m* **a destajo** payment by results
pago *m* **al contado** 1. cash terms 2. spot cash
pago *m* **anticipado** advance payment
pago *m* **anual** yearly payment
pago *m* **aplazado** deferred payment
pago *m* **atrasado** back payment
pago *m* **de una deuda** clearing
pago *m* **en efectivo** 1. cash payment 2. payment in cash
pago *m* **en especie** payment in kind
pago *m* **en exceso** overpayment
pago *m* **en metálico** payment in cash
pago *m* **inicial** down payment
pago *m* **íntegro** full payment
pago *m* **mediante cheque** payment by check
pago *m* **mínimo** minimum payment
pago *m* **parcial** partial payment
pago *m* **por adelantado** 1. prepayment 2. money up front
pagos *mpl* **a cuenta** progress payments

pagos *mpl* **de la hipoteca** mortgage payments

pago *m* **simbólico** token payment

pagos *mpl* **mensuales** monthly payments

pagos *mpl* **por etapas** staged payments

pagos *mpl* **semestrales** half-yearly payment

pago *m* **total de una deuda** full discharge of a debt

pago *m* **único** lump sum

país *m* country

país *m* **de origen** country of origin

país *m* **en vías de desarrollo** developing country

países *mpl* **exportadores de petróleo** oil-exporting countries

países *mpl* **productores de petróleo** oil-producing countries

países *mpl* **subdesarrollados** underdeveloped countries

palabras *fpl* **de agradecimiento** speech of thanks

paleta *f* pallet

panel *m* panel

pantalla *f* 1. monitor 2. screen

papel *m* **carbón** carbon paper

papel *m* **continuo** continuous stationery

papel *m* **de envolver** wrapping paper

papel *m* **de estraza** brown paper

papeleo *m* 1. paperwork 2. (*burocracia*) red tape

papeles *mpl* (*documentos*) papers

papel *m* **reciclado** recycled paper

paquete *m* 1. parcel 2. pack 3. packet 4. package 5. (*acciones*) block

paquete *m* **de sobres** pack of envelopes

par to par

parada *f* stop

parado *adj* unemployed

para entregar a *adv* care of; c/o

paraíso *m* **fiscal** tax haven

parar 1. to stop 2. to check

parecer to appear

paridad *f* parity

paro *m* 1. stoppage 2. (*desempleo*) unemployment

paro *m* **estructural** structural unemployment

paro *m* **técnico** work-to-rule

parte *f* 1. part 2. party 3. (*proporción*) proportion

parte *f* **acusadora** prosecution

parte *f* **contratante** contracting party

parte *f* **de baja** doctor's certificate

parte *f* **demandada** defendant

parte *f* **superior** top

participación *f* share

participación *f* **de beneficios** equity

participación *f* **en los beneficios** profit-sharing

particular *adj* private

partida *f* 1. batch 2. (*de un balance*) item

partidas *fpl* **excepcionales** exceptional items

partidas *fpl* **extraordinarias** 1. extraordinary items 2. non-recurring items

pasado *adj* old-fashioned

pasaje *m* fare

pasaje *m* **sencillo** one-way fare

pasante *mf* junior clerk

pasar (*tiempo*) to spend

pasar a cuenta nueva 1. to carry over a balance 2. to carry forward

pasar información a un fichero to card-index

pasar modelos to model

pasar por la criba to screen candidates

pasarse a to switch over to

pasivo *m* liability

pasivo *m* **a largo plazo** long-term liabilities

pasivo *m* **circulante** current liabilities

paso *m* **de información a un fichero** card-indexing

patentado *adj* patented

patentar un invento to patent an invention

patente *f* patent

patente *f* **de invención** letters patent

patente *f* **en tramitación** patent applied for *o* patent pending

patente *f* **solicitada** patent applied for *o* patent pending

patrimonio *m* 1. capital 2. net assets *o* net worth

patrocinado *adj* government-sponsored

patrocinador sponsor

patrocinar to sponsor

patrocinio *m* sponsorship

patrón *m* standard

peaje *m* toll

pedido *adv* on order ■ order ■ *adv* order: on order

pedido *m* **cursado al representante (comercial)** journey order

pedido *m* **no servido** unfulfilled order

pedido *m* **por correo** mail-order

pedido *m* **por servir** unfulfilled order

pedidos *mpl* **pendientes** 1. back orders 2. outstanding orders

pedidos *mpl* **por servir** dues

pedido *m* **suplementario** repeat order

pedido *m* **urgente** rush order

pedir 1. to ask 2. to ask for 3. (*solicitar*) to request

pedir información to inquire

pedir más detalles to ask for further details *o* to particulars

pedir perdón to apologize

pedir prestado to borrow

peligro *m* **de incendio** fire risk

pena *f* penalty

penalizar to penalize

pendiente *adj* 1. outstanding 2. pending

penetración *f* **en el mercado** market penetration

penetrar un mercado to penetrate a market

pensión *f* pension

pequeñas *fpl* **empresas** small businesses

pequeño *adj* small

pequeño *m* **empresario** small businessman

pequeños accionistas *mpl* minor stockholders

per *adv* (*a, por*) per

per cápita *adv, adj* per capita

perder to lose

perder (el tren/avion) to miss

perder dinero to lose money

perder el derecho a to forfeit

perder un depósito to forfeit a deposit

perder un pedido to lose an order

perder valor 1. to depreciate 2. to lose value

pérdida *f* 1. loss 2. wastage

pérdida *f* **de clientela** loss of customers

pérdida *f* **de ejercicio** trading loss

pérdida *f* **de trabajadores por jubilación** 1. attrition 2. *U.K.* natural wastage

pérdida *f* **de un pedido** loss of an order

pérdida *f* **de valor** 1. depreciation 2. loss of value

pérdida *f* **neta** net loss

pérdida *f* **parcial** partial loss

pérdidas *fpl* leakage

pérdidas *fpl* **de capital** capital loss

pérdida *f* **sobre el papel** paper loss

pérdida *f* **total** 1. write-off 2. dead loss

perecedero *adj* perishable

pericia *f* expertise

periféricos *mpl* peripherals

periódico *m* newspaper ■ *adj* periodic *o* periodical

periodo *m* period

periodo *m* **de arrendamiento** *m* tenancy

periodo *m* **de conservación de un producto** shelf life of a product

periodo *m* **de preaviso** period of notice

periodo *m* **de prueba** 1. probation 2. trial period

periodo *m* **de reembolso** payback period

periodo *m* **de reflexión** cooling off period (after purchase)

periodo *m* **de validez** period of validity

permanecer to stay

permanencia *f* stay

permiso *m* 1. permit 2. permission 3. leave

permiso *m* **de exportación** export license *o* export permit

permiso *m* **de residencia** residence permit

permiso *m* **de trabajo** work permit

permitir 1. to permit 2. to allow

permitirse un gasto to afford

perseguir 1. to chase 2. to follow up

persona *f* **autorizada** licensee

persona *f* **dedicada a las relaciones públicas** public relations man

personal *m* 1. personnel 2. staff 3. establishment ■ *adj* personal

personal *m* **administrativo** 1. office staff 2. managerial staff

personal *m* **clave** key personnel *o* key staff

personal *m* **de atención al público** counter staff

personal *m* **del hotel** hotel staff

personal *m* **de oficina** clerical staff

personal *m* **de ventas** 1. sales force 2. sales people

personal *m* **de ventas muy motivado** highly motivated sales staff

personal *m* **eventual** temporary staff

personal *m* **fijo** regular staff

personalidad *f* **jurídica** legal status

personal *m* **reducido al mínimo** skeleton staff

persona *f* **que busca clientes** canvasser

persona *f* **que toma las decisiones** decision maker

perspectivas *fpl* prospects

pertenecer to belong to

pertinente *adj* relevant

pesado *adj* heavy

pesar to weigh

pesar en exceso *adj* overweight: to be overweight

peso *m* 1. weight 2. (*moneda*) peso

peso *m* **bruto** gross weight

peso *m* **escaso** false weight

peso *m* **máximo** weight limit

peso *m* **muerto** deadweight

peso *m* **neto** net weight

petición *f* request

petición: a petición request: on request

petición *f* **de informes** inquiry

petición *f* **de informes sobre crédito** status inquiry

petición *f* **de pago (de acciones)** call

petróleo *m* oil

petrolero *m* tanker

PIB (Producto Interior Bruto) *abbr* (*gross domestic product*) GDP

pieza *f* piece

pieza *f* **de recambio** spare part

piloto *adj* pilot ■ pilot

pionero pioneer

piso *m* 1. floor 2. apartment 3. (*apartamento*) flat

plan *m* 1. plan 2. project 3. (*sistema*) arrangement

plan *m* **de emergencia** contingency plan

plan *m* **de pensiones** pension plan

plan *m* **de trabajo de una empresa** corporate plan

planear to plan

planes *mpl* **de contingencia** standby arrangements

plan *m* **general** overall plan

planificación *f* planning

planificación *f* **a largo plazo** long-term planning

planificación *f* **de la mano de obra** manpower planning

planificación *f* **económica** economic planning

planificación *f* **empresarial** corporate planning

planificación *f* **estratégica** strategic planning

planificador planner

planificar to plan

planificar las inversiones to plan investments

plano *m* plan

plan *m* **periódicamente actualizado** rolling plan

plan *m* **remunerativo** money-making plan

planta *f* 1. floor plan 2. (*fábrica*) plant

plantear to raise

plantilla *f* 1. staff 2. establishment

plata *f* **en lingotes** bullion

plaza *f* 1. vacancy 2. position 3. (*mercado*) market

plaza *f* **del mercado** 1. marketplace 2. square

plazo *m* 1. term 2. notice 3. installment 4. (*límite*) time limit 5. (*periodo*) period

plazo: a corto plazo on a short-term basis

plazo *m* **de entrega** delivery time

plazo *m* **de espera** lead time

plazo *m* **de tiempo límite** time limitation

plazo *m* **límite** *m* deadline

plazo *m* **medio** medium-term

pleito *m* lawsuit

pluriempleado moonlighter

pluriempleo *m* moonlighting

plus *m* **de carestía de vida** cost-of-living bonus

plusvalía *f* capital gains

PNB (Producto Nacional Bruto) *abbr* (*gross national product*) GNP

poder *m* 1. power 2. (*procuración*) proxy

poder *m* **adquisitivo** 1. purchasing power 2. spending power

poder *m* **de negociación** bargaining power

poderes *mpl* power of attorney

poderhabiente *mf* proxy

poder *m* **notarial** power of attorney

política *f* policy

política *f* **comercial de reciprocidad arancelaria** fair trade

política *f* **crediticia** credit policy

política *f* **de precios** pricing policy

política *f* **de precios flexibles** flexible pricing policy

política *f* **presupuestaria** budgetary policy

póliza *f* **a todo riesgo** all-risks policy

póliza *f* **de seguros** 1. insurance policy 2. *U.K.* assurance policy

póliza *f* **provisional** cover note

ponderación *f* weighting

poner 1. to put 2. to place

poner a la venta to release

poner al día to update

poner el sello to stamp

poner en contenedores to containerize

poner en la lista negra to blacklist

poner en libertad to free

poner en práctica un acuerdo to implement an agreement

poner en una caja to case

poner la dirección to address a letter *o* to a package

poner las iniciales a to initial

poner las señas to address a letter *o* to a package

poner por escrito to put in writing

poner precio a to price

poner término a un acuerdo to terminate an agreement

poner un negocio to set up in business

popular *adj* popular

por via ■ *adv* per

por adelantado *adj* up front

por asuntos de negocios on business

porcentaje *m* percentage

porcentaje *m* **de aumento** percentage increase

porcentaje *m* **de comisión** cost plus

porcentaje *m* **de descuento** percentage discount

porcentaje *m* **fijo** flat rate

por ciento *adv* percent

por cobrar *adj* receivable

por contrato *adv* contractually

por cuenta y riesgo del comprador caveat emptor

por debajo de under

por hora *adj* hourly ■ per hour

pormenores *mpl* particulars

por pagar accounts payable

por persona per head

por semana per week

por separado *adj* separate: under separate cover

portacontenedores container ship

portador 1. bearer 2. payee

portátil *adj* portable

porte *m* 1. *U.K.* carriage 2. freight

porte *m* **debido** 1. freight collect 2. freight forward 3. *U.K.* carriage forward

porte *m* **pagado** 1. freight paid 2. *U.K.* carriage paid 3. postage paid ■ *adj* postpaid

por término medio on an average

por triplicado triplicate: in triplicate

portuarios port charges *o* port duesfees

poseedor holder

poseer 1. to possess 2. to own

posesión *f* 1. possession 2. ownership 3. tenure

posfechar to postdate

posibilidad *f* possibility

posibilidad *f* **de comparación** comparability

posible *adj* possible

posible comprador prospective buyer

posición *f* 1. position 2. place 3. (*status*) status

positivo *adj* positive

posponer 1. to postpone 2. to hold over

(tarjeta) postal postcard

postal *f adj* postal ■ card

postor *m* 1. bidder 2. tenderer

postura *f* position

postura *f* **negociadora** bargaining position

potencial *adj* potential ■ potential

practicar el "dumping" to dump goods on a market

prácticas *fpl* **comerciales justas** 1. fair trading 2. fair dealing

prácticas *fpl* **restrictivas** restrictive practices

práctico *adj* handy

precauciones *fpl* safety precautions

precintar to seal

precinto *m* seal

precinto *m* **de aduana** customs seal

precio *m* 1. price 2. charge 3. (*tarifa*) rate 4. (*tarifa*) tariff

precio *m* **acordado** agreed price

precio *m* **actual** current price

precio *m* **a destajo** piece rate

precio *m* **al cierre** closing price

precio *m* **al contado** cash price

precio *m* **al detallista** trade price

precio *m* **al por mayor** wholesale price

precio *m* **al por menor** retail price

precio *m* **competitivo** competitive price

precio *m* **con entrega de artículo usado** trade-in price

precio *m* **convenido** agreed price

precio *m* **corriente** average price

precio *m* **de apertura** opening price

precio *m* **de catálogo** 1. list price 2. catalog price

precio *m* **de compra** purchase price

precio *m* **de conversión** conversion price *o* conversion rate

precio *m* **de coste** cost price

precio *m* **de descuento** discount price

precio *m* **de entrada** admission charge

precio *m* **de entrega** delivered price

precio *m* **de entrega inmediata** spot price

precio *m* **de fábrica** factory price

precio *m* **de intervención** intervention price

precio *m* **del crudo** oil price

precio *m* **de mercado** 1. market rate 2. market price

precio *m* **de ocasión** bargain price

precio *m* **de oferta** 1. offer price 2. supply price

precio *m* **de reventa** resale price

precio *m* **de subvención** support price

precio *m* **de transporte** freight rates

precio *m* **de venta** selling price

precio *m* **de venta recomendado** manufacturer's recommended price; MRP

precio *m* **en fábrica** price ex works

precio *m* **en firme** firm price

precio *m* **excesivo** overcharge

precio *m* **facturado** invoice value

precio *m* **fijo** set price

precio *m* **inicial** upset price

precio *m* **irrisorio** bargain price

precio *m* **justo** fair price

precio *m* **máximo** maximum price

precio *m* **máximo autorizado** ceiling price

precio *m* **medio** average price

precio *m* **mínimo aceptable** reserve price

precio *m* **módico** moderate price

precio *m* **neto** net price

precio *m* **por unidad** unit price

precio *m* **reducido** 1. cut price 2. reduced rate

precios *mpl* **competitivos** *U.K.* keen prices

precios *mpl* **de saldo** knockdown prices

precios *mpl* **estables** stable prices

precios *mpl* **exagerados** inflated prices

precios *mpl* **flexibles** flexible prices

precio *m* **simbólico** token charge

precio *m* **sin descuento** full price

precios *mpl* **mínimos** knockdown prices

precios *mpl* **populares** popular prices

precios *mpl* **reventados** rock-bottom prices

precio *m* **todo incluido** 1. all-inclusive price 2. inclusive charge 3. *U.K.* all-in price

precio *m* **tope** ceiling price

precio *m* **umbral** threshold price

precio *m* **vigente** going rate

precipitarse to rush

precisar to specify

predecir to forecast

preempaquetar to prepack *o* to prepackage

preferencia *f* 1. preference 2. choice

preferencial *adj* preferential

preferente *adj* preferential

preferir to prefer

prefijo *m U.K.* 1. area code 2. dialling code

prefinanciación *f* pre-financing

pregunta *f* question

preguntar 1. to ask 2. to inquire 3. to question

premio *m* award

prensa *f* press

preocupación *f* 1. concern 2. worry

preparación *f* **de pedidos** order processing

preparación *f* **de presupuestos** budgeting

preparado *adj* ready

preparar 1. to train 2. to organize 3. (*elaborar*) to process 4. (*redactar*) to draw up

prepararse to train

preparar una factura 1. to prepare an invoice 2. *U.K.* to raise an invoice

preparar un contrato to draw up a contract

preparar un horario to timetable

prescribir to prescribe

preselección *f* shortlist

preseleccionar to shortlist

presentación *f* 1. presentation 2. production 3. (*introducción*) introduction

presentar 1. to present 2. to produce 3. (*entregar*) to hand in 4. (*introducir*) to introduce 5. (*organizar*) to stage 6. (*petición, demanda*) to file

presentar excusas to apologize

presentarse to report

presentarse a una entrevista to report for an interview

presentar una cuenta to render an account

presentar una factura to render an account

presentar una letra a la aceptación to present a bill for acceptance

presentar una letra al pago to present a bill for payment

presentar una reconvención to counter-claim

presente *adj* present

presidente chairman

presidente y director gerente chairman and managing director

prestamista *mf* 1. moneylender 2. lender

préstamo *m* 1. borrowing 2. loan

préstamo *m* **a corto plazo** short-term loan

préstamo *m* **a largo plazo** long-term loan

préstamo *m* **a plazo fijo** term loan

préstamo *m* **bancario** bank loan

préstamo *m* **garantizado** secured loan

préstamos *mpl* **bancarios** bank borrowings

préstamo *m* **sin interés** soft loan

prestar 1. to lend 2. to loan

prestatario 1. borrower 2. debtor

prestigio *m* prestige

presupuestar to budget

presupuestario *adj* budgetary

presupuesto *m* 1. budget 2. (*cotización*) quote 3. (*cotización*) estimate

presupuesto *m* **de explotación** 1. operational budget 2. operating budget

presupuesto *m* **de gastos generales** overhead budget

presupuesto *m* **del Estado** budget

presupuesto *m* **de promoción** promotion(al) budget

presupuesto *m* **de publicidad** advertising budget

presupuesto *m* **de ventas** sales budget

presupuesto *m* **provisional** provisional budget

presupuesto *m* **publicitario** publicity budget

pretender (*alegar*) to claim

prevención *f* prevention

prevenir 1. to prevent 2. to preempt

preventivo *adj* preventive

prever 1. to forecast 2. to foresee 3. to anticipate 4. to tip 5. (*estipular*) to provide for

previo *adj* 1. previous 2. prior

previsión *f* 1. forecast 2. forecasting

previsión *f* **a largo plazo** long-term forecast

previsión *f* **de mano de obra** manpower forecasting

previsión *f* **de mercado** market forecast

previsión *f* **de ventas** sales forecast

previsión *f* **provisional de ventas** provisional forecast of sales

previsto *adj* projected

prima *f* bonus

prima *f* **al comisionista** del credere

prima *f* **de incentivo** incentive bonus *o* incentive payment

prima *f* **de productividad** productivity bonus

prima *f* **de renovación** renewal premium

prima *f* **de riesgo** risk premium

prima *f* **de seguros** 1. insurance premium 2. premium

prima *f* **por ausencia de siniestralidad** *U.K.* no-claims bonus

primario *adj* primary

primera opción first option

primeras entradas, primeras salidas first in first out; FIFO

primero *adj* 1. first 2. (*initial*) initial 3. (*principal*) prime

primer trimestre first quarter

principal *adj* 1. (*capital*) principal 2. chief 3. main 4. prime 5. top ■ (*capital*) principal

principio *m* 1. principle 2. (*inicio*) start

prisa *f* rush

privado *adj* private

privatización *f* privatization

privatizar to privatize

privilegio *m* **fiscal** tax concession

probar 1. to sample 2. to test

probatorio probationary

problema *m* problem

proceder to proceed

procedimiento *m* 1. process 2. procedure

procedimiento *m* **de selección** selection procedure

procedimientos *mpl* **judiciales** judicial processes

procesamiento *m* prosecution

procesamiento *m* **por lotes** batch processing

procesar to prosecute

proceso *m* 1. (*juicio*) trial 2. (*juicio*) court case 3. (*juicio*) lawsuit

proceso *m* **de datos** data processing

proceso *m* **judicial** legal proceedings

procesos *mpl* **decisorios** decision-making processes

procesos *mpl* **industriales** industrial processes

procuración *f* proxy
procurador attorney
producción *f* 1. production 2. output 3. yield
producción *f* **en serie** mass production
producción *f* **interior** domestic production
producción *f* **nacional** domestic production
producción *f* **total** total output
producir 1. to produce 2. to make 3. to bring in 4. (*dar*) to produce 5. (*devengar*) to carry 6. (*ordenador*) to output
producir en exceso to overproduce
productividad *f* productivity
productivo *adj* 1. productive 2. profitable
producto *m* product
producto *m* **defectuoso** reject
producto *m* **derivado** byproduct
producto *m* **destinado a un mercado de masas** mass market product
producto *m* **ficticio** dummy
producto *m* **final** end product
Producto Interior Bruto (PIB) gross domestic product (GDP)
Producto Nacional Bruto (PNB) gross national product (GNP)
producto *m* **prestigioso** prestige product
producto *m* **principal** staple product
productor producer
productos *mpl* produce
productos *mpl* **acabados** finished goods
productos *mpl* **competitivos** competitive products
productos *mpl* **de marca propia** 1. own label goods 2. own brand goods
productos *mpl* **de primera calidad** high-quality goods

productos *mpl* **devueltos sin vender** returns
productos *mpl* **en competencia** competing products
producto *m* **sensible a los cambios de precio** price-sensitive product
productos *mpl* **manufacturados** manufactured goods
productos *mpl* **perecederos** perishables
productos *mpl* **semiacabados** semi-finished products
profesional *adj* professional ■ professional
programa *m* program
programación *f* scheduling
programación *f* **de ordenador** computer programming
programa *m* **de investigación** research program
programa *m* **de ordenador** computer program
programador *m* **de ordenadores** computer programmer
programa *m* **informático** software
programa *m* **piloto** pilot program
programar un ordenador to program a computer
progresar to progress
progresivo *adj* 1. progressive 2. gradual 3. graduated
progreso *m* progress
prohibición *f* 1. ban 2. embargo
prohibición *f* **de hacer horas extras** overtime ban
prohibición *f* **de importar** import ban
prohibir 1. to ban 2. to forbid 3. to embargo
prohibitivo *adj* prohibitive
prolongación *f* extension
prolongar to extend
promedio *m* 1. average 2. mean
promedio *m* **ponderado** weighted average

promesa *f* 1. promise 2. undertaking

prometer to promise

promoción *f* promotion

promocionar to promote

promocionar la imagen pública de una empresa to promote a corporate image

promocionar un nuevo producto to promote a new product

promoción *f* **de un producto** promotion of a product

promoción *f* **de ventas** 1. sales promotion 2. sales drive

pronosticar 1. to forecast 2. to tip

pronóstico *m* forecast

pronto *adj* 1. early ■ *adv* prompt; soon

pronto pago *m* prompt payment

propicio *adj* favorable

propiedad *f* 1. ownership 2. property

propiedad *f* **colectiva** 1. collective ownership 2. common ownership

propiedad *f* **conjunta** multiple ownership

propiedad *f* **inmobiliaria** real estate

propiedad *f* **privada** 1. private property 2. private ownership

propietaria *f* 1. proprietress 2. landlady

propietario *m* 1. proprietor 2. landlord 3. owner

propietario legítimo rightful owner

propietario único sole owner

propina *f* tip

proponer to propose

proponer(se) to propose to

proponerse (*aspirar a*) to aim

proporción *f* proportion

proporcional *adj* proportional

proposición *f* 1. proposition 2. proposal

propósito *m* aim

propuesta *f* 1. proposal 2. proposition

prorrata *adv*, *adj* pro rata

prórroga *f* 1. renewal 2. extension

prorrogar 1. to extend 2. to renew

prorrogar un arrendamiento to renew a lease

proseguir to continue

prospecto *m* 1. prospectus 2. leaflet

prosperar 1. to flourish 2. to boom 3. to succeed

próspero *adj* 1. prosperous 2. flourishing ■ booming; flourishing trade ■ *adj* successful

protección *f* 1. protection 2. defense 3. (*cobertura*) hedging

protección *f* **al consumidor** consumer protection

proteccionista *adj* protective ■ protectionist

protector *adj* protective

proteger 1. to protect 2. to safeguard 3. to defend

protesta *f* protest

protestar contra algo to protest

protestar una letra to protest a bill

protesto *m* protest

prototipo *m* **de contrato** model agreement

proveedor supplier

proveer 1. to provide 2. to supply

provisión *f* supply

provisional *adj* provisional

provisión *f* **de fondos** 1. provision 2. allocation of funds

próximo *adj* close to

proyectado *adj* projected

proyectar 1. to project 2. to plan 3. to design

proyecto *m* 1. project 2. plan 3. (*borrador*) draft

proyecto *m* **de ley** bill

prueba *f* 1. proof 2. demonstration 3. (*ensayo*) trial 4. (*ensayo*) test

prueba: a prueba approval: on approval

prueba *f* **documentada** documentary proof

prueba *f* **gratuita** free trial

pruebas *fpl* **documentales** documentary evidence

publicación *f* **asistida por ordenador** desk-top publishing; DTP

publicación *f* **periódica** periodical

publicar 1. (*anunciar*) to advertise 2. (*divulgar*) to release

publicidad *f* 1. publicity 2. advertising

publicidad *f* **a escala nacional** national advertising

publicidad *f* **en el punto de venta** 1. point of sale material 2. POS material

publicidad *f* **por correo** 1. direct-mail advertising 2. mail shot

publicidad *f* **sin interés (por correo)** junk mail

público *adj* 1. common 2. public

puente-báscula *m* weighbridge

puerta *f* door

puerto *m* 1. port 2. harbor

puerto *m* **de contenedores** container port

puerto *m* **de embarque** port of embarkation

puerto *m* **de escala** port of call

puerto *m* **de registro** port of registry

puerto *m* **distribuidor** entrepot port

puerto *m* **franco** free port

puesta *f* **al día** updating

puesta *f* **en marcha (de un negocio)** start-up

puesta *f* **en práctica** implementation

puesto *m* 1. post 2. position 3. place

puesto *m* **aduanero** customs entry point

puesto *m* **clave** key post

puesto *m* **de trabajo** 1. (*empleo*) job 2. (*informática*) workstation

puja *f* bid

pujar más alto to outbid

punto *m* 1. point 2. (*discusión*) item

punto *m* **decimal** decimal point

punto *m* **de partida** starting point

punto *m* **de referencia** benchmark

punto *m* **de reunión** venue

punto *m* **de venta** point of sale; POS *o* p.o.s.

punto *m* **máximo** peak

punto *m* **muerto** 1. break-even point 2. deadlock

punto *m* **porcentual** percentage point

puntos *mpl* **de venta electrónicos** electronic point of sale; epos *o* EPOS

PYME (pequeñas y medianas empresas) SME (small and medium-sized businesses)

Q

que ahorra energía *adj* energy-saving

quebrado *m* bankrupt

quebrado *m* **no rehabilitado** undischarged bankrupt

quebrado *m* **rehabilitado** certificated bankrupt

quebrar 1. to crash 2. to fail

quedar 1. to remain 2. to left: be left

quedarse 1. to stay 2. to remain

quedarse atrás to fall behind

que está por llegar *adj* due

queja *f* complaint

quejarse to complain (about)

querellante *mf* plaintiff

que se repite *adj* recurrent

quiebra *f* bankruptcy

quiebra *f* **comercial** commercial failure

quitar 1. to remove 2. (*rebajar*) to take off

quórum *m* quorum

R

racionalización *f* rationalization

racionalizar to rationalize

radicar to base

rama *f* branch

rampa *f* **de carga** loading ramp

rápidamente *adv* fast

rápido *adj* 1. rapid 2. prompt 3. fast 4. (*urgente*) express

ratero *m* **de tiendas** shoplifter

ratificación *f* ratification

ratificar to ratify

raya *f* line

razón *f* 1. (*motivo*) reason 2. (*relación*) ratio

razón *f* **social** corporate name

reacción *f* 1. feedback 2. response

reactivación *f* 1. recovery 2. turnaround 3. upturn

reajustar 1. to adjust 2. to readjust

reajuste *m* 1. adjustment 2. readjustment

real *adj* 1. real 2. actual

realización *f* 1. fulfillment 2. realization

realizar 1. to realize 2. to implement

realizar activos to realize property *o* to assets

realizar una operación de cesión-arrendamiento to lease back

realizar un plan to realize a project *o* to a plan

realizar un proyecto to realize a project *o* to a plan

reanudar to resume

reanudar las negociaciones to resume negotiations

reasegurador reinsurer

reasegurar to reinsure

reaseguro *m* reinsurance

rebaja *f* 1. rebate 2. discount 3. reduction 4. (*recorte*) cut

rebajar 1. to mark down 2. to deduct 3. to take off

rebajar un precio to reduce (a price)

rebajas *fpl* sale

rebajas *fpl* **a mitad de precio** half-price sale

rebajas *fpl* **de fin de temporada** end of season sale

rebajas *fpl* **de precios** price reductions

rebatida contested takeover

recadero *m* deliveryman

recado *m* message

recargar to mark up

recargo *m* 1. surcharge 2. overcharge

recargo *m* **de importación** import surcharge

recaudación *f* take

recaudación *f* **(de un negocio)** takings

recaudación *f* **de impuestos** 1. levy 2. tax collection

recaudador collector

recaudador *m* **de impuestos** 1. tax collector 2. Excise officer

recaudar to levy

recepción *f* 1. reception 2. reception desk 3. receipt

recepcionista *mf* 1. receptionist 2. reception clerk

receptor *m* receiver (who receives)

recesión f recession

rechazar 1. to reject **2.** to turn down **3.** to refuse

rechazo m **1.** rejection **2.** refusal

recibir 1. to receive **2.** to take **3.** to get

recibir una llamada to take a call

recibo m receipt

recibo m **(de depósito) 1.** deposit slip **2.** U.K. paying-in slip

recibo m **de aduana** customs receipt

reciclaje m **profesional** retraining

reciclar 1. to recycle **2.** to retrain

recipiente m container

reciprocidad f reciprocity

recíproco adj reciprocal

reclamación f **1.** claim **2.** demand

reclamar 1. to claim **2.** to demand

recobrar 1. to recover **2.** to repossess

recoger to collect

recogida f collection

recomendación f recommendation

recomendar to recommend

reconciliación f reconciliation

reconocer a un sindicato to recognize a union

reconocer una firma to honor a signature

reconocimiento m recognition

reconocimiento m **de un sindicato** union recognition

reconvención f counter-claim

récord m record ■ adj record-breaking

recordar 1. to remind **2.** to remember

recordatorio m reminder

recortar to cut

recorte m cut

rectificación f **1.** rectification **2.** correction

rectificar 1. to rectify **2.** to correct

recuperable adj recoverable

recuperación f **1.** recovery **2.** retrieval **3.** (precios) rally

recuperación f **de datos** data retrieval

recuperar 1. (recobrar) to recover **2.** (recobrar) to repossess **3.** (rescatar) to retrieve **4.** (rescatar) to get back

recuperarse 1. (mejorar) to recover **2.** (precios) to rally

recursos mpl **1.** resources **2.** means

recursos mpl **financieros** financial resources

recursos mpl **naturales** natural resources

red f network

redactar 1. to draft **2.** to draw up

redactar una carta to draft a letter

redactar un contrato 1. to draft a contract **2.** to draw up a contract

red f **de distribución** distribution network

redimir 1. to pay off **2.** to redeem

redistribuir to redistribute

rédito m **1.** interest **2.** rate of interest

redondear por defecto to round down

redondear por exceso to round up

reducción f **1.** reduction **2.** decrease **3.** lowering **4.** shrinkage **5.** (desaceleración) slowdown

reducción f **de costes** cost-cutting

reducción f **de empleos** job cuts

reducción f **de gastos** retrenchment

reducción f **de los impuestos** tax reductions

reducir 1. to decrease **2.** (desacelerar) to slow down

reducir a escala to scale down

reducir drásticamente (los precios o las condiciones) to slash prices o to credit terms

reducir gastos 1. to reduce expenditure **2.** to cut down on expenses

reducir gradualmente to phase out

reducir los precios to lower prices

reducir un precio to reduce (a price)

redundante *adj* redundant

reelección *f* reelection

reelegir to re-elect

reembolsable *adj* **1.** refundable **2.** repayable

reembolsar 1. to refund **2.** to repay **3.** to pay back **4.** (*redimir*) to pay off

reembolso *m* **1.** repayment **2.** (*reintegro*) reimbursement **3.** (*reintegro*) rebate **4.** (*reintegro*) refund

reembolso *m* **de gastos** reimbursement of expenses

reembolso *m* **total** full refund

reemplazar to replace

reemplazo *m* replacement

reempleo *m* reemployment

reestructuración *f* restructuring

reestructuración *f* **de la compañía** restructuring of the company

reestructurar to restructure

reevaluación *f* revaluation

reexportación *f* re-export

reexportar to re-export

referencia *f* reference

referente relating to

referirse to refer

referirse a to apply to

refinanciación *f* **de un préstamo** refinancing of a loan

refinanciar una deuda to roll over credit *o* to a debt

refinanciar un crédito to roll over credit *o* to a debt

refrendar to countersign

refugio *m* shelter

regalar 1. to give **2.** to give away **3.** (*obsequiar*) to present

regalo *m* **1.** present **2.** gift **3.** free gift

regatear 1. to haggle **2.** to bargain

región *f* **1.** region **2.** area

regional *adj* regional

regir 1. to rule **2.** to run

registrado *adj* registered

registrador registrar

registrar 1. to record **2.** to register

registrarse 1. (*inscribirse*) to register **2.** (*inscribirse*) to check in

registrar una marca comercial to register a trademark

registrar una propiedad to register a property

registro *m* **1.** register **2.** registry **3.** (*informe*) record **4.** (*inscripción*) registration **5.** (*inspección*) examination

registro *m* **de compañías** companies' register

Registro *m* **Marítimo de Lloyd** Lloyd's register

Registro *m* **Mercantil** Registrar of Companies

regla *f* **1.** law **2.** rule

reglamentación *f* regulation

reglamentar to regulate

reglamentario *adj* statutory

reglamento *m* regulations

reglamento *m* **sobre incendios** fire regulations

regreso *m* return

regulación *f* regulation

regulado *adj* government-regulated

regular 1. to regular **2.** to regulate

rehusar to refuse

reimportación *f* **1.** reimport **2.** reimportation

reimportar to reimport

reintegro *m* **1.** reimbursement **2.** withdrawal

reinversión *f* reinvestment

reinvertir to reinvest

reivindicación *f* claim

reivindicación *f* **salarial** wage claim

reivindicar to claim

relación *f* 1. relation 2. connection 3. (*lista*) list 4. (*razón*) ratio

relacionar to connect

relación *f* **de directivos de una empresa** register of directors

relación *f* **de gastos** statement of expenses

relaciones *fpl* relations

relaciones *fpl* **laborales** industrial relations

relaciones *fpl* **públicas** public relations; PR

relación *f* **precio-beneficios** *abbr* (*price/earnings ratio*) P/E ratio

relación *f* **precio-ganancias** price/earnings ratio (P/E ratio)

relativo a 1. regarding 2. relating to

rematar to knock down

remate *m* distress sale

remesa *f* 1. (*envío*) consignment 2. (*partida*) batch

remite *m* return address

remitente *mf* 1. sender 2. consignor

remitir 1. to remit 2. to refer

remitir adjunto to enclose

remitir por cheque to remit by check

remontarse to soar

remuneración *f* 1. remuneration 2. payment

remunerar to remunerate

remunerativo *adj* money-making

rendimiento *m* 1. (*actuación*) performance 2. (*capacidad*) capacity 3. (*producción*) output 4. (*producción*) throughput 5. (*rentabilidad*) return 6. (*rentabilidad*) yield

rendimiento *m* **bruto** gross yield

rendimiento *m* **corriente** current yield

rendimiento *m* **de la inversión** return on investment; ROI

rendimiento *m* **efectivo** effective yield

rendimiento *m* **máximo** peak output

rendimiento *m* **neto** net yield

rendir 1. to yield 2. to bear

rendir cuentas a alguien to report to someone

renovación *f* renewal

renovación *f* **de existencias** restocking

renovación *f* **urbana** redevelopment

renovar 1. to redevelop 2. to renew

renovar existencias to restock

renovar un abono to renew a subscription

renovar una suscripción to renew a subscription

renovar un pedido 1. to reorder 2. to repeat an order

renta *f* 1. (*alquiler*) rent 2. (*ingresos*) income 3. (*rendimiento*) yield

rentabilidad *f* 1. profitability 2. cost-effectiveness

rentabilidad *f* **del dividendo** dividend yield

rentable *adj* 1. paying 2. cost-effective 3. (*lucrativo*) profit-making 4. (*lucrativo*) profitable

renta *f* **bruta** gross income

renta *f* **de inversiones** investment income

renta *f* **fija** fixed income

renta *f* **imponible** taxable income

renta *f* **nominal** nominal rent

renta *f* **personal** personal income

renta *f* **por alquiler** rental income

renta *f* **que no llega a cubrir los costes** uneconomic rent

renta *f* **real** real income *o* real wages

renta *f* **total** total income

renta *f* **vitalicia** life interest

renuncia *f* 1. renunciation 2. resignation 3. (*abandono de responsa-*

bilidad) disclaimer 4. (*desistimiento*) waiver

renunciar a to abandon

renunciar a un pago to waive a payment

reorganización *f* reorganization

reorganizar to reorganize

reparación *f* repair

reparar to repair

repartir 1. to distribute 2. to share 3. (*entregar*) to deliver

repartir un riesgo to spread a risk

reparto *m* 1. distribution 2. delivery

reparto *m* **de mercancías** delivery of goods

repercusión *f* *U.K.* knock-on effect

repertorio *m* 1. index 2. list

repetir to repeat

reponer to replace

repostar to restock

representación *f* **exclusiva** sole agency

representante *mf* 1. representative 2. agent 3. (*vendedor*) salesman 4. (*vendedor*) sales representative 5. (*vendedor*) commercial traveler 6. (*vendedor*) rep

representante *mf* **a comisión** commission rep

representante *m* **exclusivo** sole agent

representar to represent

representativo *adj* representative

repudiar to repudiate

repuesto *m* replacement

reputación *f* 1. reputation 2. standing

requerimiento *m* **de pago** demand

requerir to require

requisitos *mpl* requirements

resarcir 1. to repay 2. to indemnify 3. to compensate

resarcirse de las pérdidas to recoup one's losses

rescatable *adj* redeemable

rescatador *m* **de empresas** white knight

rescatar 1. to retrieve 2. to buy back

rescatar una póliza to surrender a policy

rescatar una prenda to redeem a pledge

rescate *m* 1. retrieval 2. recovery 3. salvage 4. (*póliza*) surrender 5. (*préstamo*) redemption

rescindir to rescind

rescindir un contrato to cancel a contract

reserva *f* 1. booking 2. reservation 3. (*almacén*) reserve 4. (*almacén*) store 5. (*provisión*) supply 6. (*provisión*) provision

reserva *f* **anticipada** advance booking

reserva *f* **en bloque** block booking

reserva *f* **en dólares** dollar balance

reservar 1. to reserve 2. to book

reservar con exceso to overbook

reservar la misma plaza a dos personas to double book

reservas *fpl* 1. reserve 2. reserves 3. stockpile

reservas *fpl* **de caja** cash reserves

reservas *fpl* **de divisas** currency reserves

reservas *fpl* **de materias primas** stock of raw materials

reservas *fpl* **ocultas** hidden reserves

reservas *fpl* **para imprevistos** emergency reserves

resguardo *m* 1. slip 2. receipt

residencia *f* residence

residente *adj* resident ■ resident

residuos *mpl* waste

resignar to resign

resolución *f* resolution

resolver to resolve

resolver un problema to solve a problem

respaldar 1. to back up **2.** to support

respaldo *m* backing

respetar to respect

responder 1. to answer **2.** to reply **3.** to respond

responder de to account for

responsabilidad *f* **1.** responsibility **2.** liability

responsabilidad *f* **contractual** contractual liability

responsabilidades *fpl* responsibilities

responsabilidad *f* **ilimitada** unlimited liability

responsabilidad *f* **limitada** limited liability

responsable *adj* responsible (for)

responsable de liable for

responsable *mf* **de la capacitación** training officer

responsable *mf* **del progreso de un trabajo** progress chaser

responsable *mf* **de relaciones públicas** public relations officer

respuesta *f* **1.** reply **2.** answer **3.** response **4.** (*reacción*) feedback

resto *m* **1.** rest **2.** remainder

restricción *f* **1.** restraint **2.** restriction

restricción *f* **a las importaciones** import restrictions

restricción *f* **comercial** restraint of trade

restrictivo *adj* restrictive

restringir to restrict

resultado *m* result

resultados *mpl* results

resultar to result in

resultar de to result from

retención *f* **de impuestos en origen** withholding tax

retención *f* **fiscal** tax deductions

retener to keep back

retirada *f* withdrawal

retirar (una oferta) to withdraw

retirar gradualmente to phase out

retirarse (*jubilarse*) to retire

retirarse (de una elección) to stand down

retirar una oferta de adquisición to withdraw a takeover bid

retiro *m* **1.** withdrawal **2.** (*jubilación*) retirement **3.** (*jubilación*) pension

retornable *adj* returnable

retrasar 1. to hold up **2.** to delay

retrasarse 1. to fall behind **2.** to late: to be late

retraso *m* **1.** hold-up **2.** delay

retroactivo *adj* retroactive

reunión *f* **1.** meeting **2.** assembly

reunión *f* **del consejo de administración** board meeting

reunión *f* **de personal** staff meeting

reunión *f* **de ventas** sales conference

reunir recursos to pool resources

reunirse to meet

revaluación *f* reassessment

revaluar 1. to revalue **2.** to reassess

revelación *f* disclosure

revelación *f* **de información confidencial** disclosure of confidential information

revelar to disclose

revelar una información to disclose a piece of information

reventa *f* resale

reverso *m* back

revertido *adj* reverse

revés *m* setback

revisar 1. to revise **2.** to inspect **3.** (*máquina*) to service

revisar las cuentas to audit the accounts

revisión *f* (*máquina*) service

revisión *f* **de cuentas** audit

revisión *f* **de sueldos** salary review

revista *f* 1. magazine 2. journal 3. periodical

revista *f* **profesional especializada** trade journal *o* trade magazine

revocación *f* reversal

revocar 1. to revoke 2. to reverse 3. to countermand

riesgo *m* 1. risk 2. exposure

riesgo *m* **financiero** financial risk

rincón *m* corner

ritmo *m* **de producción** rate of production

robo *m* theft

rollo *m* **publicitario** sales pitch

romper las negociaciones to break off negotiations

romperse to break down

romper un acuerdo to break an agreement

rotación *f* **(de mercancias)** turnover

rotación *f* **de existencias** 1. inventory turnover 2. turnaround 3. *U.K.* stock turnover

rotación *f* **de personal** turnover

rotulador *m* marker pen

rótulo *m* sign

roturas *fpl* breakages

rubricar to initial

ruego *m* request

ruptura *f* breakdown

ruta *f* **habitual** 1. run 2. regular route

rutina *f* routine

rutinario *adj* routine

S

sacar (*dinero*) to draw

sacar (*dinero*) to withdraw

sacar el título de to qualify as

saco *m* bag

sala *f* room

sala *f* **de conferencias** conference room

sala *f* **de embarque** departure lounge

sala *f* **de exposición** showroom

sala *f* **de exposiciones** exhibition hall

sala *f* **de juntas** boardroom

sala *f* **de subastas** auction rooms

sala *f* **de tránsito** transit lounge

salario *m* 1. salary 2. wage

salario *m* **inicial** starting salary

salario *m* **interesante** attractive salary

salario *m* **mínimo** minimum wage

salario *m* **mínimo interprofesional** guaranteed minimum wage

salario *m* **neto** net income *o* net salary

saldar to balance

saldar una cuenta to settle an account

saldar una factura to settle

saldo *m* 1. balance 2. balance brought down *o* balance brought forward 3. (*rebajas*) sale

saldo *m* **acreedor** credit balance

saldo *m* **a cuenta nueva** balance carried down *o* balance carried forward

saldo *m* **a favor** credit balance
saldo *m* **a (nuestro) favor** balance due to us
saldo *m* **de caja** cash balance
saldo *m* **deudor** debit balance
saldo *m* **final 1.** closing balance **2.** bottom line
saldo *m* **inicial** opening balance
saldo *m* **insuficiente** insufficient funds
saldo *m* **total** bottom line
salida *f* departure
salidas *fpl* departures
saliente *adj* **1.** retiring **2.** outgoing
salón *m* exhibition hall
salón *m* **VIP (salón de personalidades)** VIP lounge
saltarse la cola to jump the line
saltarse un plazo to miss an installment
salud *f* health
saluda *m* compliments slip
salvamento *m* salvage
salvar to salvage
salvedad *f* proviso
salvo except
salvo error u omisión 1. errors and omissions excepted **2.** e. & o.é.
sancionar to penalize
satisfacción *f* satisfaction
satisfacción *f* **del cliente** customer satisfaction
satisfacción *f* **laboral** job satisfaction
satisfacer 1. to satisfy **2.** to meet
satisfacer la demanda to keep up with the demand
satisfacer una demanda 1. to meet a demand **2.** to satisfy a demand
saturación *f* saturation
saturar to saturate
saturar el mercado to saturate the market
se admiten ofertas open to offers
sección *f* **1.** section **2.** division **3.** department
sección (de tienda) department

sección *f* **de compras** purchasing department
sección *f* **de 'marketing'** marketing division
sección *f* **de ventas** sales department
secretario secretary
secretario *m* **de una empresa** company secretary
secretario *m* **eventual** temp
secretario *m* **general** registrar
secreto *adj* secret ■ secret
sector *m* sector
sector *m* **de los servicios** tertiary sector
sector *m* **primario** primary industry
sector *m* **privado** private sector
sector *m* **público** public sector
sector *m* **terciario** tertiary sector
secuestrar 1. to sequester *o* to sequestrate **2.** to seize
secuestro *m* seizure
secundario *adj* **1.** subsidiary **2.** secondary
sede *f* headquarters; HQ
seguir 1. to follow **2.** to proceed
según *adv* depending on ■ **1.** according to **2.** under
según contrato *adv* contractually
segunda solicitud *f* reapplication
segundo *adj* second
segundo trimestre second quarter
según factura as per invoice
según muestra as per sample
según nota de expedición as per advice
seguridad *f* **1.** safety **2.** security
seguridad *f* **de empleo** security of employment
seguridad *f* **en el empleo** job security
seguridad *f* **social** social security
seguro *m* insurance ■ *adj* safe

seguro *m* **(de vida)** *U.K.* assurance

seguro *m* **a todo riesgo** comprehensive insurance

seguro *m* **contra incendios** fire insurance

seguro *m* **contra terceros** third-party insurance

seguro *m* **corriente de vida** whole-life insurance

seguro *m* **de automóviles** motor insurance

seguro *m* **de enfermedad** health insurance

seguro *m* **de la vivienda** 1. homeowners insurance 2. *U.K.* house insurance

seguro *m* **de vida** life insurance *o* life assurance

seguro *m* **general** general insurance

seguro *m* **marítimo** marine insurance

seguro *m* **temporal** term insurance

selección *f* 1. selection 2. choice

seleccionar candidatos to screen candidates

selección *f* **de artículos para un pedido** order picking

selecto *adj* choice

sellar 1. to stamp 2. (*precintar*) to seal

sello *m* stamp

semana *f* week

semanalmente *adj* weekly

semestre *m* half-year ■ *adj* semi-annual

señal *f* 1. sign 2. mark 3. (*entrada*) deposit

señalar to mark

señal *f* **de comunicar** engaged tone

señal *f* **de línea** dial tone

señas *fpl* address

sencillo *adj* single

sentada *f* sit-down protest

sentencia *f* 1. (*juicio*) judgment *o* judgement 2. (*juicio*) sentence

separado *adj* separate

separar to separate

ser despedido to get the sack

ser distinto to differ

serie *f* (*remesa*) batch

ser igual a to equal

ser responsable ante alguien to responsible to someone

ser válido (*regir*) to run

servicio *m* service

servicio *m* **de contestación** answering service

servicio *m* **deficiente** poor service

servicio *m* **de fotocopias** photocopying service

servicio *m* **de habitaciones de un hotel** room service

servicio *m* **de mantenimiento** service department

servicio *m* **de paquetes postales** parcel post

servicio *m* **de recortes de prensa** clipping service

servicio *m* **posventa** after-sales service

servicio *m* **rápido** prompt service

servicios *mpl* **de informática** computer services

servir to serve

servir un pedido to deal with an order

signatario signatory

signatario *m* **colectivo** joint signatory

significado *m* content

signo *m* **de calidad** quality label

símbolo *m* 1. symbol 2. token

símbolo *m* **de prestigio** status symbol

sin condiciones *adj* unconditional

sin confirmar *adj* unconfirmed

sin cupón de interés *adj* ex coupon

sindicalista *mf* trade unionist

sindicato *m* 1. labor union 2. union 3. *U.K.* trade union

síndico *m* 1. liquidator 2. official receiver 3. receiver

sin dinero *adj informal* broke

sin dividendo *adv, adj* ex dividend

síndrome del fénix phoenix syndrome

sin empleo *adj* out of work

sinergia *f* synergy

sin escalas *adv* non-stop

sin éxito *adj* unsuccessful

sin fecha *adj* undated

sin figurar *adj* unaccounted for

sin fines lucrativos *adj* non profit-making

sin gastos de franqueo 1. postage free 2. *U.K.* post free

siniestro *m* dead loss

sin pagar *adj* unpaid

sin papel carbón *adj* carbonless

sin parar *adv* non-stop

sin tener en cuenta regardless of

sin trabajo *adj* out of work

sin valor *adj* worthless

sin vender *adj* unsold

sistema *m* 1. system 2. (*organización*) setup

sistema *m* **de ordenador a tiempo real** real-time system

sistema *m* **de recuperación** retrieval system

sistema *m* **económico** 1. economy 2. economic system

sistema *m* **informático** computer system

Sistema Monetario Europeo (SME) European Monetary System (EMS)

sistema *m* **operativo** operating system

sistemas *mpl* **de control** control systems

sistema *m* **tributario** tax system

sitio *m* 1. (*lugar*) site 2. (*lugar*) place

sitio *m* **web** website

situación *f* 1. situation 2. position

situación *f* **financiera** financial position

situado *adj* situated

situar to place

S.(R.) L. (= sociedad (de responsabilidad) limitada) *abbr* (*limited company*) Ltd.

SME (Sistema Monetario Europeo) *abbr* (*European Monetary System*) EMS

sobornar to bribe

soborno *m* 1. bribe 2. *U.K.* backhander

sobrar to remain

sobre *m* **abierto** unsealed envelope

sobrecapacidad *f* overcapacity

sobre *m* **cerrado** sealed envelope

sobrecontratación *m* overbooking

sobregiro *m* overdraft

sobrepasar to exceed

sobreprima *f* additional premium

sobreproducción *f* overproduction

sobrepujar (*pujar*) to outbid

sobresaliente *adj* outstanding

sobrestimar 1. (*sobrevalorar*) to overestimate 2. (*sobrevalorar*) to overvalue

sobretasa *f* surcharge

sobretasa *f* **de importación** import surcharge

sobrevalorar 1. to overvalue 2. to overestimate

social *adj* social

sociedad *f* 1. society 2. (*asociación*) partnership 3. (*compañía*) company

sociedad *f* **anónima (S.A.)** Public Limited Company (Plc)

Sociedad Anónima (S.A.) *abbr* (*Public Limited Company*) PLC *o* plc

sociedad f **comercial** trading company

sociedad f **con un gran coeficiente de endeudamiento** highly-geared company

sociedad f **cooperativa** cooperative society

sociedad f **cotizada en bolsa** quoted company

sociedad f **de cartera 1.** proprietary company **2.** holding company

sociedad f **de crédito hipotecario 1.** savings and loan association **2.** *U.K.* building society

sociedad f **de responsabilidad limitada (S.R.L.)** limited (liability) company (Ltd)

sociedad f **en comandita** limited partnership

sociedades fpl **industriales** industrialized societies

sociedad f **ficticia (para la compra de acciones)** shell company

sociedad f **financiera** finance company

sociedad f **hipotecaria 1.** savings and loan association **2.** *U.K.* building society

sociedad f **limitada (S.L.)** private limited company

sociedad f **matriz** parent company

sociedad f **mercantil** corporation

socio 1. (*asociado*) partner **2.** (*asociado*) associate **3.** (*asociado*) copartner **4.** (*miembro*) member

socio m **comanditario 1.** silent partner **2.** *U.K.* sleeping partner

socio m **en comandita 1.** silent partner **2.** *U.K.* sleeping partner

socio m **principal** senior partner

socio m **subalterno** junior partner

"software" m software

solar m site

solicitación f **de votos** canvassing

solicitar 1. to apply for **2.** to ask for **3.** to request

solicitar pedidos to solicit orders

solicitar por escrito to apply in writing

solicitar una patente to file a patent application

solicitar un trabajo to apply for a job

solicitar votos to canvass

solicita votos canvasser

solicitud f **1.** application **2.** request

solicitud f **de empleo** job application

solicitud f **de trabajo** application

solución f solution

solucionar un problema to solve a problem

solvencia f solvency

solvente adj **1.** solvent **2.** creditworthy

someter a prueba to test

sondeo m **de opinión** opinion poll

soporte m holder

soslayar 1. to get around **2.** *U.K.* to get round

sostener 1. to keep up **2.** to maintain

"stand" m stand

status m status

statutario adj statutory

subalterno adj junior

subarrendador sublessor

subarrendar 1. to sublease **2.** to sublet

subarrendatario sublessee

subarriendo m sublease

subasta f **1.** auction **2.** bidding

subastar to auction

subcontratar to subcontract

subcontratista mf subcontractor

subcontrato m subcontract

subdirector 1. assistant manager **2.** deputy manager

subida *f* 1. rise 2. increase 3. appreciation

subir 1. to climb 2. to increase 3. to raise 4. to mount up 5. (*avanzar*) to rise

subir (en valor) to appreciate

subir de precio to increase in price

sub judice *adj* sub judice

subproducto *m* byproduct

subsidiario *adj* subsidiary

subsidio *m* 1. subsidy 2. benefit

subsidio *m* **de carestía de vida** cost-of-living allowance

subsidio *m* **de paro** unemployment pay

subvención *f* 1. subvention 2. subsidy 3. (*beca*) grant

subvencionar to subsidize

suceder to succeed

sucursal *f* 1. branch office 2. branch 3. division 4. (*tienda*) chain store

sueldo *m* 1. wage 2. salary

sueldo *m* **bruto** gross salary

sueldo *m* **neto** net income *o* net salary

sueldo *m* **por hora** hourly wage

suelo *m* floor

suelto *adj* 1. loose 2. (*desparejado*) odd

suficiente *adj* sufficient

sufragar to defray

sufrir daños to suffer damage

sujetapapeles *m* paperclip

sujetar to attach

sujeto a 1. liable to 2. subject to

sujeto a impuesto *adj* taxable

suma *f* 1. sum 2. addition

suma *f* **global** lump sum

sumar to total

sumar una columna de cifras to add up a column of figures

suma *f* **total** grand total

suministrador supplier

suministrar to supply

suministro *m* supply

superar 1. to exceed 2. to top

superávit *m* surplus

superficie *f* surface

superficie *f* **útil** floor space

superior *adj* 1. superior 2. senior 3. top

supermercado *m* supermarket

supervisar to supervise

supervisión *f* supervision

supervisor supervisor

suplementario *adj* 1. supplementary 2. additional

suplemento *m* supplement

suplemento *m* **de póliza** endorsement

suplemento *m* **por el servicio** service charge

suplente *mf* deputy

suprimir 1. to delete 2. to remove 3. to lift 4. (*extirpar*) to excise

suprimir controles to decontrol

surtido *m* 1. choice 2. range 3. selection

suscribir una opción to take up an option

suspender 1. to suspend 2. to cancel 3. (*interrumpir*) to discontinue

suspender pagos to stop payments

suspender un acuerdo to call off a deal

suspendido *adj* off

suspensión *f* 1. suspension 2. stoppage

suspensión *f* **de entregas** suspension of deliveries

suspensión *f* **de pagos** 1. suspension of payments 2. stoppage of payments

sustituir 1. to replace 2. to take over

sustituir a alguien to deputize for someone

sustituto replacement

T

tablas *fpl* **actuariales** actuarial tables

tablas *fpl* **de mortalidad** actuarial tables

tablero *m* panel

tablero *m* **de hojas sueltas** flip chart

tabulación *f* tabulation

tabulador tabulator

tabular to tabulate

tachar to cross off *o* to cross out

tacógrafo *m* tachograph

talla *f adj* stock size

talla *f* **muy grande** outsize; OS

taller *m* workshop

talonario *m* **de cheques** check book

talonario *m* **de recibos** receipt book

tamaño *m* size

tamaño *m* **corriente** *adj* stock size

tamaño *m* **normal** regular size

tangible *adj* tangible

tanteo *m* trial and error

tanto *m* **alzado** flat rate

tanto *m* **por ciento** percentage

taquilla *f* **1.** ticket office **2.** *U.K.* booking office

taquillero 1. ticket clerk **2.** booking clerk

tara *f* **1.** tare **2.** (*defecto*) defect **3.** (*defecto*) fault **4.** (*defecto*) imperfection

tarado *adj* damaged

tarde *adv* late

tarea *f* **1.** assignment **2.** task **3.** job

tarifa *f* **1.** tariff **2.** rate

tarifa *f* **de horas extras** overtime pay

tarifa *f* **de mercado** market rate

tarifa *f* **horaria 1.** hourly rate **2.** time rate

tarifa *f* **nocturna** night rate

tarifa *f* **por horas** time rate

tarifa *f* **postal** postage

tarifa *f* **preferencial** preferential duty *o* preferential tariff

tarifa *f* **preferente** preferential duty *o* preferential tariff

tarifa *f* **reducida 1.** cheap rate **2.** reduced rate

tarifas *fpl* **de carga aérea** air freight charges *o* rates

tarifas *fpl* **de flete** freight rates

tarifas *fpl* **de seguros** insurance rates

tarifas *fpl* **diferenciadas** differential tariffs

tarifas *fpl* **postales** postal charges *o* postal rates

tarifas *fpl* **publicitarias** advertising rates

tarjeta *f* **1.** card **2.** business card

tarjeta *f* **de cajero automático 1.** ATM card **2.** *U.K.* cash card

tarjeta *f* **de crédito 1.** credit card **2.** check (guarantee) card **3.** charge card

tarjeta *f* **de desembarque** landing card

tarjeta *f* **de dinero 1.** ATM card **2.** *U.K.* cash card

tarjeta *f* **de embarque 1.** embarkation card **2.** boarding pass

tarjeta *f* **de saludo** compliments slip

tarjeta *f* **inteligente** smart card

tarjeta *f* **oro** gold card

tarjeta *f* **postal** card

tasa *f* rate

tasación *f* valuation

tasación *f* **de acciones** stock market valuation

tasa *f* **de amortización** depreciation rate

tasa *f* **de cambio** exchange rate

tasa *f* **de conversión** conversion price *o* conversion rate

tasa *f* **de crecimiento** growth rate

tasa *f* **de descuento** discount rate

tasa *f* **de errores** error rate

tasa *f* **de impuestos normal** standard rate (of tax)

tasa *f* **de inflación** rate of inflation

tasa *f* **de interés** interest rate

tasa *f* **de rendimiento** rate of return

tasador valuer

tasar to value

tasas *fpl* **de aeropuerto** airport tax

techo *m* ceiling

techo *m* **crediticio** credit ceiling

tecla *f* key

tecla *f* **de control** control key

tecla *f* **de mayúsculas** shift key

teclado *m* keyboard

teclado *m* **numérico** numeric keypad

tecleado *m* keyboarding

teclear to keyboard

tecleo *m* keyboarding

técnica *f* 1. skill 2. technique

técnica *f* **asesora** consulting engineer

técnicas *fpl* **de dirección de empresas** management techniques

técnicas *fpl* **de 'marketing'** marketing techniques

técnicas *fpl* **de sondeo** canvassing techniques

técnico *m* **asesor** consulting engineer

Telaraña *f* **mundial** World Wide Web

telefax *m* fax

telefonear 1. to telephone 2. to phone

telefonista *mf* 1. telephone operator 2. *U.K.* telephonist

teléfono *m* 1. telephone 2. phone

teléfono *m* **celular** cellular telephone

teléfono *m* **de conferencias** conference phone

teléfono *m* **de tarjeta** card phone

teléfono *m* **interno** internal telephone

teléfono *m* **móvil** 1. cell phone 2. *U.K.* mobile phone

teléfono *m* **público** pay phone

teletarjeta *f* phone card

teletrabajo *m* teleworking

télex *m* telex

tema *f* subject

temporada *f* season

temporada *f* **baja** off-season

temporero casual worker

temprano *adj* early

tendencia *f* trend

tendencia *f* **alcista** upward trend

tendencias *fpl* **del mercado** market trends

tendencias *fpl* **económicas** economic trends

tendero storekeeper

tenedor holder

tenencia *f* tenure

tenencia *f* **de acciones** shareholding

tener 1. to hold 2. to have 3. to own

tener como objetivo to target

tener en cuenta to allow for

tener en existencia to carry

tener existencias to stock

tener éxito to succeed

tener lugar to take place

tener tiempo to afford

tener una discusión to hold a meeting *o* to hold a discussion

tercero *m* third party

tercer trimestre *m* third quarter

terminación *f* 1. termination 2. expiration

terminado *adj* finished

terminal *adj* terminal

terminal *f* **de aeropuerto** air terminal

terminal *f* **de contenedores** container terminal

terminal *f* **del aeropuerto** airport terminal

terminal *m* **de ordenador** computer terminal

terminar 1. to end 2. to terminate 3. to wind up

terminar de trabajar to knock off

término *m* 1. time limit 2. term

términos *mpl* terms

terna *f* shortlist

territorio *m* territory

Tesoro *m* treasury

testigo *mf* witness

testimonio *m* witness

texto *m* 1. text 2. wording

tiempo: a tiempo time: on time

tiempo *m* **de preparación (de una máquina)** make-ready time

tiempo *m* **invertido por el ordenador** computer time

tiempo *m* **libre** spare time

tiempo *m* **muerto** down time

tienda *f* 1. store 2. *U.K.* shop

tienda *f* **de barrio** corner store

tienda *f* **de fábrica** factory outlet

tienda *f* **de rebajas** 1. cut-price store 2. discount store 3. discount house

tienda *f* **de regalos** gift store

tienda *f* **de una cadena** chain store

tienda *f* **libre de impuestos** duty-free store

tiendas *fpl* **al detall** retail outlets

tierra *f* land

timador racketeer

timbrar to stamp

timbre *m* stamp

timo *m* fiddle

tipo *m* discount rate

tipo *m* **base de interés bancario** bank base rate

tipo *m* **de cambio** 1. rate of exchange 2. exchange rate

tipo *m* **de cambio actual** current rate of exchange

tipo *m* **de cambio cruzado** cross rate

tipo *m* **de cambio desfavorable** unfavorable exchange rate

tipo *m* **de cambio estable** stable exchange rate

tipo *m* **de cambio para operaciones a plazo** forward rate

tipo *m* **de gravamen** tax rate

tipo *m* **de interés** 1. interest rate 2. rate of interest

tipo *m* **impositivo** tax rate

tipo *m* **preferencial de interés bancario** prime rate

tipos *mpl* **de cambio flotantes** floating exchange rates

tipos *mpl* **de interés** money rates

tirada *f* circulation

titulado *adj* certificated

título *m* 1. deed 2. *U.K.* (*acción*) share certificate 3. (*acción*) unit 4. (*acción*) bond

título *m* **al portador** bearer bond

títulos *mpl* 1. equities 2. securities

títulos *mpl* **del Estado** 1. government stock 2. gilt-edged securities 3. government bonds

títulos *mpl* **profesionales** professional qualifications

todo incluido *adv* 1. all-inclusive 2. *U.K.* all-in

todos los gastos pagados all expenses paid

toma *f* **de decisiones** decision making

tomar to take

tomar la iniciativa to take the initiative

tomar medidas 1. to act 2. to take action 3. to make provision for

tomar nota 1. to take note 2. to minute

tomar posesión to take over

tomar prestado to borrow

tomarse tiempo libre (durante el trabajo) to take time off work

tomar una decisión to reach a decision

tonelada f ton

tonelada f **métrica** tonne

toneladas fpl **de peso muerto** deadweight tonnage

tonelaje m tonnage

tonelaje m **bruto** gross tonnage

total m 1. total 2. sum ■ adj total

total m **acumulado** running total

totalidad f total

totalizar to total

total m **parcial** subtotal

trabajador worker

trabajador m **a domicilio** homeworker

trabajador m **a tiempo parcial** part-timer

trabajadores mpl **pagados por horas** hourly-paid workers

trabajador m **eventual** casual worker

trabajador m **por libre** freelancer

trabajar to work

trabajo m 1. labor 2. work 3. job

trabajo m **a contrata** contract work

trabajo m **a destajo** piecework

trabajo m **a tiempo completo** full-time employment

trabajo m **bien remunerado** well-paid job

trabajo m **de campo** field work

trabajo m **de oficina** clerical work

trabajo m **en curso** work in progress

trabajo m **eventual** casual work

trabajo m **manual** manual work

trabajo m **por horas** part-time work o part-time employment

trabajo m **por turnos** shift work

trabajo m **rutinario** routine work

trabajo m **urgente** rush job

traducción f translation

traducir to translate

traductor translator

traer to bring

tramitación f procedure

tramitación f **del pago de un cheque** clearance of a check

tramitar to process

tramitar el pago de un cheque to clear a check

trámite m 1. formality 2. procedure 3. business transaction

trampa f fiddle

transacción f 1. deal 2. business transaction 3. transaction

transacción f **en efectivo** cash deal

transacción f **global** package deal

transbordador m ferry

transbordo m transfer

transferencia f transfer

transferencia f **bancaria** bank transfer

transferencia f **de fondos** transfer of funds

transferible adj transferable

transferir to transfer

transigir to compromise

tránsito m transit

transmisión f **del título de propiedad** conveyance

transmisión f **de títulos de propiedad** conveyancing

transportar 1. to transport 2. to carry

transportar en contenedores to containerize

transporte m 1. transport 2. freight 3. *U.K.* carriage

transporte m **en contenedores** containerization

Transporte Internacional por Carretera abbr (*Transports Internationaux Routiers*) TIR

transporte *m* **por carretera** 1. road transportation 2. road haulage 3. trucking

transporte *m* **por carretera o por vía marítima** surface transportation

transporte *m* **por ferrocarril** rail transportation

transporte *m* **público** public transportation

transporte urgente to express

transportista *mf* 1. road hauler 2. carrier 3. shipper

trasladar 1. to transfer 2. to remove

trasladar(se) to move

trasladar temporalmente to second

traslado *m* 1. transfer 2. (*mudanza*) removal

traspaso *m* 1. premium 2. transfer fee 3. key money

tratado *m* **comercial** trade agreement

tratamiento *m* **de textos** word-processing

tratante *mf* dealer

tratar to handle

tratar con alguien to deal with someone

trato *m* 1. bargain 2. deal

trato *m* **difícil** hard bargaining

tren *m* train

tren *m* **de mercancías** 1. freight train 2. goods train

tren *m* **de mercancías de contenedores** freightliner

tribunal *m* court

tribunal *m* **de arbitraje** arbitration board *o* arbitration tribunal

tribunal *m* **de arbitraje laboral** industrial arbitration tribunal

tribunal *m* **de justicia** adjudication tribunal

tribunal *m* **de rentas** rent tribunal

tribunales *mpl* **de justicia** law courts

tributación *f* **progresiva** progressive taxation

trimestral *adj* quarterly

trimestralmente *adv* quarterly

trimestre *m* 1. quarter 2. term

triple *adj* triple

triplicar 1. to triple 2. to treble

trocar to barter

trueque *m* 1. barter 2. bartering

turno *m* shift

turno *m* **de día** day shift

turno *m* **de noche** night shift

U

UE (= **Unión Europea**) *abbr* (*European Union*) EU

último *adj* 1. last 2. latest 3. (*final*) final

último requerimiento de pago final demand

últimos en entrar, primeros en salir last in first out; LIFO

último trimestre last quarter

umbral *m* threshold

único *adj* 1. (*exclusivo*) sole 2. *U.K.* (*fuera de serie*) one-off 3. (*sencillo*) single

unidad *f* unit

unidad *f* **de almacenaje** storage unit

unidad *f* **de producción** production unit

unidad *f* **monetaria** monetary unit

uniforme *adj* flat

unilateral *adj* 1. unilateral 2. one-sided

unión *f* **aduanera** customs union

Unión Europea (UE) European Union (EU)

unir 1. to join **2.** to unite

urgencia *f* emergency

urgente *adj* **1.** urgent **2.** (*correo*) express

usado secondhand

usar to use

uso *m* **1.** use **2.** utilization

usual *adj* usual

usuario user

usuario *m* **final** end user

usufructo *m* **vitalicio** life interest

útil *adj* **1.** useful **2.** handy

utilización *f* utilization

utilizado employed

utilizar 1. to use **2.** to run

utilizar capacidad ociosa to use up spare capacity

V

vacaciones *fpl* **reglamentarias** *U.K.* statutory holiday

vacante *adj* **1.** free **2.** vacant ■ vacancy

vaciar to empty

vacío *adj* empty ■ gap

vagón *m* **(de ferrocarril)** truck

vale *m* voucher

vale *m* **de caja** cash voucher

valedero *adj* valid

vale *m* **para un regalo** gift voucher

valer 1. to cost **2.** to worth: be worth

validez *f* validity

válido *adj* valid

valla *f* **publicitaria 1.** billboard **2.** *U.K.* hoarding

valor *m* **1.** value **2.** worth

valoración *f* **1.** valuation **2.** assessment **3.** estimation **4.** estimate **5.** (*apreciación*) appreciation

valoración *f* **de daños** assessment of damages

valoración *f* **de existencias 1.** inventory valuation **2.** *U.K.* stock valuation

valoración *f* **de resultados** performance rating

valor *m* **actual** present value

valor *m* **a la par** par value

valorar 1. to value **2.** to assess **3.** to estimate **4.** (*apreciar*) to appreciate

valor *m* **contable** book value

valor *m* **de activo** asset value

valor *m* **declarado** declared value

valor *m* **de escasez** scarcity value

valor *m* **de mercado** market value

valor *m* **de reposición** replacement value

valor *m* **de rescate** surrender value

valores *mpl* securities

valores *mpl* **convertibles en acciones** convertible loan stock

valor *m* **neto** net worth

valor *m* **nominal 1.** face value **2.** nominal value

valor *m* **total de factura** total invoice value

variación *f* **1.** variation **2.** variance

variaciones *fpl* **estacionales** seasonal variations

vehículo *m* vehicle

vehículo *m* **de transporte** carrier

vencer 1. to mature **2.** to fall due **3.** to expire

vencido *adj* **1.** overdue **2.** due

vencimiento *m* **1.** expiration **2.** expiry

vendedor 1. sales clerk **2.** seller **3.** vendor **4.** salesman

vendedor *m* **a domicilio** door-to-door salesman

vendedor *m* **de seguros** insurance salesman

vender 1. to sell **2.** to market **3.** to retail

vender a futuros to sell forward

vender al por menor to retail goods

vender a precio más bajo que un rival to undercut a competitor

vender con entrega aplazada to sell forward

vender las existencias sobrantes to dispose of excess stock

vender más barato to undersell

venderse al por menor to retail

vender un bono to redeem a bond

vender un negocio to sell out

vendible *adj* **1.** salable **2.** marketable

venirse abajo to fall through

venta *f* **1.** sale **2.** selling **3.** disposal

venta *f* **a domicilio 1.** house-to-house selling **2.** door-to-door selling

venta *f* **agresiva** hard selling

venta *f* **al contado** cash sale

venta *f* **al por menor** retail

venta *f* **a prueba 1.** sale or return **2.** sale on approval **3.** *U.K.* see-safe

venta *f* **con tarjeta de crédito** credit card sale

venta *f* **detalle** retail

venta *f* **directa** direct selling

venta *f* **en depósito 1.** sale or return **2.** consignment sale **3.** *U.K.* see-safe

venta *f* **en la bolsa** bargain

venta *f* **en subasta** sale by auction

venta *f* **forzosa 1.** forced sale **2.** distress sale

ventana *f* window

ventanilla *f* counter

venta *f* **por correo** direct mail

ventas *fpl* sales

ventas *fpl* **a plazo** forward sales

ventas *fpl* **bajas** low sales

ventas *fpl* **estimadas** estimated sales

venta *f* **sin presionar al cliente** soft sell

ventas *fpl* **nacionales 1.** domestic sales **2.** home sales

ventas *fpl* **netas** net sales

ventas *fpl* **por teléfono** telesales

ventas *fpl* **previstas** projected sales

ventas *fpl* **registradas** book sales

verbal *adj* verbal

verdadero *adj* **1.** real **2.** true

verificación *f* verification

verificar to verify

vetar una decisión to veto a decision

vía via

viabilidad *f* feasibility

viable *adj* viable

viajar diariamente al trabajo to commute

viaje *m* **de negocios** business trip

viaje *m* **de regreso** homeward journey

viajera diaria *f* commuter

viajero diario *m* commuter

videoconferencia *f* videoconference

viejo *adj* old

vigente *adj* ruling

vigilante *m* security guard

vigor *m* energy

vigoroso *adj* strong

vinculante *adj* binding

vínculo *m* **1.** connection **2.** link

violación *f* **de contrato** breach of contract

violación *f* **de garantía** breach of warranty

violación *f* **de patente** infringement of patent

violar 1. to violate **2.** to infringe

violar una patente to infringe a patent

visado *m* visa

visado *m* **de entrada** entry visa

visado *m* **de entradas múltiples** multiple entry visa

visado *m* **de tránsito** transit visa

visita *f* **1.** visit **2.** call

visita *f* **comercial sin cita previa** cold call

visita *f* **de negocios** business call

visitar 1. to visit **2.** to call on

vista *f* sight

vitalidad *f* strength

vitrina *f* **1.** display case **2.** showcase

vitrina *f* **de exposición** display stand *o* display unit

volumen *m* **1.** volume **2.** bulk

volumen *m* **comercial** volume of trade *o* volume of business

volumen *m* **de negocios** volume of trade *o* volume of business

volumen *m* **de ventas 1.** volume of sales **2.** sales volume **3.** turnover

voluminoso *adj* bulky

voluntaria voluntary redundancy

volver a comprar to buy back

volver a nombrar to reappoint

volver a presentarse to reapply

volver a telefonear to phone back

voto *m* **de calidad** casting vote

voto *m* **de gracias** vote of thanks

voto *m* **por poderes** proxy vote

vuelo *m* flight

vuelo *m* **chárter** charter flight

vuelo *m* **de correspondencia** connecting flight

vuelo *m* **de larga distancia** long-distance flight *o* long-haul flight

vuelo *m* **regular** scheduled flight

vuelta *f* **1.** (*cambio*) change **2.** (*regreso*) return

W-Z

website *f* website

zona *f* **1.** (*distrito*) area **2.** (*región*) area

zona *f* **comercial peatonal** shopping precinct

zona *f* **del dólar** dollar area

zona *f* **de libre cambio** free trade area

zona *f* **euro** eurozone

zona *f* **franca 1.** free trade zone **2.** free zone

zona *f* **industrial 1.** industrial park **2.** *U.K.* industrial estate

Business correspondence

Sample résumé

Sample covering letter for job application

Sample letter making a job offer

Sample letter of complaint

La correspondencia comercial

Curriculum vitae

Carta de presentación

Oferta de empleo

Carta de reclamación

Sample Résumé

CURRICULUM VITAE – Jacinta Terradas Bello
C/ Veza 3, 5° A, 28028 Barcelona
Teléfono: (020) 8868 9854   Móvil: (07914) 248553
e-mail: jterradasbello@hotmail.com

Objetivo:
Ser gerente de recursos humanos desempeñando el papel de responsable de
equipo en una empresa puntera. En el futuro, gestionar las relaciones laborales
a nivel nacional en España o a nivel internacional.

Experiencia laboral:
2002 – actualidad   **ONDEA Sociedad Mercantil, Barcelona**
Asesora del departamento de recursos humanos:
*Asesoramiento profesional en todos los temas del departamento de recursos
humanos, entre ellos las relaciones laborales y la formación de los
empleados. Creación de un programa para España y puesta en práctica de
cambios en el programa de la empresa.*

1998 – 2001   **ONDEA Sociedad Mercantil, Barcelona**
**Asesora de recursos humanos: navegación, transporte marítimo y
aviación comercial**
*Asesoramiento en la selección de personal en tres departamentos del grupo
TEASA: productos de navegación, transporte marítimo y aviación comercial.
Coordinación de varios procesos de selección de personal internos y externos
en todas las fases, desde el anuncio publicitario hasta la selección del
candidato.*

1995 – 1997   **ONDEA Producción, Barcelona**
Asesora de recursos humanos: ingeniería de explotación petrolera
*Asesoramiento en una serie de temas, entre otros la gestión de una
reubicación empresarial a gran escala.*

Educación/Títulos:
2001 – 2003	Máster en Relaciones Laborales, *Universidad Autónoma de Madrid*
1998 – 2000	Graduada por la Facultad de Personal y Desarrollo
1992 – 1995	Licenciada en Psicología Experimental, *Universidad de Salamanca*
1984 – 1992	Bachillerato y COU (ciencias y letras), *Instituto de Bachillerato La Esperanza, Salamanca*

RÉSUMÉ for Josephine Catterall
21 Washington Drive, Indianapolis, Indiana 56261
T: (316) 972 49 63   M: (301) 602 24 11   e-mail: jfcatterall@boohoo.com

Objective:
To become a professional Human Resources manager with a team-leader role within a blue-chip company. Future positions to involve managing employee relations on a national or global basis.

Work History:
Dec 1999 – present   GP International Trading and Shipping Co., Inc., Indianapolis
Human Resources Policy Adviser
Provided professional advice on all HR policy matters including employee relations and training. Developed policy and implemented policy changes within the business.

May 1996 – Nov 1999 GP International Trading and Shipping Co., Inc., Indianapolis
Human Resources Adviser: Marine, Shipping, and Aviation
Provided recruitment advice to 3 departments of the Global Businesses group: Marine Products, Shipping, and Aviation. Coordinated several internal and external recruitment processes through all stages from advertising to candidate selection.

Sept 1993 – Apr 1996 GP U.S. Exploration and Production, Indianapolis
Human Resources Consultant: Oil-well Engineering
Provided advice on a range of issues, including helping to manage a large-scale company relocation.

Education/Qualifications:

1999 – 2001	M.Sc. in Employee Relations, *University of Indiana*
1996 – 1998	Graduate of the Chartered Institute of Personnel and Development
1990 – 1993	B.A. (Hons) Experimental Psychology (Class Iii), *University of Bristol, U.K.*
1982 – 1990	A-Levels: Biology (A), French (A), German (B), *St Stephen's School, Cambridge, U.K.*

Sample covering letter for job application

Adriana García Seoane
C/ Ramón Cabanillas, N° 20
28020 Barcelona

> Sra./Srta. Sonia Ibero Fernández
> Jefa de personal
> ALFATEC
> Columela 15
> 28002 MADRID

> 25 de marzo de 2004

Estimada Sra./Srta. Ibero Fernández:

Estoy muy interesada en el puesto de Jefa de ventas de ALFATEC que se ha anunciado el día 20 de marzo en el periódico *El País*.

Durante el año pasado en mi actual puesto de Delegada de ventas de InfoSoria he contribuido a aumentar en un 15% nuestra cuota de mercado. He podido apreciar en su página web y en su informe anual que ALFATEC también ha aumentado su cuota de mercado y pretende conseguir el mismo objetivo el próximo año fiscal. Creo que mis títulos y experiencia encajarían bien en este plan de desarrollo.

Tal como se indica en el anuncio, le envío adjunto una copia de mi Currículum Vitae en el que se incluyen todos los datos sobre mis títulos y experiencia laboral. Me sería muy grato poder ser considerada para este puesto.

Sin otro particular, quedo a la espera de sus noticias.

Le saluda atentamente,

Adriana García Seoane

Anexo

Carta de presentación

Adrienne Griffiths
20 Oak Drive
Houston
Texas 77065

Jane Nichol
Senior Personnel Officer
DataTech Inc.
Suite 205, 2900 Butterfield Rd
Houston
Texas 77096

March 25 2004

Dear Ms. Nichol

I am very interested in the position of sales manager at DataTech Inc. as described in your advertisement of March 20.

In my current position of deputy sales manager for Parker Smith Inc. I have helped to increase our market share by 15% in the past year. I see from your Web site and annual report that DataTech have also increased their market share this year and are aiming to do the same in the next financial year, and I feel my track record and qualifications would fit in well with these plans for growth.

As requested in the advertisement, I enclose a copy of my résumé which gives full details of my qualifications and work history. I would be very pleased to be considered for this position and I look forward to hearing from you.

Yours sincerely

Adrianne Griffiths

Encl.

Sample letter making a job offer

ALFATEC
Columela 15
28002 MADRID

Sra./Srta. Adriana García Seoane
C/ Ramón Cabanillas, Nº 20
28002 Madrid

10 de abril de 2004

Estimada Sra./Srta. García Seoane:

Asunto: Puesto de Jefa de ventas

Con relación a la entrevista mantenida la semana pasada, me complace poder ofrecerle el puesto de Jefa de ventas, dependiendo directamente de Francisco Aramburu Laguna, Director de ventas de la empresa.

Su salario inicial será de 31.600 euros, con una revisión del mismo al año de haberse incorporado a la empresa. Las demás condiciones serán según se han acordado en la entrevista.

Si desea aceptar esta oferta, le estaría muy agradecida que comunicara su confirmación por escrito. A continuación se podrán ultimar los detalles de su contrato, la fecha de comienzo y estudiar los gastos que pueda ocasionar el cambio a su nuevo puesto.

Sin otro particular, reciba un cordial saludo,

Sonia Ibero Fernández
Jefa de personal
ALFATEC

Oferta de empleo

DataTech Inc.
Suite 205, 2900 Butterfield Rd
Houston
Texas 77096

Ms. Adrienne Griffiths
20 Oak Drive
Houston
Texas 77065

April 10 2004

Dear Ms. Griffiths

Re: Post of Sales Manager

Further to your interview last week I am pleased to be able to offer you the post of Sales Manager, reporting directly to David Wardlock, our Company Sales Director.

Your starting salary will be $45,000, with an annual salary review on the date of your joining the company. Other terms and conditions will be as outlined in the interview.

If this offer is acceptable to you I would be grateful if you could send me confirmation in writing. We can then finalize details of your contract and starting date and discuss any relocation expenses you may have to claim.

Yours sincerely

Jane Nichol
Senior Personnel Officer
DataTech Inc.

Sample letter of complaint

C/ Labastida 3, 47
20010 San Sebastián

> Sra./Srta. Marina Blanco Requejo
> INFOTÉCNICA
> Avda. Sancho el Sabio, 30 Bajo
> 20010 San Sebastián
>
> 20 de marzo de 2004

Estimada Sra./Srta. Blanco Requejo:

Impresora de chorro de tinta defectuosa (número de modelo A1234)

El jueves 13 de marzo hice la compra de una impresora de chorro de tinta (número de modelo A1234) en su establecimiento (adjunto copia del recibo). Desafortunadamente, la impresora no funciona y dos de los técnicos de su establecimiento no han podido establecer la causa del problema. Por consiguiente, le agradecería que se procediese lo antes posible a realizar el reintegro completo del importe de la impresora defectuosa.

No dude en ponerse en contacto conmigo en la dirección arriba indicada para poder acordar una fecha para el reintegro del importe y la recogida de la impresora.

Sin otro particular, quedo a la espera de sus noticias.

Le saluda atentamente,

Isabel Sandoval Ochoa